AS MINISTERS OF CHRIST

The Christological Dimension of Ministry in the New Testament

AN EXEGETICAL AND THEOLOGICAL STUDY

by

J.T. Forestell, C.S.B.

PAULIST PRESS
New York/Mahwah

ACKNOWLEDGMENTS

The publisher gratefully acknowledges use of the following materials: brief excerpts from *Galatians* (Hermeneia Series) by H.D. Betz; *The New Testament as Canon* by B.S. Childs; *The Acts of The Apostles* (Hermeneia Series) by H. Conzelmann, all published by Augsburg Fortress, Minneapolis, Minnesota; the following quotes from *Theological Dictionary of the New Testament*: 2.566 (W. Foerster); 4.230 (H. Strathmann); 6.682–83 (G. Bornkamm); 9.406 (H. Conzelmann); 9.433 n. 55 (E. Lohse). Detail verso; and the following quote from E. Käsemann, *Commentary on Romans* (1980): ". . . here he is calling himself the priest of the Messiah Hesus to the whole of the Gentile world," published by Wm. B. Eerdmans Publishing Company, Grand Rapids, Michigan; quotations from "The Ministry in the Church: Reflections on a Recent Publication, I—Data of the New Testament," *Clergy Review*, vol. 8 (1983), reproduced by permission of The Tablet Publishing Company Ltd. 48 Great Peter Street, London SW1P 2HB.

Library of Congress Cataloging-in-Publication Data

Forestell, J. Terence.
    As ministers of Christ : the christological dimension of ministry in the New Testament : an exegetical and theological study / by J. T. Forestell.
        p. cm.
    Includes bibliographical references and index.
    ISBN 0-8091-3220-6
    1. Clergy—Office—Biblical teaching. 2. Priests—Biblical teaching. 3. Bible. N. T.—Criticism, interpretation, etc. 4. Jesus Christ—Person and offices. 5. Catholic Church—Clergy. 6. Catholic Church—Doctrine. I. Title.
BS2545.C56F67   1991
262'.1'09015—dc20
                                                                    90-25363
                                                                        CIP

Published by Paulist Press
997 Macarthur Boulevard
Mahwah, New Jersey 07430

Printed and bound in the
United States of America

CONTENTS

iii

TO THE PRESBYTERS
OF THE ROMAN CATHOLIC CHURCH

LIST OF ABBREVIATIONS

AB	Anchor Bible
ACW	Ancient Christian Writers
Adv.Haer.	Irenaeus, *Adversus Haereses*
AnBib	Analecta Biblica
BAG	W. Bauer, W.F. Ardnt and F.W. Gingrich, *Greek-English Lexicon of the NT*
Bib	*Biblica*
b.Moʻed Qat.	Babylonian Talmud, Tractate *Moʻed Qaṭan*
CBQ	*Catholic Biblical Quarterly*
C.E.	Common Era (= A. D., *Anno Domini*)
chap.	chapter
1 Clem.	1 Clement
Did.	Didache
EBib	Etudes Bibliques
ed., eds.	editor, editors
Herm.Vis.	Hermas, *Visions*
Hist.eccl.	Eusebius, *Historia ecclesiastica*
HNT	Handbuch zum Neuen Testament
HTKNT	Herders theologischer Kommentar zum Neuen Testament
ICC	International Critical Commentary
Int	*Interpretation*
JBL	*Journal of Biblical Literature*
LCL	Loeb Classical Library
LPGL	G.W.P. Lampe, *Patristic Greek Lexicon*
l.v.	*lectio varians*
LXX	Septuagint
Moulton-Milligan	J.H. Moulton and G. Milligan, *The Vocabulary of the Greek New Testament. Illustrated from the Papyri and Other Non-Literary Sources*

MT	Masoretic Text
n., nn.	note, notes
NRT	*Nouvelle Revue Théologique*
NT	New Testament
NTAbh	Neutestamentliche Abhandlungen
OED	*Oxford English Dictionary*
OT	Old Testament
p., pp.	page, pages
Proceedings CTSA	*Proceedings of the Catholic Theological Society of America*
RB	*Revue Biblique*
RelSRev	*Religious Studies Review*
RSV	*The Holy Bible*. Revised Standard Version. Catholic Edition, 1966
SANT	Studien zum Alten und Neuen Testament
SBT	Studies in Biblical Theology
Str-B	[H. Strack and] P. Billerbeck, *Kommentar zum Neuen Testament*
TDNT	G. Kittel and G. Friedrich (eds.), *Theological Dictionary of the New Testament*
Tg.Ps.-J.	*Targum Pseudo-Jonathan*
TS	*Theological Studies*
v, vv	verse, verses
WUNT	Wissenschaftliche Untersuchungen zum Neuen Testament

INTRODUCTION

It is a fact that every grouping in human society recognizes certain individuals as its leaders. These leaders are responsible for directing the group toward its goals and for providing the services which the group requires to achieve those goals. Political and social history records many ways in which such leaders come to attain the positions they hold. Sometimes it is what might be called a process of natural selection, whereby the group automatically recognizes the leadership potential of certain individuals because of their wisdom, their strength, their courage or their concern for others. In less favorable circumstances a serious crisis in the group may be the occasion for a highly endowed person or group of persons to assume leadership, with or without the consent of the larger group, for the purpose of solving the immediate crisis; such situations then give rise to more or less permanent forms of government such as monarchies, dictatorships, oligarchies, juntas or tyrannies in which the rule of one or of a few is established without explicitly seeking the consent of those being governed. In democratic systems, both ancient and modern, leaders are selected by the free votes of those being governed, regardless of whether suffrage is universal or not. Contemporary sociological studies have examined the process whereby leaders are selected, installed and empowered in any group, regardless of its size. In well-organized groups there are also procedures for calling the leaders to account for the discharge of their responsibilities.

In the British parliamentary system of government, and in other democratic systems dependent on the British system, such leaders are called "ministers." The word designates someone who works under the authority of a superior and who provides services of some kind to others. In the NT the word "minister" and its cognates "ministry" and "to minister" are commonly used to render the Greek words *diakonos, diakonia,* and *diakoneō* respectively.

1

Until recently, in church circles, the word "minister" was reserved for the ordained clergy of Protestant churches, while leaders in the Roman Catholic, Orthodox and Anglican communions were called "priests" and "bishops." Since the Second Vatican Council (1962–65) which reaffirmed the NT teaching that all leadership in the church is service and that all Christians are called to service, the word "minister" is being applied to anyone who performs any service whatsoever for others in a Christian community, whether such individuals are formally ordained or not. Such generalizations in the use of the "ministry" word group emphasize the call of Christ to all his disciples to become servants of one another and of the world after his example. At the same time, however, the specific difference between the ministry of all the faithful and the specialized ministry of the ordained, especially in the Roman Catholic Church, has become obscured. It is my hope that this study may contribute to a clarification of this distinction between general ministry and specialized or ordained ministry, a distinction which is traditional not only in episcopal communions but also in many major Protestant churches.

Other interrelated reasons have led me to undertake this study at the present time. Much of my teaching career has been devoted to the preparation of young men for priestly ordination in the Roman Catholic Church. As student bodies have become more diversified in the years following the Second Vatican Council, the problem of priestly identity has become more acute. Lay women and lay men are now receiving the same academic formation as candidates for the priesthood in many centers of theological education. Pastoral tasks which were once performed exclusively by the ordained are now being legitimately assumed by the non-ordained, not simply to compensate for a lack of priests, but especially in recognition of the universal call to ministry contained in the sacraments of baptism and confirmation. Paul reminded his Christians at Corinth that all ministries are for the good of the whole community and urged them not to allow the diversity of gifts within the community to become a cause for competition, jealousy and dissension. If the present study contributes to greater unity within today's diversity of gifts in the church, I shall be amply rewarded.

Over the years, too, I have often been asked to speak to priests about their ministry in the light of the gospels and the letters of the NT. These talks have been generally well received and priests have asked me to write something on ministry to help them in their work. Consequently, it is partially in response to their requests that I have undertaken this work.

Besides my desire to help priests and candidates for the priesthood in the Roman Catholic Church, I was also motivated to write by Edward Schillebeeckx's study entitled *Ministry, Leadership in the Community of Jesus Christ* (New York: Crossroad, 1981). Schillebeeckx's work is the fruit of a long theological and pastoral career. It is motivated by a profound pastoral desire to provide the contemporary church with an adequate ministry, especially as regards the eucharist, in face of an ever-growing shortage of priests, at least in certain parts of the world. In this wide-ranging study of the practice of ministry over the centuries, Schillebeeckx rightly insists that practice should mirror theological reflection upon ever new and evolving human and cultural situations.[1] Schillebeeckx distinguishes what comes from below and what comes from above.[2] He argues that "On each occasion official documents sanction a church practice, concerning the ministry in the church, developing from below," and that "At the present moment we can again see new alternatives or parallel views and practices, concerning the ministry in the church, developing from below."[3] Since the church is the body of Christ and the temple of the Holy Spirit, Schillebeeckx asserts that "it is obvious that what developed spontaneously from below (as we would now put it, in accordance with the sociological laws of group formation) was recognized and explicitly interpreted by the communities, naturally and with good reason, indeed spontaneously, as a 'gift from the Lord' (Eph. 4:8–11; I Tim. 4:14; II Tim. 1:6)."[4]

In theory this thesis is very attractive, but in writing 1 Corinthians Paul used the theological criterion of the church as the body of Christ precisely to check the dissensions and abuses which were developing spontaneously in the Christian community of Corinth. Existentially it will always be difficult to distinguish between what comes from below and what comes from above; there are sociological laws which explain not only the emergence of leaders within groups, but also the rise of factions and misunderstandings. In the present tension of the "already" and the "not yet," which is the existential situation of the church in the present time, it will always be difficult to judge what is of "the spirit" from what is of "the flesh"; discernment is required to decide in every case. When Paul used the Greco-Roman metaphor of the human body in 1 Cor 12, he recognized with his pagan contemporaries that what is spontaneous in a social group sometimes has to be corrected by appeal to higher principles which the self-serving attitudes of individuals or factions within the group are not always ready to acknowledge. Paul, however, is not satisfied with using the Greco-Roman metaphor without qualification; he argues in 1 Cor 12:12–13 that the metaphor applies *a fortiori* in a Christian community precisely because the Christian community is the body of Christ. "For just as the body is one and has many members, and all the members of the body, though many, are one body, so it is with Christ (RSV; the Greek is more pointed: "So also Christ" [*houtōs kai ho Christos*]). For by one Spirit we were all baptized into one body—Jews or Greeks, slaves or free—and all were made to drink of one Spirit."[5]

The church, therefore, is more than a human society; it is the body of Christ by reason of the union of each baptized Christian with the person of the risen Christ. As a human society it needs its own procedures for providing itself with the leaders necessary to further its goals and objectives; in this respect sociological laws of group formation will be operative in the church as in any human society. As the body of Christ, however, the church's task is to continue the mission of Christ himself and bring it to fulfillment. This understanding of the church's mission finds it fullest expression in the epistle to the Ephesians.[6] Ministry in the church, therefore, derives its specificity from the ministry of Christ himself.

In a review of Schillebeeckx's book, Walter Kasper[7] questions whether the priority which Schillebeeckx gives to the "pneumatological-ecclesial foundation for the ministry" does "justice to the fundamental evidence in the New Testament" and "to the christological concreteness of salvation history" (187). Kasper continues:

> The christological foundation of the Church's ministry means that salvation has been given to the Church through Jesus Christ, that the Word of God is not derived from below but rather is graciously bestowed . . . and that, as a result, it requires a commission in order for it to be officially announced. Thus the Church and the ministry have a given norm—namely, Jesus Christ—to which they must constantly redirect themselves. The christological foundation for the ministry is thus not only an ideological legitimization of the ministry, under certain circumstances, but also a criterion for and, on certain occasions, a critique of the concrete practice of the ministry. Understood in this

way it has a good biblical basis. We need only recall Luke 10:16: "The one who hears you hears me," and 2 Cor 5:20: "We are Christ's ambassadors . . . We entreat you in Christ's name" (188).

Later in the review Kasper speaks of Schillebeeckx's "minimizing of the christological basis of the Church" (191). He calls for an integrating of the pneumatological and the christological foundation of the ministry (194).

In another review Albert Vanhoye[8] has questioned the manner in which Schillebeeckx presents the NT data as the foundation of his thesis. Vanhoye takes issue with Schillebeeckx "in minimizing the part the apostles played and in establishing the organization of the Church on 'what arises spontaneously from below' " (155); he continues, ". . . each time the New Testament expresses itself clearly, it confirms that, in the church of Christ, ministry comes from above and not from below. Such was the case for the Twelve: it was the same for the heads of the communities" (160). In response to these substantial critiques of Schillebeeckx's book,[9] I have undertaken to take a closer look at the NT data.

Finally, I should like to consider this study to be a contribution to the wider discernment process which is now engaging the Roman Catholic Church concerning the ordination of women. Writing in *Chicago Studies* in 1983 Agnes Cunningham, SSCM[10] commented on the reception given the 1976 *Declaration on the Question of the Admission of Women to the Ministerial Priesthood*, issued by the Sacred Congregation for the Doctrine of the Faith in Rome. Cunningham considers that, if this document is perceived as the major stumbling block on the road to women's full participation in the ministry of the church, theologians have themselves to blame:

A careful reading of both the declaration and its accompanying commentary leads to the conclusion that this document was never meant to be taken as seriously as it was in the theological community. The document, it would seem, was meant to convey a single message to three audiences: to the bishops of the United States; to those persons who were fearful that women would be ordained to priesthood in the Roman Catholic Church; to those women and men who seemed convinced that it was only a matter of time before Rome would admit women to the ordained priesthood. The message was meant to affirm a position; to allay

fears; and to demonstrate the ineffectiveness of agitation
and pressure.

There is no sign in the document that it had been intended as a scholarly, theologically sophisticated text. That
it was blamed for its failure to be such is regrettable. The
talent and energy expended in its analysis and critique
might have produced, rather, what is desperately needed
today: a definitive, interdisciplinary study that takes Apostolic Tradition seriously; that reflects on the existential
praxis of women throughout the ages; that is credible because of its scholarship and persuasive because of its wisdom (279).

As I hope to show in this present study, it is precisely the
christological dimension of the ministries of preaching, teaching
and healing which has theologically conditioned the *praxis* of the
church in ordaining only men. Any reconsideration of this practice
will have to give serious attention to this tradition which has its
roots in the NT. It is, therefore, as one contribution to the interdisciplinary study called for by Agnes Cunningham that I conceive the
present project. That ministry in the church has its specificity from
the ministry of Christ himself is apparent from John 17:18: "As thou
didst send me into the world, so I have sent them into the world,"
and from John 20:21: "As the Father has sent me, even so I send
you." The primary mission of ministers in the church is from the
Father through the Son. It is this christological dimension of ministry which I wish to examine in this present study.

Methodological Considerations

Historically, it is clear that the ministerial structures of the
early church developed and were largely in place by the beginning
of the third century when all but seven of the twenty-seven books
of the NT attained canonical status. It would be a mistake, therefore,
to affirm that the NT as we know it today governed the shape of
ministry in the church. The development of ministerial structures
in local communities and general adoption of the three-tiered ministry of bishop, presbyters and deacons, as in Ignatius of Antioch
(about 110 C.E.), developed gradually out of a living tradition inherited from the apostles of Jesus Christ, and not on the basis of any
received texts.[11] This point is important because too often far more

weight is given to NT documents in considerations of ministry than is justified by the nature of the texts and the history of the canon.

The structuring of ministry is not the purpose of any NT document except perhaps the pastoral epistles. Yet even the pastoral epistles are not church order documents; they are written as exhortations for Timothy and Titus and include instructions for organizing local communities; they are in no way to be construed as juridical documents. Those responsible for producing the literature which now constitutes the NT of the Christian church were primarily interested in fostering the Christian life in those for whom they wrote. Only indirectly and by the way does this literature reflect the internal structure of these local communities. In the course of this study it will become evident that some form of local leadership existed in all these early Christian communities, but the texts tell us practically nothing about how these leaders were selected and commissioned nor what their precise functions actually were. Biblical scholars, historians and theologians extrapolate from hints in the text and from silence to reconstruct the organization of early Christian communities and the development of church structures in the first and early second centuries, prior to the emergence of the three-tiered ministry which is clearly evident in the letters of Ignatius about 110 C.E.[12] Valuable as these studies are, it must be recognized that they are based on conjecture; they are reconstructed in the light of later organizational patterns in the church and on analogy with modern patterns of social organization; they are not based on unambiguous and contemporary documentary evidence. It is important to keep these limitations of historical research in mind in constructing a theology of ministry on the basis of the NT texts.[13]

While the structures of ministry developed in the first two centuries under the guidance of the Spirit and in accordance with the needs and socio-cultural patterns peculiar to the day, subsequent theological reflection upon ministry in the church was based on the inspired texts of the NT which had been canonized in the meantime. Thus a dialectical relationship arose between the actual practice of ministry and its reflection in the apostolic writings. It is the NT as canon rather than the NT as history which has shaped theological reflection on the ministry.[14]

Consequently, no attempt will be made in the present study to reconstruct the authentic teaching of Jesus on ministry or the historical development of ministry in the first century. The witness of the texts will be examined in the light of contemporary exegesis with the hope of discerning certain theological principles governing the understanding and *praxis* of ministry in the church of Christ. For it is the inspired text in its present form which conditions theological reflection in the church, and not the problematic historical reconstructions of the authentic teaching of Jesus or of the life of the early church.

Every attempt, therefore, will be made to let the texts speak for themselves and no attempt will be made to make them say more than can be justified by the texts themselves. Ultimately it is the *praxis* of the living community of the faithful under the guidance of the Spirit which determines the normative character of the scriptures. In the present time of the "already" and the "not yet," however, the work of the Spirit always needs to be discerned; several criteria come into play in that work of discernment; contemporary needs and experience are certainly among such criteria; the witness of the apostolic churches as reflected in the NT writings is another important criterion. In the Roman Catholic Church the magisterium of the pope and bishops is the final judge of the work of the Spirit in the whole church. My ambition in this study is simply to bring the witness of the NT writings to the fore in a new way in the hope that the christological dimension of ministry may play a larger role in contemporary discussions concerning the shape and structures of ministry in the Roman Catholic Church. While I recognize the need for radical reforms in the structure of ministry, I would not like to see those reforms dictated solely by socio-cultural facts which are operative only in more advanced western societies.

Presuppositions

The critical study of the NT over the past two hundred years has achieved certain results which enjoy a wide consensus among exegetes, historians and theologians. As in any historical discipline which deals with ancient texts, such results are subject to revision in the wake of new criticism and methodologies. On the other hand, theological reflection in the church always rests upon the contemporary state of scientific and historical learning. Although there remain in the church those who still resist the use of historical criticism in exegesis and theology,[15] the intellectual challenge of our day is to integrate the new historical learning into theological reflection upon the faith.

Consequently, in the present study, certain acquired results of biblical criticism will be presupposed. Although the classical two-source theory of synoptic relationships does not resolve all the literary problems and is being challenged from different quarters in contemporary scholarship, it has not yet been replaced and still governs the vast majority of gospel studies. Mark, therefore, will be considered to be the earliest of the canonical gospels and a source for Matthew and Luke. Matthew and Luke are also dependent upon a hypothetical collection of the sayings of Jesus, referred to as "Q," for the material they have in common apart from Mark. "Q" may be dated earlier than Mark. It is likewise presupposed that Matthew and Luke did not know each other's work and that each may have had access to their own written sources, designated "M" and "L" respectively.

It will also be taken for granted that our written gospels are not direct, eyewitness accounts of the life and ministry of Jesus, but reflect a long process of preaching, teaching and pastoral experience in the early church between the time of Jesus' death and resurrection about 30 C.E. and the composition of Mark shortly before or after 70 C.E. The witness of the written gospels is indeed rooted in the eyewitness experience of Jesus' original disciples, but it is refracted through the prisms of post-Easter understanding and the pastoral needs of the communities to which the original message was preached and taught.

As the Pontifical Biblical Commission indicated in its 1964 *Instruction Concerning the Historical Truth of the Gospels*,[16] three stages are to be recognized in the development of the gospel traditions: the first stage is the life and ministry of Jesus; the second stage is the oral preaching and teaching of the apostles, illumined as they were by the experience of the risen Lord and the gift of the Holy Spirit; the third stage is that of the gospel writers themselves who selected from the tradition what was suitable to the needs of their communities and presented it in a manner which they considered effective to attain their pastoral goals. As a consequence of this complex development, the gospels as we read them today are primarily a dialogue between the evangelist and his community; behind the evangelist's text lies a witness to the life and teaching of the early church about Jesus and to the life and teaching of Jesus himself.

The difficulties involved in reconstructing a reliable picture of the historical ministry of Jesus and of his authentic teaching are notorious, but do not need to be discussed here. It may be affirmed, however, that a wide consensus has been reached concerning the basic shape of Jesus' life and ministry, without it being possible to reach consensus concerning the authenticity or non-authenticity of all the sayings attributed to him in the gospel tradition. There is nonetheless a real continuity between the way Jesus was experienced by his first disciples and the way in which he was portrayed in the oral period after the resurrection and in the written gospels.

The eyewitness tradition of the first disciples was nonetheless profoundly affected by the experience of the resurrection and the gift of the Holy Spirit; their knowledge of Jesus has, therefore, been communicated to believers as they came to understand its significance in the light of Jesus' resurrection; the material contained in the gospels is selected out of this enriched tradition according to the pastoral needs of given communities. The way the tradition has been communicated is in itself important for our knowledge of Jesus and for the continuing life of the church living in the presence of the risen Lord and under the guidance of his Spirit.

While our knowledge of the life and ministry of Jesus is totally dependent on gospels written forty to seventy years after his death and resurrection, we have in the authentic letters of Paul documentary evidence about Christian faith and life which can be dated twenty to thirty years after the time of Jesus. The letters of Paul which are universally recognized as authentic, namely, 1 Thessalonians, Galatians, 1 and 2 Corinthians, Philippians, Romans and Philemon, were all written between 50 and 60 C.E. The other NT letters attributed to Paul, namely, Colossians, Ephesians, 2 Thessalonians, 1 and 2 Timothy and Titus, are considered to have been written by disciples of Paul after his death. Such pseudonymity was a way of invoking the authority of Paul and of his teaching to deal with new problems as they arose in the churches founded by him or his co-workers. There is by no means agreement among commentators concerning the authorship and date of these letters; some scholars would still argue for the Pauline authenticity of all these letters; a few more would maintain the Pauline authenticity of Colossians and/or 2 Thessalonians; the deutero-Pauline character of Ephesians and the pastorals is acknowledged by the majority today. These literary judgments do not affect the canonical authority of these writings, but they do condition the chronology of development in the early church. In this study Paul's own thought will be sought only in those letters which are universally accepted as authentic. The witness of the deutero-Paulines will be used to show how Paul's understanding of his ministry continued to affect the tradition of the Pauline churches. This example of tradition at work should help us to understand how the NT tradition as a whole may still inform a contemporary understanding of ministry without requiring a purely juridical or slavish conformity to the past.

The historical value of the Acts of the Apostles as a witness to the life of the early church immediately after Pentecost and to the life and ministry of Paul depends upon how one resolves the question of sources and assesses the way the author's theology and apologetics have affected his presentation of history. In case of conflict between Acts and the authentic letters of Paul, preference will always be given to the letters of Paul. In cases of conflict within Acts itself or with reference to other biblical and non-biblical sources, a judgment must be made in consideration of the literary and ideological purposes of the authors concerned. Where no such contradictions are apparent, there is no reason for not accepting the historical value of Acts, even though in some cases the theological and apologetic purposes of the author may color the way certain data is presented.

With these presuppositions in mind, the witness of the texts themselves may now be approached with the purpose of discovering the way in which the ministry of Jesus himself has affected the understanding of ministry in the church. A first chapter will be devoted to the way in which the ministry of Jesus is presented in the synoptics and in the fourth gospel. A second chapter will deal with the way the gospels portray Jesus sharing his ministry with his disciples, especially with the twelve and the seventy. The third chapter will undertake to synthesize the way Paul considers his own ministry in the authentic letters. In a fourth chapter the attempt will be made to determine what motivates the various provisions for ministry which are reflected in the other writings of the NT. For while no one pattern of church organization emerges from the pages of the NT, certain theological interests will appear to be common to all particular arrangements. It is these common theological interests discovered in the literature of the NT which, to my mind, need to inform all projects for the reformation of ministry in the Roman Catholic Church. In a concluding chapter, therefore, I shall reflect upon the implications of what has been learned for the exercise of ministry, and especially for ordained ministry, in the church today.

I

THE MINISTRY OF JESUS

The English word "ministry" and its cognates "minister" and "to minister" are used to translate the corresponding Greek words *diakonia, diakonos* and *diakoneō* in the NT. The word group conveys the notion of service and is used of all who serve the gospel in any way whatsoever. Only in 1 Tim 3:8, 12 does the personal noun *diakonos* clearly have the technical meaning of a church official, namely, that of the deacon. The technical use of *diakonos* for certain individuals in the church at Philippi (Phil 1:1) and for Phoebe, the *diakonos* at Cenchreae, is still debated among exegetes. The generic sense of service applies in the other twenty-five occurrences of the noun *diakonos* in the NT. Only twice in the gospels does this language of service appear on the lips of Jesus with reference to himself. When a dispute arises among his disciples concerning which of them is the greatest, Jesus asks them in the course of his reply, "For which is the greater, one who sits at table, or one who serves? Is it not the one who sits at table? But I am among you as one who serves" (Luke 22:27). A similar situation occurs when James and John, the sons of Zebedee, seek the places of honor when Jesus comes in his glory; when the other ten become indignant at their ambition Jesus tells them that "the Son of man also came not to be served but to serve, and to give his life as a ransom for many" (Mark 10:45).[1] A third occurrence of the verb *diakoneō* with reference to Jesus may be found in the parable of the master who girds himself and serves his reliable servants (Luke 12:37). In the first two instances Jesus is presenting his own service as an example to the twelve apostles. This evidence in itself is sufficient to justify speaking of the ministry of Jesus and to see in Jesus the paradigm for ministry in the church.

The Mission of Jesus in the Synoptic Gospels

The pattern of Jesus' ministry, as it is presented in the first three gospels, is the fulfillment of a mission from God. He proclaims the coming and the presence of the kingdom of God and calls his contemporaries to repentance.[2] He teaches those who will listen the true understanding of God's will, but insists at the same time that the kingdom of God is above all a new and enabling power which will make this new obedience possible. The healings and the exorcisms which he performs are demonstrations of that power of God. In this way Jesus reveals the triumph of God's kingly rule over all forms of evil, including sin, sickness and death. He himself lives in total fidelity to this new vision of God's kingdom. Because he does so, he faces criticism, opposition and finally death itself. His resurrection is the victory of that power by which he lived. A more detailed examination of synoptic texts will justify this portrait of the ministry of Jesus in the synoptic gospels.

A first, but by no means the only indication of how Jesus' activity is understood and presented by the evangelists is the vocabulary found on the lips of Jesus speaking about himself and his work. The use of the verbs "to send" (apostellō) and "to come" (erchomai) points to a mission which Jesus has from God. The divine necessity which surrounds Jesus' life and destiny is also expressed by the use of the Greek verb dei.

Sufficient notice is not often given to the fact that even in the synoptic gospels Jesus is the one who has been sent by the Father; this idea is regularly considered to be characteristic of the gospel according to John. In Mark, the first of the synoptic gospels and a source for Matthew and Luke, Jesus also refers to God as the one who sent him. "Whoever receives one such child in my name receives me; and whoever receives me, receives not me but him who sent me" (9:37). A similar saying appears in the second synoptic source, "Q"; in Matthew's missionary discourse Jesus says with reference to the twelve: "He who receives you receives me and he who receives me receives him who sent me" (10:40).[3]

Three other sayings of Jesus in the synoptic gospels refer explicitly to his mission from God. In the synagogue at Nazareth he applies to himself the text of Is 61:1–2: "The Spirit of the Lord is upon me, because he has anointed me to preach good news to the poor. He has sent me to proclaim release to the captives and recovery of sight to the blind, to set at liberty those who are oppressed, to proclaim the acceptable year of the Lord" (Luke 4:18–

19). In Luke's presentation of Mark 1:35–38, Jesus replies to the importunate crowds: "I must preach the good news of the kingdom of God to the other cities also; for I was *sent* for this purpose" (4:43). According to Matt 15:24 Jesus rejects the appeals of the Canaanite woman with the words, "I was *sent* only to the lost sheep of the house of Israel."[4] The use of the passive voice in the last two texts implies that it was God who sent Jesus; the so-called "divine" passive was a Jewish circumlocution to avoid naming God. The sending of Jesus by God is expressed allegorically in the parable of the wicked husbandmen (Mark 12:1–12). It is not difficult for the Christian reader to see God behind the owner of the vineyard,[5] the OT prophets behind the servants sent for the fruit, and Jesus behind the beloved son whom the owner sent (12:6) and whom the husbandmen killed (12:8). The reference to Israel's rulers as the husbandmen was certainly not lost on the chief priests, scribes, and elders to whom Jesus was speaking: ". . . for they perceived that he had told the parable against them" (12:12).[6]

The use of the verb "to come" is another indicator of Jesus' mission from God in the synoptic gospels. The sayings in which this verb appears express an inner necessity which is driving Jesus. When Simon and those with him find Jesus at prayer and try to bring him back to the enthusiastic crowds, Jesus replies, "Let us go on to the next towns, that I may preach there also for that is why I *came out*" (Mark 1:38).[7] "I *came* not to call the righteous but sinners" (Mark 2:17).[8] "For the Son of man *came* to seek and save the lost" (Luke 19:10). "Think not that I have *come* to abolish the law and the prophets; I have not *come* to abolish them but to fulfill them" (Matt 5:17). "Do not think that I have *come* to bring peace, but a sword. For I have *come* to set a man against his father, and a daughter against her mother, and a daughter-in-law against her mother-in-law; and a man's foes will be those of his own household" (Matt 10:34–36). "I *came* to cast fire upon the earth; and would that it were already kindled. I have a baptism to be baptized with; and how I am constrained until it is accomplished" (Luke 12:49–50). "For the Son of man *came* not to be served but to serve, and to give his life as a ransom for many" (Mark 10:45).[9] In all these sayings Jesus clearly appears as a man on a mission, without the source of his mission being made clear. The Christian reader, however, easily recognizes how these texts point to the mysterious origin of Jesus and his mission from God.

The verbal form *dei* is another way in which the divine necessity of Jesus' mission is expressed: "I *must* preach the good news of the kingdom of God in the other cities also; for I was sent for this purpose" (Luke 4:43). "And he began to teach them that the Son of man must suffer many things, and be rejected by the elders and the chief priests and the scribes, and be killed, and after three days rise again" (Mark 8:31).[10] The other passion predictions in Mark 9:30–32 and 10:32–34, with their parallels in Matthew and Luke, convey the same notion of necessity but without the use of dei. Similarly in Luke 17:25 the Son of Man "must suffer many things and be rejected by this generation." At the last supper Jesus says to his disciples: "For I tell you that this scripture must be fulfilled in me, 'And he was reckoned with transgressors'; for what is written about me has its fulfillment" (Luke 22:37). In the garden at his arrest Jesus rebukes the disciple who uses force to defend him, referring to the divine necessity of fulfilling the scriptures: "But how then should the scriptures be fulfilled, that it must be so" (Matt 26:54). After the resurrection the same language is used three times in Luke 24 to express the divine necessity of Jesus' suffering as a pathway to glory, once by the two men in the tomb (24:6–7) and twice by the risen Lord himself (24:26, 44–46). The divine necessity that governed Jesus' life was already anticipated in Luke's infancy narrative: "Did you not know that I must be in my Father's house?" (2:49). Even Jesus' visit to the house of Zacchaeus appears to have been under the same necessity: "For I must stay at your house today" (Luke 19:5). Finally, the very place of Jesus' suffering and death was predetermined: "Nevertheless I must go on my way today and tomorrow and the day following; for it cannot be that a prophet should perish away from Jerusalem" (Luke 13:33).

It is evident from these texts that Jesus is presented in the synoptic gospels as a person who lives under a divine necessity to preach the good news of the kingdom of God to the lost sheep of the house of Israel, but especially to the poor; to seek out and to save sinners by bringing them to repentance; and to suffer, die and rise again in Jerusalem.

The Works of Jesus in the Synoptic Gospels

The total picture of Jesus' ministry, however, is not discovered by the examination of pertinent vocabulary alone. The other aspects of his activity may now be considered in the light of this wider mission. Matthew conveniently summarizes the activity of Jesus under three headings, namely, preaching, teaching and healing:[11]

"And he went about all Galilee, *teaching* in their synagogues and *preaching* the gospel of the kingdom and *healing* every disease and infirmity among the people" (4:23).

a) Preaching

The object of Jesus' preaching is clearly the kingdom of God: "Now after John was arrested, Jesus came into Galilee, preaching the gospel of God, and saying, 'The time is fulfilled, and the kingdom of God is at hand; repent and believe in the gospel' " (Mark 1:14–15). In Mark the object or content of Jesus' preaching is not otherwise specified. Matthew reproduces the substance of Mark 1:14–15: "From that time Jesus began to preach, saying, 'Repent, for the kingdom of heaven is at hand' " (4:17) and speaks of "the gospel of the kingdom" in 4:23; 9:35; at 11:5 the words of Jesus "the poor have the gospel preached to them" reflect Is 61:1, but like Mark, Matthew does not further specify the content of this gospel. Luke uses the verb *kēryssō*, "to proclaim as a herald" or "to preach," in parallel with the expression "to bring the good news of the kingdom of God" (*euaggelizomai tēn basileian tou theou*; 8:1).[12]

This parallelism is doubtlessly based on Is 61:1–2 as cited in Jesus' preaching in the synagogue at Nazareth. "The Spirit of the Lord is upon me, because he has anointed me to preach good news to the poor (*euaggelisasthai ptōchos*). He has sent me to proclaim (*kēryxai*) release to the captives and recovery of sight to the blind, to set at liberty those who are oppressed, to proclaim (*kēryxai*) the acceptable year of the Lord" (Luke 4:18–19). In the "Q" saying of Matt 11:4–6 the healing activity of Jesus is closely associated with the preaching of the good news to the poor. Responding to the disciples of John the Baptist, Jesus says, "Go and tell John what you hear and see: the blind receive their sight and the lame walk, lepers are cleansed and the deaf hear, and the dead are raised up, and the poor have good news preached to them. And blessed is he who takes no offense at me." This same connection between the kingdom of God and the healing activity of Jesus is nowhere more clearly expressed than in the "Q" saying of Luke 11:20: "If it is by the finger of God that I cast out demons, then the kingdom of God has come upon you."

All that the gospels tell us about the content of Jesus' preaching may be summed up in three points: 1) the presence of the kingdom of God, 2) the call to repentance or conversion, and 3) the proclamation of release coming from God to all who are oppressed.

b) Healing

As it is implied in Luke 11:20 the exorcisms of Jesus are signs of a new power in the world to overcome the power which the devil exercises over men and women. The parallel text of Matt 12:28 replaces "the finger of God" with "the Spirit of God"; both these expressions refer to the power of God. The same power is manifest in the healing of the sick, the raising of the dead and the forgiveness of sins. When the woman with a hemorrhage touches Jesus' garment and is healed, Jesus is aware that power (dynamis) has gone out from him (Mark 5:30). Introducing the sermon on the plain Luke describes the enthusiastic crowds who come to hear Jesus and to be healed of their diseases: "And all the crowd sought to touch him, for power (dynamis) came forth from him and healed them all" (Luke 6:19). Luke also tells us that it was the power of God which was operative in Jesus' healing activity (5:17).[13] When Jesus raises the widow's son at Nain, the people recognize a visitation from God, but Jesus is seen only as a prophet: "A great prophet has arisen among us! God has visited his people" (Luke 7:16). The common word used in the synoptics for what are commonly called the miracles of Jesus is dynameis, that is, acts of power;[14] according to Luke 19:37, they are occasions for praising God, not Jesus. Herod attributes Jesus' acts of power to John the Baptist raised from the dead (Mark 6:14); the scribes attribute his exorcisms to Beelzebul (Mark 3:22). For the evangelists and the believer, however, the power which is manifest in Jesus' exorcisms and healings is a power that comes from God and is closely associated with the creative power of the Holy Spirit. The parallelism is evident in Luke's narrative of the virginal conception of Jesus: "The Holy Spirit will come upon you and the power of the Most High will overshadow you; therefore the child to be born will be called holy, the Son of God" (1:35). Jesus' very existence is the work of the power and spirit of God; this same power and spirit is manifest in his healing activity.

The forgiveness of sins should also be associated with the healing activity of Jesus as the most important of his healing works. The forgiveness of sins is also an exercise of divine power, but instead of being exercised against the devil, sickness and death, it is exercised against sin itself. This relationship between physical healing and the forgiveness of sins is clearly seen in the healing of the paralytic in Mark 2:1–12: "But that you may know that the Son of man has authority (exousia) on earth to forgive sins—he said to the paralytic—I say to you, rise, take up your pallet and go home" (Mark 2:10).[15] Mark 2:1–12 and Luke 7:36–50 are the only two narratives in the synoptic gospels in which Jesus forgives sins; on both occasions the scribes and Pharisees present are scandalized on the grounds that God alone can forgive sins; Jesus is guilty in their eyes of exercising a divine prerogative. Jesus certainly recognizes the authority of God to forgive sins. This recognition is evident in the prayer which Jesus gives to his disciples (Matt 6:9–13), in his teaching on forgiveness and reconciliation (Mark 11:25; Matt 5:23–26; 6:14–15; 18:21–22), in the parable of the merciless servant (Matt 18:23–35) and in the three parables of the lost sheep, the lost coin and the generous father in Luke 15. In the case of the paralytic and the sinful woman, however, Jesus is exercising that authority himself. This same authority to forgive is also exercised by Jesus when he associates with the toll collectors and sinners before receiving any signs of repentance from them. By eating with them he restores them to the community of God's people from which they were excluded by the self-righteous attitudes of the scribes and Pharisees.[16] Jesus' attitude to those whom correct society disdains never fails to provoke the hostility of the authorities.

The gifts of healing and of forgiveness bear a deeper meaning. On the one hand, they are a response to faith in the power of God present in Jesus, and on the other hand, they are a foreshadowing of eschatological salvation. On four occasions, Jesus says to those whom he heals or forgives, "Your faith has saved you."[17] This connection between physical and spiritual healing on the one hand, and eschatological salvation on the other follows from the way in which the verb sōzō is used for physical healing or for preservation from death,[18] for the forgiveness of sins[19] and for eschatological salvation.[20] In the synoptic gospels Jesus is called "savior" only in Luke 2:11, and the abstract noun sōtēria, "salvation," only appears in an eschatological sense in Luke 1:69, 71, 77 and perhaps in Luke 19:9! Physical healing and the forgiveness of sins are integral parts of that total salvation which Jesus brings and which the prophets had promised for the last days. Healing and forgiveness are therefore signs and first-fruits of the eschatological kingdom of God.

c) Teaching

Teaching is also an exercise of divine power and authority. According to Mark 1:21–28 Jesus is teaching in the synagogue at Capernaum and the people are astonished at his teaching, "for he taught them as one who had authority (*exousia*), and not as the scribes" (1:22). A demoniac enters the synagogue; the evil spirit challenges Jesus but is cast out by Jesus with the words, "Be silent, and come out of him" (1:25). "And they were all amazed, so that they questioned among themselves saying, 'What is this? A new teaching! With authority (*exousia*) he commands even the unclean spirits, and they obey him' " (1:27). The parallel text in Luke adds *dynamis*: "What is this word (*logos*)? For with authority and power he commands the unclean spirits, and they come out" (4:36). These texts imply that the teaching or the word of Jesus has a power to bring about what he commands.

The teaching activity of Jesus receives more emphasis in all three gospels than does his preaching. Indeed, the distinction between preaching and teaching may be a modern one imposed upon the gospel texts.[21] Preaching is a public proclamation to gain attention; the teaching of Jesus is generally offered either in the synagogues or to a group of disciples already disposed to listen; some teaching, such as that contained in the parable of the wicked tenants (Mark 12:1–12) and in the controversy stories, is nonetheless presented to a hostile audience.

"Teacher" is the most common term used by others to address or to refer to Jesus.[22] The content of Jesus' teaching is usually evident from the context. In Mark 1:21–22 Jesus' teaching is contrasted with that of the scribes; this reflection suggests that his teaching concerned the interpretation of the law. This inference is confirmed by Matthew, for he uses Mark 1:21–22 after the sermon on the mount in which Jesus reinterprets the law of Moses and expounds the new righteousness (7:28–29). In the discussions over ritual purity (Mark 7:1–23) Jesus contrasts the true understanding of God's commandment (7:9) with human teachings and commandments (7:7), thereby rejecting the intricacies of the oral law which was so dear to the Pharisees. Under the rubric of teaching Mark presents Jesus repealing the Mosaic provision for divorce and reinstating God's original purpose for marriage (10:1–12).

In the parables Jesus teaches about the kingdom of God. The parables are illustrations of the mystery of the kingdom of God (Mark 4:11); they describe in story form how things happen when

God is in charge. The need to use parables to teach about the kingdom suggests its mysterious character; it cannot be explained, it must be experienced; the story communicates the reality of the kingdom more adequately than straightforward, rational discourse. Mark 4:14 identifies the sower as the one who sows the word (*logos*). The reference must be to Jesus himself, at least in the first instance; the ministry of Jesus is the sowing of the seed of the kingdom. Elsewhere Jesus demonstrates his compassion for the crowds, who were like sheep without a shepherd, by teaching them before feeding them (Mark 6:34); Luke 9:11 tells us that on this occasion Jesus speaks to them about the kingdom of God. Besides feeding the crowd from five loaves and two fish, Matthew (14:14) and Luke (9:11) also record that he heals their sick. Here teaching, healing and feeding are all manifestations of the compassion Jesus shows toward those who are "like sheep without a shepherd" (Mark 6:34). In this way Jesus brings to fulfillment the promises of God contained in Ez 34 to shepherd his people himself.

In the latter half of Mark's gospel Jesus' teaching is directed primarily to his disciples and deals with his forthcoming passion, death and resurrection. This teaching is first presented in Mark 8:31 as a qualification to Peter's confession of Jesus as the Christ; in 8:32 this teaching is referred to simply as "the word" (*ton logon*). Jesus' teaching about little children and the kingdom of God (Mark 10:13–16) and about the dangers of riches (10:17–31) are presented by Mark after Jesus repeals the Mosaic provision for divorce. After cleansing the temple, Jesus teaches, "Is it not written, 'My house shall be called a house of prayer for all the nations'? But you have made it a den of robbers" (Mark 11:17). In speaking this way about the temple Jesus is using words attributed to God in Is 56:7 and Jer 7:11. The text of Jeremiah is part of a call to repentance addressed by the prophet to the people in the temple of Jerusalem. The text of Isaiah is part of an eschatological oracle inviting the foreigners to Jerusalem to worship God; the Jerusalem temple of Jesus' day excluded Gentiles from the inner courts under pain of death.[23]

Finally, there is a concentrated presentation of Jesus' teaching in the temple addressed to the authorities in contemporary Judaism (Mark 11:27—12:44). The authority of Jesus is at issue from the very beginning of his teaching in Jerusalem. The chief priests and the scribes and the elders, that is, the membership of the Sanhedrin, ask Jesus by what authority (*exousia*) he acts (Mark 11:28),[24] and who gave him this authority. The question is a juridical one and is asked by the supreme authority in contemporary Judaism. By asking them about John's baptism Jesus turns the question into a theological one about discernment between divine authority and human authority: "Was the baptism of John from heaven or from men?" (Mark 11:30). The people already acknowledged the divine authority of John by holding him to be a real prophet (11:32). The popular reaction to Jesus was that he too was a prophet, that is, someone in whom the power of God was active. On the occasion of the raising of the widow's son at Nain, "Fear seized them all; and they glorified God, saying, 'A great prophet has arisen among us!' and 'God has visited his people' " (Luke 7:16). "To glorify God" is to recognize God as the source of Jesus' power and authority. All three synoptic gospels testify to the fact that the people attributed Jesus' healing activity to God (Mark 2:12; Matt 15:31; Luke 5:25–26; 13:13; 18:43; 19:37). Jesus agrees with this assessment when he responds to the Samaritan leper: "Was no one found to return and give praise to God except this foreigner" (Luke 17:18). By refusing to answer Jesus' question the members of the Sanhedrin show their unwillingness to admit the truth, namely, that God does not speak only through them.

The parable of the wicked husbandmen is a judgment upon the authority of the Sanhedrin and they recognize it to be such (Mark 12:1–12). In the matter of tribute to Caesar Jesus foils the attempt of the Pharisees and their counterparts, the Herodians, to enlist him for their respective causes (Mark 12:13–17). In teaching the Sadducees about the resurrection Jesus reminds them of the power (*dynamis*) of God, the same power that was at work in Jesus' own miracles (*dynameis*; Mark 12:18–27). Responding to the scribe about the first commandment, Jesus cuts through the casuistry of the schools and affirms the primacy of the two commandments of love, love of God and love of neighbor (Mark 12:28–34). The riddle about the messiah and David's son is a challenge to the adequacy of their exegetical principles (Mark 12:35–37), indeed the adequacy of any text to express the mystery of the messiah's identity. Finally, Jesus contrasts the self-righteous piety of the scribes with the self-sacrificing piety of the widow (Mark 12:38–44).

Matthew emphasizes the role of Jesus as a teacher in the five great discourses which are the primary literary feature of his gospel. Luke also highlights the teaching activity of Jesus in the ways he handles his sources in Mark and "Q". The healing of the paralytic and the forgiveness of sins is set by Luke in a context of teaching (5:17–26). Healing on the sabbath is presented by Luke as an example of teaching (6:6–11; 13:10–17); Jesus responds to his disciples' request, "Lord, teach us to pray, as John taught his disciples" (11:1). Here Luke includes not only the Lord's prayer but other material from "Q" and the narrative of the friend at midnight (11:1–13). Other "Q" material is presented as teaching in Luke 13:22–30. It is clearly in the context of teaching that Jesus enters into conflict with the religious authorities of Judaism. The formation Jesus gives his disciples will be discussed explicitly later. As presented in the synoptic gospels, however, the teaching of Jesus is more than formal instruction about the proper interpretation of the law of Moses and about the kingdom of God; his healing activity and his personal example are also presented as forms of teaching.

Another important aspect of Jesus' teaching activity is his constant effort to direct people's attention not to himself but to the Father and to foster obedience to the Father's will. Jesus is not the proper object of faith in the synoptic gospels. "These little ones who believe in me" (Matt 18:6) is the only textually certain saying of Jesus in which he himself is the object of the verb "to believe."[25] The context of Matthew's community discourse suggests that this form of the saying is the work of the early church. Faith is generally associated with Jesus' healing activity in the synoptic gospels, but in these cases neither the noun nor the verb has an object.[26] Jesus indeed asks the two blind men, "Do you believe that I am able to do this?" (Matt 9:28), but he does not ask for faith in his own person. In the healing narratives the implied object of faith is not Jesus but God and the kingdom of God present in Jesus.

After calming the storm at sea Jesus challenges the faith of his disciples: "Have you no faith?" but they said to each other, "Who then is this, that even wind and sea obey him?" (Mark 4:40–41); it is more likely that Jesus is asking about faith in the power of God to protect them from danger. In Mark's narrative of the withered fig tree the faith that works wonders is explicitly said to be faith in God: "Have faith in God (pistin theou)" (11:22). The object of the verb "to believe" in Luke's interpretation of the parable of the sower is implicitly "the word of God" (8:11–15). In the parallel text of Matthew the seed is interpreted as "the word of the kingdom" (13:19). In Mark the teaching of Jesus is often referred to simply as "the word" (ho logos; 2:2; 4:13–20; 8:32). Luke prefers the expression "the word of God" (5:1; 8:11, 21; 11:28). This identification of Jesus' word with the word of God and the word of the kingdom is clear from the interpretation of the parable of the sower. In other synoptic texts the words of Jesus are treated as if they had the authority of the word of God; for example, the saying of Jesus in Mark

13:31, "Heaven and earth will pass away but my words will not pass away," recalls Is 40:8: "The grass withers, the flower fades; but the word of our God will stand for ever."[27] When asked by the Sanhedrin whether he is the Christ, Jesus answers, "If I tell you, you will not believe" (Luke 22:67); here the object of the verb is implicitly the teaching of Jesus, not his person. In Luke 24:25 the object of the verb "to believe" is "all that the prophets have spoken." In short, according to the synoptic gospels Jesus does not call for faith in his own person, but rather for faith in God and in the power of the kingdom operative in his words and deeds.

Throughout the synoptic gospels Jesus' teaching is characterized by the primacy he gives to God, his will and his kingdom. Jesus does not proclaim himself, but God his Father. The clearest expression of this fact is to be found in the narrative of the rich young man. According to Mark, who is followed here by Luke, he addresses Jesus with the words "Good teacher," but Jesus replies, "Why do you call me good? No one is good but God alone" (Mark 10:18 = Luke 18:19). In the controversy over the ritual laws of purity Jesus shows that his primary interest is the proper understanding and fulfillment of the commandments of God (Mark 7:8–13).

After the first prediction of the passion and Peter's protestations Jesus does not rebuke him for not understanding himself, but for not giving his prime attention to the things of God (Mark 8:33). In the same vein, "You cannot serve God and mammon" (Matt 6:24). The prohibition of divorce is rooted in the fact that it is God himself who has united a man and a woman in marriage (Mark 10:9). It is only by the power of God that Jesus' disciples will be able to follow his teaching and be saved (Mark 10:26–27). It is the power of God that makes resurrection possible (Mark 12:24). Nor does Jesus let family relationships, even those with his mother, interfere with the primacy of God's will in his life (Mark 3:31–35). He places the highest value on those disciples who both hear the word of God and keep it. In Luke 11:27–28 Jesus may very well imply that his mother fulfills those conditions, but blood relationship alone does not give anyone a claim upon Jesus. The same point is made to the false prophets who claim a special relationship to Jesus at the judgment: "Not every one who says to me, 'Lord, Lord,' shall enter the kingdom of heaven, but he who does the will of my Father who is in heaven" (Matt 7:21).[28]

The sermon on the mount (Matt 5—7) in its entirety is an instruction on the true understanding of the will of God. Radical obedience to the will of God is a new righteousness which surpasses the observance of the scribes and Pharisees (5:20). The reinterpretations of the law of Moses in Matt 5:21–48 are illustrations of the new righteousness.[29] The good works of almsgiving, prayer and fasting are not to be performed with a view to human praise or recognition, but solely for the Father who is in heaven (6:1–6, 16–18). Faith in the Father's care should remove anxiety (6:25–34) and inspire confidence in prayer (7:7–11). The so-called "golden rule" (7:12) sums up the law and the prophets; later in Matt 22:34–40 it is the twofold commandment of love which sums up the law and the prophets; in this latter case the primacy is given to the love of God.[30] In short, in the sermon on the mount, Jesus calls all his disciples to live as sons and daughters of their Father in heaven (Matt 5:44–48) and to perform good works in such a way that others will acknowledge the Father in heaven (Matt 5:16). Later, in the controversy over taxes to Caesar Jesus is recognized, albeit ironically, as one who truly teaches the way of God, and in his reply he affirms the prior claims of God (Mark 12:13–17).

Jesus is not satisfied only to teach his disciples the primacy of God and of his kingdom in their lives. He demonstrates by his own life the centrality of God and of his will. He does not falter before the objections of the scribes and Pharisees or of the Sadducees. He defends the practices of his disciples against their criticism. His personal devotion to the Father is best illustrated in his own practice of prayer. The prayer of Jesus is noted in Mark and Matthew, but it is especially highlighted in Luke.[31] It is Jesus' commitment to the will of God as he understands it that eventually leads to his death. Even when he comes face to face with the prospect of suffering and dying for his commitment he prays, "Not what I will, but what thou wilt" (Mark 14:36). Consequently, the kingly rule of God is the central object of Jesus' ministry as preacher, healer and teacher and the primary motivation of his personal life.

Authority in Jesus' Ministry

In the course of examining the way the synoptic gospels present the preaching, healing and teaching of Jesus, it has become apparent that in these activities he is exercising power and authority. The Greek word used for this authority in the synoptic gospels is *exousia*. The word is not reserved exclusively to the divine power or authority given to Jesus. It is used of the authority of the devil (Luke 4:6; 22:53). It is also used of any political authority, be it the authority of kings or governors (Luke 12:11; 20:20; 23:7), military officers (Matt 8:9) or commissioned slaves (Mark 13:34; Luke 19:17). Analogously we are dealing with the same type of authority,[32] even though Jesus insists that whatever authority is to be exercised by any of his disciples be exercised in the same way that he does, that is, in service. "Whoever will be great among you will be your servant (*diakonos*), and whoever would be first among you must be slave (*doulos*) of all. For the Son of man also came not to be served but to serve, and to give his life as a ransom for many" (Mark 10:45). "I am among you as one who serves (*ho diakonōn*)" (Luke 22:27).[33] Jesus thereby establishes himself as the paradigm for the exercise of all authority and ministry in the church.

At the same time, however, it is not a personal power or authority that is at work in Jesus in the synoptic gospels. It is the power of God and of his kingdom breaking into the world through the ministry of Jesus. The object of faith is not the person of Jesus nor his identity, but rather the power of the kingdom present in Jesus. The good news of the kingdom is simply the power of God to overcome evil and to give life. Paul offers a similar definition of the gospel in Rom 1:16: "For I am not ashamed of the gospel: it is the power of God for salvation to every one who has faith, to the Jew first and also to the Greek." In Jesus it was the same power of God that ultimately raised him from the dead, thus vindicating his own understanding of commitment to the cause of God and at the same time revealing the eschatological salvation which God had promised to his people in the law and the prophets.

The Mission of Jesus in the Fourth Gospel

The striking contrast between the synoptic gospels and the gospel according to John has been noticed at least from the time of Clement of Alexandria in the third century. At first sight it would appear that the portrait of Jesus in the fourth gospel is incompatible with that of the synoptics. On closer examination, however, many of the synoptic themes appear in John in a different key. The most obvious difference is the way in which the fourth gospel focuses on the person of Jesus rather than on the proclamation of the kingdom of God; the phrase "the kingdom of God" appears only twice in John (3:3, 5) compared to fifty times in the synoptics. Already in the fourth gospel the proclaimer has become the proclaimed.[34] Nonetheless, this emphasis on the person of Jesus is always in relationship to and in dependence upon the Father; more prominently than in the synoptics, Jesus is "the one sent by the Father."[35]

The Greek verbs used to express Jesus' mission from the Father are *apostellō* and *pempō*. *Apostellō* always appears in a finite form[36] and *pempō* generally as an active participle.[37] God for Jesus is simply "the Father who sent me." The proverb of John 13:16 could apply equally to Jesus and to the disciples: "A servant is not greater than his master; nor is he who is sent (*apostolos*) greater than he who sent (*pempsantos*) him."[38] Jesus also makes it clear that his mission is to do the will of the Father who sent him.[39] This will of the Father is explained in John 6:39–40: "This is the will of him who sent me, that I should lose nothing of all that he has given me, but raise it up at the last day. For this is the will of my Father, that everyone who sees the Son and believes in him should have eternal life; and I will raise him up on the last day." In John 10:10 it is phrased somewhat differently: "I came that they may have life, and have it abundantly." The most succinct expression of the Father's will is found in John 12:50: "His commandment is eternal life."

The verb "to come" also appears in John as an indicator of Jesus' mission from God. Nicodemus recognizes Jesus as a teacher *come* from God (3:2). He is presented as the light that has *come* into the world (3:19; 12:46). He is the one who has *come* from above or from heaven (3:31). He has not *come* for judgment, but for the salvation of the world (12:47; 3:17).[40] "I *came* that they may have life, and have it abundantly" (10:10). He has *come* in the name of his Father (5:43). After the multiplication of the loaves he is recognized by the crowd as the prophet who is *coming* into the world (6:14). He did not *come* on his own, but on the authority of the one who sent him (7:28–29); indeed, he *came forth* from God in a saving role (8:42).[41] Jesus knows where he *came* from and where he is going (8:14). Martha confesses Jesus as the Christ who is to *come* into the world (11:27). Anticipating his passion Jesus himself declares that he *came* to this hour in order to glorify the Father's name (12:27–28). He told Pilate that he *came* into the world to bear witness to the truth; only in that sense is he really a king (18:37). In short, Jesus *comes* from God (13:3) and he returns to God (16:27–30; 17:8) to give life to all who believe in him.

The language of "sending" and "coming" can, of course, be used to describe the mission of any OT prophet. Indeed it is also used to describe the mission of John the Baptist (John 1:6, 33; 3:28). Prophets, too, speak the words of God. What distinguishes Jesus from the prophets and from John the Baptist is his claim to have come down from heaven (John 3:13, 31; 6:33–58). This claim is precisely the cause of Jewish murmuring in John 6:41. The claim is also associated with the title "Son of man" (John 3:13; 6:27, 53, 62).

Salvation and Eternal Life

Elsewhere in the fourth gospel Jesus' mission is described as the salvation of the world (John 3:17; 4:42), speaking the words of God (John 3:34) and completing the works the Father has given him (John 4:34; 5:36; 9:4). The work which the Father has given Jesus is best described as giving eternal life to those who believe in him; to possess eternal life is salvation in the fourth gospel. That eternal life is described by the evangelist as the knowledge of God and of Jesus Christ whom he has sent.[42] Jesus' devotion to the will of the Father is even more prominent in John than in the synoptic gospels.[43] The paradox of John's presentation of Jesus is that his dependence on the Father in his teaching, his words, his works and his action is as prominent as his equality with the Father.[44] Jesus recognizes that his very own life is the Father's gift (John 5:26; 6:57). More specifically, the work the Father gave him involves the laying down of his very own life; this self-giving is the Father's commandment for Jesus (John 10:18; 12:50; 14:31). The Father's love for Jesus is rooted precisely in his readiness to lay down his life for his sheep (John 10:17). Yet Jesus is able to accomplish this work because of the authority (exousia) he has received from God (John 10:18; 17:2; 5:27). In his death and resurrection Jesus reveals his own love for his friends (John 15:13), but also the Father's love for himself (John 17:23, 26). It can be said that eternal life is the commandment Jesus received from the Father (John 12:50) because by his death and resurrection he hands on to his disciples the same life and love which the Father has in himself and which he bestows on Jesus (John 5:26; 6:57; 15:9–10).

Included among the works of Jesus in the fourth gospel are the miracles or what the evangelist prefers to call "signs" (sēmeia). In the synoptic gospels the so-called miracles were acts of power (dynameis) demonstrating the presence of the kingdom of God in the activity of Jesus. In John they are signs which point to the glory of God revealed in Jesus (2:11; 11:4, 40; 1:14). In this way Jesus is identified with the new temple as the new place of God's presence and action in the world (John 2:19, 21; 4:21–24).

The Object of Faith

In striking contrast to the synoptic gospels where the object of faith is the power or kingdom of God present and active in Jesus, the object of faith in John is almost exclusively Jesus himself. The noun "faith" (*pistis*) does not appear; the verbal formula "to believe in" (*pisteuō eis*) is characteristic of John;[45] it has Jesus as its object thirty-four out of thirty-six times. In the other two cases faith in Jesus is parallel to and practically identical with faith in God (John 12:44; 14:1).[46] This characteristic formula, with the Greek preposition *eis* followed by the accusative case, connotes commitment to the person of Jesus, and not simply acceptance of his formal teaching. Of the thirty cases where the verb appears absolutely, in practically all cases the context suggests that Jesus is the personal object of faith, not just his words or his teaching but his very self.[47] God himself is clearly the object of the verb in only three cases.[48] When followed by a *hoti* clause, the act of faith regularly concerns Jesus and his relationship to the Father.[49] This unity of Jesus with the Father as an object of faith is more clearly expressed in texts such as John 12:44–45: "He who believes in me, believes not in me, but in him who sent me. And he who sees me sees him who sent me"; and 14:9: "He who has seen me has seen the Father." In this Johannine context, the synoptic-type saying of John 13:20 takes on added meaning: "He who receives anyone whom I send receives me; and he who receives me, receives not me but him who sent me." This last text has three parallels in the synoptic gospels: "Whoever receives one such child in my name receives me; and whoever receives me, receives not me but him who sent me" (Mark 9:37). "He who receives you receives me, and he who receives me receives him who sent me" (Matt 10:40). "He who hears you hears me, and he who rejects you rejects me, and he who rejects me rejects him who sent me" (Luke 10:16).[50] Salvation and eternal life depend upon the recognition of this relationship between Jesus and the Father: "He who hears my word and believes him[51] who sent me has eternal life; he does not come to judgment, but has passed from death to life" (John 5:24). A similar idea is expressed in the text of Matt 11:6: "Blessed is he who takes no offense at me"; and in the parallel text of Luke 12:8–9 and Matt 10:32–33, in which future judgment is dependent upon reception of Jesus in the present.

Only in the "Q" saying of Matt 11:27 and Luke 10:22 does Jesus appear explicitly in the synoptic gospels as one who reveals the

Father: "All things have been delivered to me by my Father; and no one knows the Son except the Father, and no one knows the Father except the Son and any one to whom the Son chooses to reveal him" (Matt 11:27). The ideas expressed in this "Q" saying are developed extensively in the fourth gospel; the absolute use of "the Father" and "the Son" is characteristic of John's gospel:[52] "the Father" appears absolutely seventy-nine times;[53] "the Son" is used absolutely of Jesus sixteen times; the expressions appear in direct relation to one another seven times.[54] The same relationship is referred to some sixteen times elsewhere in the gospel but the expression used for "the Father" is either "my Father" (fourteen times),[55] God (3:17), or simply "you" (17:1, 2, 4 etc.). Jesus justifies his life-giving activity on the sabbath by claiming that the Father bestowed on the Son the divine prerogative of giving life and of judging (5:17–30). The closest Johannine parallel to the "Q" saying of Matt 11:27 is to be found in 5:21: "For as the Father raises the dead and gives them life, so also the Son gives life to whom he will." For John the life-giving activity of Jesus is his revelation of the Father, and it reaches its climax in his glorification. Jesus also maintains that the divine quality of his works is rooted in the union of the Father and the Son: ". . . believe the works that you may know and understand that the Father is in me and I am in the Father" (10:38).[56]

The presentation of Jesus in the fourth gospel is dominated by the conviction, already suggested in the "Q" saying of Matt 11:27, that Jesus as the Son reveals the Father. In the fourth gospel this conviction carries with it an eschatological dimension. The vision and/or the knowledge of God is an eschatological good. "Philip said to him, 'Lord, show us the Father, and we shall be satisfied' " (14:8). In Ex 33:18 Moses addressed a similar request to God: "I pray thee, show me thy glory." In the OT it was understood that no one could see God and live.[57] Nonetheless, certain individuals like Jacob, Moses, Manoah and his wife, Elijah, Isaiah and Ezekiel approached such a vision without incurring death.[58] This same conviction is expressed in the fourth gospel;[59] but since Jesus himself has seen the Father (John 6:46b) and knows the Father (John 7:29; 8:19, 55), he alone is in a position to offer a vision or knowledge of God that does not bring death, but eternal life. This knowledge or vision comes through faith in Jesus (John 6:40); it requires the drawing of the Father (John 6:44), but this drawing power is revealed in the "lifting up" of Jesus (John 12:32). He is both the door of the sheep (John 10:7–10) and the way to the Father (John 14:6–7). The glory of Jesus is also the glory of the Father (John 1:14); it is to this same glory that he wants to introduce his disciples (John 12:26; 17:24). In the Matthaean parable of the last judgment, the glorious Son of man (25:31) invites the sheep, "Come, O blessed of my Father, inherit the kingdom prepared for you from the foundation of the world" (25:34). The theological reality behind both texts is identical.

In the synoptic gospels the object of faith is the kingdom of God present in Jesus; there Jesus heals both bodily and moral ills in response to this faith; such healings are proleptic tokens of eschatological salvation: "Your faith has saved you." In the fourth gospel Jesus himself is the object of faith and he offers to those who believe in him a vision and/or knowledge of God which, far from bringing death, is the gift of eternal life (John 17:3) now and resurrection on the last day (John 6:39, 40, 44, 54). In both the synoptics and in John, though in different ways, Jesus is presented as the source of eschatological salvation through faith.

General Conclusion

This examination of the synoptic gospels and of John has shown that Jesus is on a mission from God. In the synoptics this mission consists in preaching the coming of God's kingdom, in teaching about its nature, its demands and its fruits, and in inaugurating that kingdom by moral and bodily healing. Jesus' teaching is tantamount to a new revelation of the will of God; this revelation is not new in the sense of being other than the Mosaic law; it is new because it involves a more radical understanding of God's will than the understanding that was being mediated in contemporary Judaism: "Unless your righteousness exceeds that of the scribes and Pharisees, you will never enter the kingdom of heaven" (Matt 5:20). The healing activity of Jesus is a partial revelation of the power of God to destroy the effects of sin in human society. Like the prophets of the OT, Jesus issues an urgent call to repentance and an invitation to faith in the eschatological kingdom of God; the power of God's rule or kingdom is already breaking into the world in Jesus' threefold ministry of preaching, teaching and healing. Jesus sees his own life as one that is totally lived under the power of that rule of God. The purpose of his ministry is to win his listeners for the Father and to teach and empower them to live as "the sons of your Father who is in heaven" (Matt 5:45).

In one "Q" text of the synoptics (Matt 11:27) Jesus' ministry is presented as a revelation of the Father by the Son. The fourth gospel offers a similar description of Jesus' ministry but in a totally different key. The synoptic emphasis on the kingdom of God is replaced by Jesus' gift of eternal life to those who believe in his own person. This gift of eternal life is the knowledge and vision of God. This knowledge and vision are accompanied by an obedience to and dependence on God's will which is totally manifest in the Son because of his personal relationship to the Father. Jesus' gift of eternal life is an eschatological good because it makes available in the present a knowledge and vision of God never before accessible to humankind in general. Jacob, Moses, Manoah and his wife, Elijah, Isaiah and Ezekiel approached a vision of God without incurring death. Jesus' gift is a vision of God which is eternal life.

The power of God's kingdom that was at work in Jesus' ministry on earth brought Jesus to his personal fulfillment in the resurrection and the ascension. In Johannine terms the glory which Jesus revealed through his works and signs during the public ministry reached its culmination in Jesus' hour, the hour of his glorification and exaltation to the Father through the cross. In his risen or glorified state Jesus has become the source of power to bring others into the same state as himself. That power is otherwise spoken of as the Holy Spirit. As risen Lord, however, Jesus is no longer visible to subsequent generations. It is clear from the fourth gospel that the gift of the Holy Spirit, the Paraclete or Spirit of truth, to the disciples was intended by Jesus to guarantee the continuity of his own ministry: ". . . he will bear witness to me; and you also are witnesses, because you have been with me from the beginning" (John 15:26–27); "He will glorify me, for he will take what is mine and declare it to you" (John 16:14).[60] These texts about the Paraclete make it abundantly clear that Jesus intends his own personal ministry to continue in his disciples. Provision for the continuation of that ministry is the next object of this investigation.

II

THE MINISTRY OF JESUS' DISCIPLES

The purpose of this chapter is to examine the ways in which the gospels portray Jesus providing for the continuation of his own mission from the Father. The most explicit texts to this effect are found in the fourth gospel. In the course of his prayer at the last supper Jesus says, "As thou didst send me into the world, so I have sent them into the world" (John 17:18). Later after the resurrection Jesus appears to the disciples and says to them, "Peace be with you. As the Father has sent me, even so I send you" (John 20:21). In the synoptic gospels the mission of Jesus' disciples is clarified by the way in which Jesus chooses the twelve and empowers them to carry on his own mission of preaching, healing and teaching. The commissioning of the twelve by Jesus is certainly a paradigm for ministry in the church. What is more difficult to establish on the basis of the biblical texts alone is whether this empowering by Jesus is restricted to a small group of his disciples or whether it belongs indiscriminately to all the disciples.

The Identity of Jesus' Disciples

All four gospels show people responding to Jesus in different ways. Even among those who respond positively there is considerable diversity. The largest group is the crowds.[1] Outside the passion narratives their response is generally favorable,[2] although there is some evidence of division among them, especially in the fourth gospel.[3] The crowds are regularly distinguished from Jesus' disciples,[4] but there is no indication of their numbers except in the feeding narratives: In the first feeding narrative the crowd numbers five thousand men (*andres*; Mark 6:44); in the second feeding narrative the number is four thousand (Mark 8:9); in both cases Matthew adds that women and children are not included in these figures (14:21; 15:38). Since there is a legendary element in these numbers, no certain conclusions can be based on them. Luke speaks twice (6:17; 19:37) of a large crowd of disciples, but does not specify any number. This intimation of a large group of disciples would be confirmed if it were certain that the division among the disciples which is recorded in John 6:66 took place within the public ministry of Jesus; it has been cogently suggested that this text reflects rather a division of Christians within the Johannine community over the understanding of the eucharist.[5] Luke does not identify the acquaintances of Jesus who witness the crucifixion (23:49) but they certainly include more than the women from Galilee.[6] The presence of about one hundred and twenty, including women, in the upper room after Jesus' ascension (Acts 1:12–15) is the only evidence we have of the actual number of Jesus' disciples either before or after the crucifixion. It is nonetheless clear that the disciples are a larger group than either the twelve mentioned in all the gospels or the seventy mentioned in Luke 10:1.

There is likewise no way of knowing whether all these disciples were personally called by Jesus as were Peter, Andrew, James, John, Levi (Matthew), Philip, Nathanael and the second, anonymous disciple mentioned in John 1:35–40.[7] Vocation narratives appear in all the gospels toward the beginning of Jesus' public ministry.[8] The stylizing of these narratives, with little historical or psychological information, suggests that they are intended by the evangelists as paradigms of Christian discipleship for their own communities. Discipleship of Jesus is not a matter of personal initiative but a response to a call from Jesus. The Gerasene demoniac wants to accompany Jesus but is sent by Jesus on another mission (Mark 5:18–20); perhaps he is to prepare the post-Easter Gentile mission—the time of Jesus' public ministry is the time of Jewish privilege.[9] The rich man in Mark 10:17–22 rejects Jesus' call because he is not prepared to part with his riches. The sayings on discipleship collected in Matt 8:19–22 and Luke 9:57–62 indicate that following Jesus may mean different things for different individuals: For one, to follow Jesus means accepting the itinerant life of Jesus (Matt 8:19–20); for another, Jesus' call involves the severing of family ties (Luke 9:61–62); for yet another who is already a disciple, the following of Jesus requires neglecting a solemn obligation of religion and piety, namely, burying his very own father (Matt 8:21–22)![10]

These examples show that discipleship is not a purely personal decision. It is primarily a response to a call. Would-be disciples must at least be accepted by Jesus, but must also be prepared to change personal plans because Jesus does not hesitate to impose conditions upon those who would follow him. General conditions of discipleship are presented elsewhere throughout the gospels. "If any man would come after me, let him deny himself and take up his cross and follow me. For whoever would save his life will lose it; and whoever loses his life for my sake and for the gospel's will save it" (Mark 8:34–35). "If any one comes to me and does not hate his own father and mother and wife and children and brothers and sisters, yes, and even his own life, he cannot be my disciple. Whoever does not bear his own cross and come after me, cannot be my disciple . . . whoever of you does not renounce all that he has cannot be my disciple" (Luke 14:25–27, 33). "Every one who acknowledges me before men, I also will acknowledge before my Father who is in heaven; but whoever denies me before men, I also will deny before my Father who is in heaven" (Matt 10:32–33). "No one who puts his hand to the plough and looks back is fit for the kingdom of God" (Luke 9:62). According to Mark 8:34 and Luke 14:25 these conditions are presented to the crowds as well as to the disciples. Luke emphasizes the radical and enduring character of the renunciation demanded by Jesus by his use of the word "all" in 5:11, 28 and 14:33 and by referring to the daily cross in 9:23.[11] The effective renunciation Peter speaks of in Mark 10:28 was probably limited to the twelve during the public ministry of Jesus, but has become a paradigm for the disciple in the life of the church.[12]

The Disciples and the Twelve

In the synoptic gospels and in John the verb "to follow" (akoloutheō) is used in the ordinary spatial sense of both crowds and disciples,[13] but also of the personal commitment which is proper to the following of Jesus as a disciple.[14] In some cases the spatial use carries with it the symbolic sense of discipleship.[15] The committed followers of Jesus are called "disciples" (mathētēs) in all the gospels, but outside the gospels the word only appears in the Acts of the Apostles, where it is used as a designation for Christians.[16] The group of Jesus' disciples is obviously wider than the twelve.

From this larger group of disciples Jesus chooses twelve for special tasks during his earthly ministry,[17] but it is practically impossible to discern in the gospels when Jesus is speaking to all his disciples in general and when he is speaking only to the twelve with reference to their special tasks. The twelve are generally referred to as *hoi dōdeka*.[18] Only Matthew uses the expression "the twelve disciples."[19] Luke refers to the twelve as "the apostles."[20] In some cases the text, the context or some other clue indicates that only the twelve are being addressed by Jesus. The first clear case is the missionary discourse in Mark 6:7–13 and the parallel texts in Matt 10:1–42 and Luke 9:1–6; some of the sayings in Matthew's discourse, however, apply to disciples in general and not exclusively to the twelve as missionaries.[21] A second case in which the twelve are exclusively involved is in the narratives of the feeding of the crowds. The matter is clear for the first narrative from the reference to the apostles in Mark 6:30 and Luke 9:10; Luke specifies "the twelve" in 9:12; it can therefore be legitimately inferred that Matthew's use of *mathētai* in 14:15 likewise refers to the twelve; the twelve baskets of fragments may be an additional confirmation of the exclusive role of the twelve. Since the second narrative is a doublet of the first, the term "disciples" in this narrative should also be understood of the twelve.[22] Third, it is also clear from the synoptic gospels that it is exclusively the twelve who share the last supper with Jesus and are present for the institution of the eucharist.[23] In addition, the instruction on true greatness (Mark 9:33–37), the third prediction of the passion (Mark 10:32–34 = Luke 18:31–34 = Matt 20:17–19) and the instruction on the exercise of authority (Mark 10:35–45 = Matthew 20:20–28)[24] are addressed explicitly to the twelve. The "Q" saying about the twelve thrones (Matt 19:28 = Luke 22:28–30) is obviously directed only to the twelve.[25] According to Matt 28:16–20 the risen Jesus gives the universal teaching mission to the eleven—that is, the twelve less Judas—in virtue of the fullness of authority (*exousia*) which has been given to him.

The situation is not so clear in the fourth gospel. The twelve are only mentioned directly once (6:66–71); they are the disciples who have been especially chosen by Jesus and appear to be the only ones who remain with him after the crisis in Galilee. At the narrative level, therefore, it should probably be understood that they are Jesus' only companions at the last supper and the only witnesses to his resurrection appearances in 20:19–29.[26]

Given this ambiguity in the texts, it must be recognized that it is not always possible, from an exegetical point of view, to discern adequately those instructions which Jesus gives to the twelve as disciples and those which he gives to them precisely as leaders among his disciples. The juridical questions raised subsequently in the church do not preoccupy the evangelists. Matthew's peculiar expression "the twelve disciples" may suggest that the leadership role of the twelve presupposes the fact that they are first of all disciples. What is addressed to them should, therefore, be understood as addressed to all the disciples of Jesus, except where the context and the content of the text clearly point to a leadership role involving responsibility for other disciples of Jesus; this is obviously the case in the instruction on the exercise of authority (Matt 20:20–28). The exclusive presence of the twelve with Jesus at the feeding of the crowds implies a leadership role; this role is made explicit in the first feeding narrative by Jesus' words, "You give them something to eat" (Mark 6:37). By placing the instructions of Jesus on the proper use of authority and the saying about the thrones of judgment within the narrative of the last supper (Luke 22:24–30), Luke indicates that the twelve are present at the last supper and at the institution of the eucharist not simply as disciples but in a leadership capacity. The words of Jesus addressed to Simon in Luke 22:31–34 explicitly involve some form of responsibility with respect to the others at table with them. In the instructions about the swords (Luke 22:35–38) Jesus refers to the earlier mission of the twelve and prepares them for a subsequent mission. In this context Luke's addition to the words over the bread, "Do this in remembrance of me" (22:19), clearly makes the twelve responsible for repeating what Jesus did at the last supper.

It is clear from the gospel texts that Jesus chooses the twelve out of a larger group of disciples to exercise leadership in the community of his disciples. On the other hand, the twelve chosen by Jesus had previously answered the call to discipleship. Moreover, the leadership for which they are chosen by Jesus is to be exercised as a service of the disciples and not according to the pattern of secular authority. In such a situation, both disciples and leaders should share the same goals, namely, the continuation of the mission of Jesus. These exegetical considerations alone, however, are not sufficient of themselves to explain texts such as Matt 18:18 and John 20:23,[27] nor to resolve later doctrinal and juridical questions associated with specialized ministry in the church. Such questions can only be resolved by the actual practice of the Spirit-guided community of faith.

The Commissioning of the Twelve

The mission texts of the public ministry of Jesus and the mission instructions of the risen Jesus are the places to seek Jesus' own provisions for the continuation of his work among his disciples as well as his understanding of the relationship of their ministry to his. Even though it is not always exegetically possible to determine the authenticity of all these instructions, nonetheless they do bear witness to the way the early church and the evangelists viewed the relation of ministers in the community to the ministry of Jesus.

The choice of the twelve is recounted in all three synoptic gospels (Mark 3:13–19; Matt 10:1–4; Luke 6:12–16; cf. Acts 1:13) and implied in John 6:66–71.[28] Eleven of the names are identical in all three lists; in place of Thaddeus in Mark and Matthew, Judas the son of James appears in Luke's list; this Judas is likely identical with the Judas mentioned in John 14:22. On the other hand, there is no independent biblical evidence for the popular identification of Nathanael (John 1:45–50) with Bartholomew or for the identification of Thaddeus with the Judas of John 14:22 and Luke 6:16.[29] Seven of these eleven, namely, Simon Peter, Andrew, the sons of Zebedee, Philip, Thomas and Judas Iscariot, appear in the gospel according to John together with Judas, the son of James, from Luke's list. Five of these individuals, Simon Peter, Andrew, James and John the sons of Zebedee, and Matthew, are the objects of special vocation narratives in the synoptic gospels.[30] Renunciation of business and family accompanies the disciples' response to Jesus' call in these synoptic narratives.[31] Peter, Andrew, Philip, Nathanael and one other unidentified disciple are specially called by Jesus in different circumstances in John 1:35–50; at least Andrew and the anonymous disciple were previously disciples of John the Baptist. Such calls to discipleship, however, are distinct from and prior to Jesus' choice of the twelve.

Jesus' choice of these twelve from a larger group of disciples is completely gratuitous. In a separate narrative Mark tells his readers that Jesus "called to him those he desired" (3:13). Luke marks the solemnity of this choice by telling his readers that Jesus spent the previous night in prayer to God (6:12).[32] No criteria for this choice are indicated; the inclusion of Judas Iscariot, who throughout the gospels is always characterized as the one who would betray Jesus,[33] confirms the unmerited character of Jesus' choice. That Jesus' choice does not depend upon any expression of intent on the part of the twelve is also confirmed by John 15:16: "You did not choose me, but I chose you and appointed you that you should go and bear fruit and that your fruit should abide."

Mark also specifies the reasons for Jesus' choice of the twelve: "He appointed twelve [whom also he named apostles][34] to be with him and to be sent out to preach and to have authority to cast out demons" (3:14–15). Two roles are intended for the twelve. In the first place they are established as the privileged eyewitnesses of Jesus' life and work.[35] Luke is particularly sensitive to the role of eyewitnesses in establishing continuity between the ministry of Jesus and the emerging church: In the Acts of the Apostles Peter requires of Judas' replacement that he be a man who accompanied the others "during all the time that the Lord Jesus went in and out among us, beginning from the baptism of John until the day when he was taken up from us—one of these must become with us a witness to his resurrection" (1:21–22); in this case the gratuity of the choice is guaranteed by the use of lots (1:24–26).[36] On the other hand, when James is killed (12:1–2), there is no question of replacing him in the group of the twelve. As eyewitnesses of Jesus' public life and resurrection the role of the twelve is unique and cannot be repeated in subsequent generations.

The second reason given by Mark for Jesus' choice of the twelve is for a mission which is identical with his own: ". . . to be sent out to preach and to have authority to cast out demons." At this point in Mark's gospel the preaching activity of Jesus has already been mentioned three times (1:14, 38, 39); exorcisms have likewise been highlighted (1:23–28, 34; 3:11). Jesus has also been shown teaching (Mark 1:21; 2:13; cf. 2:2), but the twelve are not explicitly commissioned to teach. The commissioning of the eleven by the risen Jesus in Matt 28:16–20 is the only gospel text in which a teaching mission is explicitly given to any of Jesus' disciples. Mark does record that the twelve taught on their preaching mission: "The apostles returned to Jesus, and told him all that they had done and taught" (6:30); but teaching was not explicitly included in their original mission, nor is it elsewhere recorded that the twelve taught during the public ministry of Jesus. The evangelists, however, may not have made the same distinction between preaching and teaching which modern commentators make between these two activities. Nonetheless, when the risen Jesus does commission the eleven to teach, the content of their teaching is defined in terms of Jesus' own teaching: ". . . make disciples of all nations, baptizing them in the name of the Father and of the Son and of the Holy Spirit, teaching them to observe all that I have commanded you . . ." (Matt 28:19–20).[37] According to Luke 24:27, 44–48 the risen Jesus instructs his disciples about the way in which the Jewish scriptures are fulfilled in him. According to John 14:25–26 and 16:12–15 post-resurrection teaching is attributed to the Paraclete, but here again the teaching of the Paraclete is defined in terms of Jesus himself: "He will glorify me, for he will take what is mine and declare it to you. All that the Father has is mine; therefore I said that he will take what is mine and declare it to you" (16:14–15).

In discussing the ministry of Jesus it was shown that Jesus' activity of preaching, healing and teaching was the exercise of an authority (exousia) which he had received from God. In all the synoptic accounts of Jesus' commissioning of the twelve it is clearly stated that he gave them authority (exousia) to cast out unclean spirits and to heal.[38] Similarly, when the risen Jesus commissions the eleven to teach, he does so in virtue of the universal exousia which he has received from God: "All authority (exousia) in heaven and on earth has been given to me. Go therefore and make disciples of all nations . . . teaching them to observe all that I have commanded you . . ." (Matt 28:18–20). The mission of the twelve is thus the exercise of a divine authority received from Jesus. Nowhere in the synoptic gospels is this type of authority given indiscriminately to all Jesus' disciples.[39] In other words, Jesus commissions some of his disciples for responsibilities which he does not give to all.

The word exousia is not used in any exclusive sense in the gospels; it is used of civil authority, military authority and demonic authority as well as being used of the divine authority which Jesus has from God and which he communicates to the twelve.[40] Consequently, it is highly significant that Jesus also instructs the twelve that they are not to exercise this authority after the manner of civil and political leaders: "You know that those who are supposed to rule over the Gentiles lord it over them, and their great men exercise authority (katexousiazousin) over them. But it shall not be so among you; but whoever would be great among you must be your servant, and whoever would be first among you must be slave of all. For the Son of man also came not to be served but to serve, and to give his life as a ransom for many" (Mark 10:42–45). While it is true that all Christians are called to serve Jesus and one another,[41] in this case the twelve have a real and distinctive authority to exercise which is analogous to that of civil and political leaders. The manner in which they are to exercise this authority is nonetheless radically different. We are presented here with one of those paradoxical reversals which characterize the kingdom of God as revealed in the parables: Power over others is really service of others in love. The same point is made in the Lucan parable of the master waiting upon his servants (Luke 12:35–38) and in the paradoxical sayings of Luke

22:26–27: "Let the leader (hēgoumenos) become as one who serves!
. . . I am among you as one who serves!" Jesus is presenting himself
to the twelve as a model for the exercise of authority over others.[42]

The text of the commission as it appears in the three synoptic
gospels[43] presupposes that the twelve are not only doing God's
work but are also following the itinerant lifestyle of Jesus. They are
not to make provision for their own food, clothing or shelter, but are
to depend on what God provides through people who welcome the
kingdom: "The laborer deserves his food" (Matt 10:10).[44] Their mission has the same urgency as Jesus' own preaching: "Salute no one
on the road" (Luke 10:4). Rejection of their mission has the same
consequences as the rejection of Jesus' mission. This judgment is
implied in the instruction to shake the dust off their feet in Mark
6:11 and explicitly stated in Matt 10:15: "It shall be more tolerable
on the day of judgment for the land of Sodom and Gomorrah than
for that town." Appearing as it does between vv 1–14 and vv 16–42
this "Q" saying may be understood both of the pre-Easter and the
post-Easter missions of the twelve, and of those who will continue
the mission after them in the church. In Matt 11:20–24 Jesus addresses a similar judgment upon Chorozain, Bethsaida and Capernaum because they did not repent when confronted with his own
mighty works (dynameis): ". . . it shall be more tolerable on the day
of judgment for Tyre and Sidon than for you . . . it shall be more
tolerable on the day of judgment for the land of Sodom than for
you." The same "Q" saying is used by Luke in the commissioning
of the seventy (10:12–15). A similar "Q" saying is addressed to the
contemporaries of Jesus who ask him for a sign (Matt 12:38–42 =
Luke 11:16, 29–32).

Teaching excluded, the mission of the twelve during the public
ministry of Jesus is identical with what he himself has already been
doing. The grant of authority first mentioned in Mark 3:15 is repeated in Mark 6:7: "And he called to him the twelve and began to
send them out two by two, and gave them authority (exousia) over
the unclean spirits." The sequence in Matthew is very instructive
on this point. In Matt 9:35 the evangelist summarizes the activity of
Jesus: "And Jesus went about all the cities and villages, teaching in
their synagogues and preaching the gospel of the kingdom, and
healing every disease and every infirmity (therapeuōn pasan noson
kai malakian)." In the next verse Matthew explains that Jesus' activity is motivated by compassion for the crowds who are like sheep
without a shepherd. Then, after inviting the disciples to pray for

needed laborers, "he called to him the twelve disciples and gave them authority (exousia) over unclean spirits to cast them out, and to heal every disease and every infirmity (therapeuein pasan noson kai malakian)" (10:1).[45] Jesus specifies the mission even further: "Preach as you go, saying, 'The kingdom of heaven is at hand.'[46] Heal the sick, raise the dead, cleanse lepers, cast out demons. You received without pay, give without pay" (10:7–8). Their mission is not a remunerative profession, but a gratuitous service, just as their initial choice by Jesus was entirely gratuitous. Matthew's literary presentation is a powerful witness to the direct continuity that was understood to exist between the ministry of Jesus and that of the twelve. After Jesus finishes speaking, Mark summarizes the activity of the twelve: "So they went out and preached that men should repent. And they cast out many demons, and anointed with oil many that were sick and healed them" (6:12–13).[47] The return of the twelve from their mission is only briefly narrated, but Mark does state that they also taught (Mark 6:30). It is possible that by mentioning teaching here Mark wants to create a literary inclusio with 6:6, just prior to the commission of the twelve, where it is said of Jesus, ". . . he went about the villages teaching."

The Commissioning of the Seventy

It is peculiar to Luke's gospel that the commissioning of the twelve in 9:1–6 is paralleled in 10:1–16 for a second group of seventy (or seventy-two). This text has been constructed out of material from "Q", most of which appears in the commissioning of the twelve in the longer missionary discourse of Matt 10:1–42.[48] A few sayings appear only in Luke 10, but may easily have been in "Q". "Salute no one on the road" (10:4). "Peace be to this house" (10:5). "Remain in the same house, eating and drinking what they provide . . . do not go from house to house. Whenever you enter a town and they receive you, eat what is set before you" (10:7–8). Finally, the instruction about shaking the dust from their feet (10:10–11), which is also found in Mark 6:11, is presented here as a direct address to the townspeople.

Since the commissioning of the seventy is composed entirely of "Q" texts which Matthew uses in chap. 10,[49] these sayings must have appeared in "Q" independent of any particular audience. Matthew includes them in the missionary discourse to the twelve; Luke uses them for the commissioning of the seventy.[50] At the time Luke composed his gospel, the twelve were most likely all dead and the

Lord had not yet returned. What had been committed to the twelve had to be continued. There could be no more eyewitnesses to the public ministry and resurrection of Jesus, but the work of evangelization was not yet complete; Luke makes this clear by the saying which introduces the instruction: "The harvest is plentiful, but the laborers are few; pray therefore the Lord of the harvest to send laborers into his harvest" (10:2).[51] No doubt the discourse has been positioned here because of Luke 9:51–53: "And he sent messengers ahead of him, who went and entered a village of the Samaritans, to make ready for him; but the people would not receive him, because his face was set toward Jerusalem."[52] The symbolism of the number seventy has been variously explained: Some commentators would see a reference to the seventy nations of the world in Gen 10:2–31;[53] others suggest the seventy offspring of Jacob (Ex 1:5; Deut 10:22), the seventy elders of Israel who assisted Moses, Aaron, Nadab and Abihu (Ex 24:1), or the seventy elders with whom the Lord shared the spirit of Moses (Num 11:16–17). If the seventy are intended as symbols of the nations of the world as the twelve are for the tribes of Israel, Luke would then be referring to the Gentile mission. Lacking a clear indication to this effect, there is a greater similarity between the function of the seventy in Luke and the role of the elders who assisted Moses and shared his spirit. By constructing this second commission out of "Q" material Luke wants to show that the work of the twelve is being carried on in his day by a larger group, and that this development is according to the intention of Jesus.[54]

Jesus expects both the twelve and the seventy to receive the same welcome or rejection that he received. He also gives their reception or rejection the same eschatological significance. "A disciple is not above his teacher, nor a servant above his master; it is enough for the disciple to be like his teacher and the servant like his master. If they have called the master of the house Beelzebul, how much more will they malign those of his household" (Matt 10:24–25).[55] "He who receives you receives me, and he who receives me receives him who sent me" (Matt 10:40).[56] In the same context of mission Matthew inserts the saying about judgment: "So every one who acknowledges me before men, I also will acknowledge before my Father who is in heaven; but whoever denies me before men, I also will deny before my Father who is in heaven" (Matt 10:32–33). In the context of the missionary discourses, the reception of Jesus' envoys has the same significance for salvation and for judgment as the reception of Jesus himself.

Thus Jesus' mission from the Father is continued in the twelve during Jesus' ministry and after the resurrection. It is also continued in a wider group after the resurrection and throughout the history of the church.

Some Difficult Texts

a) Matthew 9:1–8—The Healing of the Paralytic

In addition to the commissioning of the twelve and the seventy, there are other texts in the synoptic gospels which have been traditionally seen as relating to ministry in the church. The healing of the paralytic demonstrates Jesus' power to forgive sins. In the Marcan narrative (2:1–12) Jesus defends his power as Son of man to forgive sins by healing the paralytic, thus offering visible evidence of the same divine power. Moral and bodily healing are closely related; by offering forgiveness first, Jesus shows that the moral healing is more important, but it remains invisible. The bodily healing is the visible sign of the internal, moral renewal. Although it is customary to read Mark 2:10 on the lips of Jesus, it is more likely a parenthetical remark of the evangelist:[57] ". . . that you may know that the Son of man has authority (exousia) to forgive sins on earth (literal order of the Greek text) . . ." The authority (exousia) exercised by Jesus is the same power of God which is evident in Jesus' teaching and by which he heals the sick and casts out demons. Apart from the scribes, the other bystanders recognize that Jesus' power came from God: ". . . they were all amazed and glorified God, saying, 'We never saw anything like this' " (Mark 2:12). "To glorify God" means to acknowledge publicly that God is the source of the benefit received. The use of the title "the Son of man" in this context may either identify Jesus as a human being or may already be a reference to the eschatological judge who is exercising his power to save even now.[58] Luke gives the incident a more solemn setting; he mentions explicitly that Jesus was teaching and that the power of God was with him to heal (5:17). In Luke's narrative, both the paralytic and the bystanders recognize that the healing came from God: ". . . (the paralytic) went home, glorifying God . . . amazement seized them all, and they glorified God and were filled with awe, saying, 'We have seen strange things today' " (5:25–26).

Matthew (9:1–8) follows Mark substantially, but the conclusion is significantly different: "When the crowds saw it, they were afraid, and they glorified God who had given such authority (ex-

ousia) to men (*anthrōpois*)" (9:8). It is both logically and exegetically possible that Jesus appears in this narrative simply as a man among men, a member of the human race, but the literary and theological presentation of Matthew's gospel renders this minimal exegesis inadequate. Jesus is clearly the messiah, the Son of God, Lord and eschatological Son of man for the author and the reader of the gospel.[59] There is also general agreement among commentators that Matthew's gospel was written for a structured Christian community. Consequently, the deliberate change which Matthew has introduced into the Marcan narrative at 9:8 must refer to the fact that Christ's ministry of forgiveness was being continued in Matthew's community. The use of the generic noun *anthrōpos* does not permit us to specify who in the Christian community was exercising this authority. It is nonetheless the same divine power which Jesus exercised in forgiving and healing the paralytic.

A later narrative in this same gospel, Matt 18:15–20, contains instructions for reconciling sinners in the community; here the binding or loosing of the sinner may be the work of any individual, of two or three, or of the whole community. The Christian community of Matthew is a community of forgiveness; when Christians forgive one another in private or in public, their action is the exercise of a divine power or authority (*exousia*) received from the Son of man. On exegetical grounds alone we cannot say that the text of Matt 9:8 refers exclusively to an authority possessed only by the twelve.

b) Matthew 18:15–20—Binding and Loosing in the Community

The community discourse of Matt 18 includes procedures for mutual correction and reconciliation within the church; on occasion, the application of such procedures may lead to the isolation of the unrepentant sinner (18:15–20). From an exegetical point of view, it is impossible to determine Jesus' audience in this discourse. At this point in his gospel, Matthew has been following Mark.[60] Beginning with 7:24, Mark's narrative concentrates on Jesus instructing his disciples; this intention of Jesus is made clear in Mark 9:30–31a: "They (i.e. Jesus and his disciples) went on from there and passed through Galilee. And he would not have anyone know it; for he was teaching his disciples . . ." The community discourse in Matt 18 begins with a question of the disciples about greatness in the kingdom of God (18:1–5); the parallel narrative in

Mark 9:33–37 involves Jesus and the twelve. In Matthew, however, the private instructions of Jesus are addressed to the disciples in general, except when the text or context specifies the twelve. Consequently, no juridical conclusions can be drawn from the narratives which Matthew has gathered together in the community discourse.

On the other hand, throughout Matt 18, a structured community is presupposed. Pastoral exhortations about caring for "little ones" and lost sheep (18:6–14) suppose that some members of the community have responsibility for others. The instructions on mutual correction and reconciliation (18:15–17), however, are addressed to all members of the community as individuals.[61] If the phrase "against you" in v 15 is omitted with Vaticanus and Sinaiticus, mutual correction is not limited to personal offenses. Every member of the community has this responsibility toward other members. The offense is made known to the church, that is, the local community of believers, only after private efforts at correction and reconciliation have failed. There is no indication in the text about how the denunciation is made or about how the local community reproves the sinner; a juridical process is not necessarily involved. Nor is it clear that an official excommunication follows upon the sinner's failure to acknowledge his fault and be reconciled; the advice given in v 17b, "let him be to you as a Gentile and a tax collector," is in the singular and applies directly only to the individual; in other words, the sinner who refuses to acknowledge his or her fault and be reconciled should now be avoided until such time as he or she repents. It is impossible to speak of a formal excommunication on the basis of this text. The instruction to this point is a practical application of the previous parable of the lost sheep (18:12–14).

The next three sayings (18:18–20) are in the plural and are appended by Matthew to the previous instructions on correction and reconciliation. The mention of "two" in v 19 and "two or three" in v 20 connects these sayings with vv 15–16. The evangelist, therefore, is using these sayings to reinforce the instructions given to individual Christians in the previous verses. The binding and loosing of v 18 is consequently restricted in application to the action of Christians in seeking reconciliation with each other and with the local community. Decisions to reconcile or to withhold reconciliation, if taken prayerfully and in Jesus' name, will be ratified by God. The rabbinic formula of "binding and loosing" normally concerns authoritative decisions regarding halakâ, but it is also used for releasing from vows or the forgiveness of sins.[62] The context must determine the meaning of the formula in each case.

In conclusion, Jesus' instructions in Matt 18 are addressed to the whole community of disciples. The procedures for correction and reconciliation in 18:15–20 may be an illustration of Matt 9:8, but this text tells us nothing about the specific role of leaders in the work of reconciliation. The agreement of two or more disciples who prayerfully seek the will of God in Jesus' name is a sign of the presence and action of Christ among them and the work of the Holy Spirit in all concerned.[63]

c) Matthew 16:17–19—Peter and the Power of the Keys

The words of Christ to Peter in Matt 16:17–19 have, of course, been the object of an enormous literature and controversy. For the purpose of this study it will be sufficient to discuss the meaning the text has for Matthew's community. If, as is generally agreed, Matthew's gospel was written in Antioch between 80 and 90 C.E., this text among others is a witness to the way Peter's role was remembered there over twenty years after his death.[64] The text says nothing about the significance of Peter's historical ministry for the church beyond his death, but it does acknowledge the high regard in which he was held in the tradition of the Antioch church.[65] First of all, it needs to be recognized that the context in which this text appears is quite different from the context of 18:18; for this reason it is exegetically unjustified to play 18:18 off against 16:19, as is frequently done.[66] In the context of Matthew's literary and theological presentation, Peter's confession is formulated as a full profession of post-Easter faith: "You are the Christ, the Son of the living God" (16:16).[67] In Matthew's narrative sequence, Jesus replies that Peter's understanding is not an inference of unassisted human reason ("flesh and blood"), but a revelation of the Father,[68] and promises to make him the foundation of his church with the necessary power and authority.

All commentators agree that the text of Matt 16:17–19 is an intrusion into the Marcan sequence at this point; it creates an unresolved tension with the charge of secrecy inherited from Mark (Matt 16:20) and with Peter's subsequent rejection of a suffering messiah (16:21–23). Oscar Cullman who defended the authenticity of the saying suggested a setting at the last supper, parallel to Luke 22:31–34. Others prefer a post-Easter setting similar to John 21:15–17.[69] Regardless of the historical circumstances in which the saying may have been delivered by Jesus, this promise, addressed to Peter alone, designates him as the foundation stone of Jesus' own *ekklē-sia*. This is the only appearance of the expression "my church" in the whole of the New Testament.[70] The formula may correspond to another Matthaean expression, "the kingdom of the Son of man."[71] Christ's church, like the kingdom of the Son of man, is the place where the kingly rule of the risen Lord is visible in this world until such time as he has brought all things under his feet and the kingdom of God is realized in all its fullness.

Christ promises Peter that this church of his[72] will not succumb to the power of sin, death or Satan[73] because of the victory already won by the risen Lord over these powers. By receiving the keys of the kingdom of heaven Peter becomes the majordomo of the kingdom after the manner of Eliakim, the son of Hilkiah, to whom the Lord God spoke in Is 22:22: "I will place on his shoulder the key of the house of David; he shall open and none shall shut; and he shall shut and none shall open." The imagery used here implies that Peter is given authority to admit to and to exclude from the kingdom of heaven in Jesus' name.[74] This commissioning of Peter makes Jesus' *ekklēsia* a gateway to the kingdom of heaven where God's plan of universal salvation will find its eschatological fulfillment. This personal authority[75] goes beyond anything contained in Matt 18:18; the latter text in its context only deals with the work of reconciliation within the local community of Jesus' disciples.

The second half of 16:19 must be read in the light of the authority conferred personally on Peter by the bestowal of the keys: "Whatever you bind on earth shall be bound in heaven, and whatever you loose on earth shall be loosed in heaven." The power to bind and to loose in this context is similar to the power to open and to shut that was given to Eliakim. Consequently, the better attested meaning of the rabbinic formula of binding and loosing, namely, authoritative decisions in matters of *halakâ*, applies more properly here than in Matt 18:18.[76] A similar responsibility is given to Peter in Luke 22:31–34 and John 21:15–17. All three texts, recorded after the death of Peter, bear witness to the way his role was remembered. The only biblical argument that may be offered for a continuing Petrine ministry is the delay of the Lord's coming and the ensuing necessity for Jesus' *ekklēsia* to continue throughout time.

The Mission of the Disciples in the Fourth Gospel

It has already been pointed out at the beginning of this chapter that the texts of John 17:18 and 20:21 clearly express the relationship of the mission of Jesus' disciples with the mission which Jesus himself received from the Father. "As thou didst send me into the world, so I have sent them into the world" (17:18; apostellō in both clauses). "As the living Father has sent (apostellō) me, even so I send (pempō) you" (20:21).[77] It is more difficult to determine on exegetical grounds whether this mission is limited to the twelve. The twelve appear as such only at John 6:66–71, where Peter is their spokesperson. The departure of the other disciples at this juncture in the Galilean ministry would seem to imply that, in terms of the narrative, only the twelve remained as disciples of Jesus throughout the rest of the gospel.[78] Judas Iscariot who is identified as "one of the twelve" in 6:71[79] is called "one of his disciples" in John 12:4. The verb eklegomai is used of the twelve as Jesus' chosen ones in John 6:70 and 13:18; the context and the last supper setting do not justify a wider meaning in John 15:16–19.[80] On this basis the instructions of Jesus at the last supper and in the post-resurrection narratives would be addressed to the twelve and the eleven respectively.

Other texts, however, suggest that even after the crisis narrated in John 6:66–71, the term "disciple(s)" may refer to more than the twelve. The brothers of Jesus refer to his disciples in Judea in John 7:3; the reference is probably to the believers and the disciples mentioned in John 2:23, 3:22 and 4:1. At John 8:31 Jesus invites Jews who have believed in him to become true disciples.[81] The disciple whom Jesus loved who is present at the last supper (John 13:23), at the foot of the cross (John 19:26) and in the resurrection narratives (John 20:2, 21:7, 20) may not have been one of the twelve. Then there is "the other disciple" who was known to the high priest (John 18:16) and Joseph of Arimathea, the secret disciple of Jesus (John 19:38). It may also be argued that Martha, Mary and Lazarus whom Jesus loved (John 11:5) were disciples, but the word "disciple" is not used in their regard.[82] These texts may all be exceptions to the general narrative pattern of the gospel according to which only the twelve remain as disciples after the crisis of John 6:66–71.[83] In the absence of any clear indication to this effect, it is probably safer to recognize that discipleship is the primary category under which the twelve should be considered in all the gospels, but especially in Matthew and John. Mission and leadership in the community are an

important part of their responsibility, but juridical distinctions concerning the prerogatives of leaders cannot be established on a
purely exegetical basis. In the final analysis, appeal must be made
to the continuous and lived practice of the post-Easter communities
of Jesus' disciples.

The continuity between Jesus' mission from the Father and the
mission of Jesus' disciples is also expressed in the saying of John
13:20: "He who receives any one whom I send receives me; and he
who receives me receives him who sent me." This saying has its
parallels in Matt 10:40 and Luke 10:16.[84] The negative side of this
saying is found in John 15:18–20: "If the world hates you, know that
it has hated me before it hated you. If you were of the world, the
world would love its own; but because you are not of the world, but
I chose you out of the world, therefore the world hates you. Remember the word that I said to you, 'A servant is not greater than
his master' (cf. John 13:16). If they persecuted me, they will perse-
cute you; if they kept my word, they will keep yours also." Another
mission saying of Jesus appears at John 4:37–38: "For here the saying holds true, 'One sows and another reaps.' I sent (*apostellō*) you
to reap that for which you did not labor; others have labored and
you have entered into their labor." The interpretation of this saying
in the context of chap. 4 is the object of much debate, and there is
no agreement as to whom the "others" may be.[85] It seems best to
understand the present text of John as a general principle for Christian missionary activity: Jesus is the first missionary; all other missionaries are sent by Jesus and build on the work of those who have
preceded them.[86] A third mission instruction after the washing of
the feet also expresses a real continuity between the service of Jesus
and that of his disciples; in content the text parallels the instruction
on the exercise of authority in Mark 10:42–45: "Do you know what
I have done to you? You call me Teacher and Lord; you are right,
for so I am. If I then, your Lord and Teacher, have washed your feet,
you also ought to wash one another's feet. For I have given you an
example, that you also should do as I have done for you. Truly,
truly, I say to you, a slave (*doulos*; RSV: servant) is not greater than
his master; nor is he who is sent (*apostolos*, only here in John)
greater than he who sent him" (John 13:12–16). All these texts
clearly state that Jesus sends his disciples on a mission which is
identical with his own and which is to be carried out in the same
manner and with the same results.

Other metaphors are used throughout the gospel to express the
relationship of the disciples to Jesus. Each of these metaphors must

be understood in its own context; otherwise, a conflicting picture is created of Jesus and his disciples. As slaves (*douloi*) they are not greater than their master (John 13:16). As servants (*diakonoi*) they follow Jesus, will be honored by the Father and will eventually be where Jesus himself now is (John 12:26).[87] The servants (*diakonoi*) of the first Cana sign, who know where the water made wine is from, may also be symbols for discipleship (John 2:9); for throughout the gospel a major question is where Jesus is from (John 8:14, 9:29–30; 19:9). As one whom Jesus sends (*apostolos*), the disciple of Jesus is not above the one who sent him (John 13:16).

On the other hand, those who believe in Jesus are no longer sinful slaves (*douloi*) but free sons (*huioi*; John 8:34–36); nor are they ignorant slaves (*douloi*) but Jesus' friends (*philoi*); as such, Jesus tells them all he has heard from the Father and lays down his life for them (John 15:13–15). They are his own and he loves them to the end (John 13:1).

These diverse metaphors suggest a complex relationship between Jesus and his disciples. On the one hand, they are entirely dependent upon Jesus, and unlike the disciples of other teachers, they cannot expect to outdo their master or be treated any better than he. On the other hand, they are taken completely into his confidence, are called to a free and equal association with him and are the object of a total self-sacrificing love: "Greater love has no man than this, that a man lay down his life for his friends" (John 15:13). Indeed, there is a real parallel between Jesus' relationship with his Father and the disciples' relationship with Jesus; it is paradoxically a relationship both of dependence and of equality.

The Mission in John 17:18 and 20:21–23

The clearest statements in the fourth gospel of the mission Jesus gives to his disciples are those of John 17:18 and 20:21: "As thou didst send me into the world, so I have sent them into the world" (17:18) and "As the living Father has sent me, even so I send you" (20:21).

The first statement appears within the context of Jesus' prayer at the last supper. In this prayer Jesus speaks of revealing the Father's name to his disciples and of teaching them that he himself came from God; this revelation is not just a new way of referring in speech to the reality of God, but it is the self-manifestation of the Father through Jesus' own person: "He who has seen me has seen the Father" (John 14:9). This knowledge of God and of Jesus is eternal life (John 17:3).

Jesus then prays that his disciples may persevere in this knowledge in face of evil and of the world's hatred (John 17:9–16). In v 17 this fidelity to Jesus' revelation of God is described as sanctification or consecration in the truth. Thus enlightened and encouraged by Jesus' prayer the disciples are sent into the world as Jesus was sent into the world: "As thou didst send me into the world, so I have sent them into the world" (John 17:18). The use of a past tense here implies that the mission has already been given to the disciples.[88]

Jesus then declares that his commitment or consecration to his mission is ordered to their consecration and commitment to a similar mission. Consecration is the setting aside of things or persons for the special service of God or for a special mission on behalf of God. According to John 10:36 God himself has consecrated Jesus and sent him into the world; he is the holy one of God (John 6:69), the one on whom God has set his seal (6:27),[89] the one in whom God's love for the world is concretely visible (John 3:16).

Jesus who is himself the word of God and the truth (John 14:6) sets his disciples apart from the world for the same mission by his own self-consecration. The self-consecration of Jesus is his own commitment to the will of the Father by the gift of his life upon the cross.[90]

Finally, Jesus prays for all those who will believe in him through the word of his disciples (John 17:20–23). The word of the disciples is not simply a matter of formal preaching and teaching but also of action.[91] It is the lived unity and love of Jesus' disciples for one another that will lead the hostile world to understand that Jesus is not only the one sent by the Father, but also the one in whom God's love for the world has been revealed. A mission such as this cannot be confined to a few leaders within a larger community; it is necessarily a mission to which all Jesus' disciples indiscriminately must be committed. Whatever leadership roles the twelve may have in the community of Jesus' disciples are ordered to forming the whole community for its mission to the world.

The commissioning narrated in John 20:21–23 is the post-resurrection realization of what was referred to as already completed in the setting of the last supper. After the glorification of Jesus the disciples are equipped for continuing his mission of revealing the Father and the Father's love to the world. Although the narrative context of the gospel implies that only ten of Jesus' original twelve are the witnesses of this appearance of the risen Jesus,[92] the gift of the Holy Spirit (John 20:22) brings to fulfillment the promise of the Spirit throughout the gospel narrative.[93]

The evangelist does not envisage an outpouring of the Spirit fifty days later as does Luke in Luke-Acts. The pentecostal gifts of the Spirit come to a group of one hundred and twenty, and in accordance with the citation of Joel 3:1–5 (LXX) in Acts 2:16–21 this gift is not limited to the twelve, but is universal. There is no exegetical justification for the harmonizing of the two accounts, whereby the gift of John 20 would be reserved to the apostles and the gift of Acts 2 extended to all.[94] The forgiveness of sins accompanies the gift of the Spirit both in Acts 2:38 and in John 20:23.[95]

This narrative is the only place in the fourth gospel where the forgiveness of sins is mentioned.[96] Unlike Acts 2:38, however, the forgiveness of sins is not presented in John as a simple complement of the gift of the Holy Spirit; it is granted on the basis of a discernment on the part of the disciples: "If you forgive the sins of any, they are forgiven; if you retain the sins of any, they are retained" (John 20:23).[97]

Formally, Matt 18:18 is the closest parallel to this text in the gospels; there it is a question of reconciling a fellow Christian to the community, and a discernment has to be made concerning the individual's readiness to acknowledge his or her fault and be reconciled. In Matt 18 the context does not distinguish the role of leaders from the role of the community, but a structured community is presupposed. It may likewise be presupposed here that the evangelist or editor who so formulated the narrative belongs to a community in which structures for this discernment already exist.[98]

It would be forcing the text beyond its original intent to expect an answer to later ecclesiastical problems, such as the process by which this discernment is to be made and the designation of individuals in the community who have the authority to make the discernment. The risen Lord is fulfilling the promise of the gospel narrative itself and communicating to the community of his disciples, in the persons of the ten gathered behind closed doors, the gift of the Spirit for communication to others. Through the Spirit Jesus' mission from the Father will be continued in his disciples. The Spirit of Jesus is a power of sinlessness; it includes the forgiveness of sins of its very nature. Further juridical specifications can not be determined by exegesis, but only by the practice of the Spirit-guided church. In the gift of the Spirit is Jesus' gift of eternal life.

General Conclusion

Jesus is portrayed in all the gospels providing for the continuation of the ministry which he received from the Father. In the synoptic gospels that provision is made through the twelve apostles and the seventy, to whom is given the power and authority to preach, heal and eventually to teach. The twelve are first of all disciples of Jesus and thereby paradigms for all future disciples. The primary leadership in the church is that of discipleship. At the same time, however, the twelve are called by Jesus to have power and authority in the community of his disciples. That power and authority is to be exercised in service after the pattern of Jesus' own ministry, but it is a real power and authority from God to preach, to heal and to teach as Jesus preached and healed and taught. This power and authority is not given to all Jesus' disciples indiscriminately, but only to the twelve and the seventy. As far as the gospel texts permit us to determine, Jesus' choice of the twelve is completely gratuitous and is not based on any prior social or cultural considerations or on any native ability. If Jesus acts according to the pattern of the God of Israel, it may even be argued that he deliberately eschews such considerations so that the results may be more clearly seen to be the work of God. If after Easter the early Christian communities organize their internal life according to existing social and cultural patterns, they nonetheless remain inspired by the necessity of continuing Jesus' ministry of preaching, healing and teaching, and by Jesus' own example in the choice and commissioning of the twelve. The fact that the twelve are presented in the gospels as they are is not simply an historical recollection; it is testimony to the early church's recognition of the twelve as a paradigm for ministry in the church.[99]

III

PAUL'S UNDERSTANDING
OF HIS MINISTRY

The NT offers very little information about the activity of the twelve or the seventy after the ascension of Jesus and nothing at all about the way they viewed their own ministry. Of the twelve only Judas, Peter, James and John are mentioned outside the gospels. Judas is mentioned by name in Acts 1:16. James, the son of Zebedee and brother of John, was put to death by Herod Agrippa I (Acts 12:2). Something may be learned about Peter's attitudes and activities from Acts 1—12 and from Paul's letters,[1] but the texts of Acts and Paul contain no first-hand information about Peter's own understanding of his ministry. Since 1 and 2 Peter are generally considered pseudonymous, these two letters cannot provide reliable historical information about Peter. John appears with Peter in Acts 3—4 and 8:14–25, but nothing distinctive is said of him. Modern scholars are skeptical about the ecclesiastical tradition which attributes the fourth gospel and the three letters of John to John, the son of Zebedee.[2] James, the brother of the Lord was neither one of the twelve nor one of the seventy, and cannot be considered to be a disciple of Jesus during the public ministry.[3] The seventy have left little trace in the history of the early church.[4] If they represent an historical group, they may well have been among the wider group of apostles known to Paul.[5] Joseph Justus Barsabbas and Matthias (Acts 1:23) and the other men who fulfilled the qualifications necessary to replace Judas (Acts 1:21–22) might have been among the seventy.[6]

As a consequence, only Paul, the apostle who was untimely born (1 Cor 15:8), provides first-hand information about the way the initial disciples of Jesus understood their ministry. Although Paul was not an eyewitness to the public ministry of Jesus and was neither called nor commissioned by Jesus prior to the ascension, he nonetheless considered his ministry to be identical with that of the other Jerusalem apostles (1 Cor 9:1–2). He did not consider himself subject to the twelve or to those who were apostles before him, but he was at pains to see that there was agreement between them and himself in the gospel they preached (Gal 1:6—2:10). "Whether then it was I or they, so we preach and so you believed" (1 Cor 15:11). Paul's understanding of his ministry, therefore, is crucial to all further understanding of ministry in the church. This chapter will be devoted primarily to Paul's own understanding of his ministry and apostolate as it appears from the proto-Pauline or certainly authentic Pauline letters. Brief consideration will then be given to the way Paul's self-understanding has been preserved and developed in the deutero-Pauline letters.[7]

Paul as *Diakonos*

Among the many Greek words Paul uses to describe his work on behalf of the gospel, *diakonos* and *apostolos* are the most significant.[8] It was Paul who popularized the vocabulary of service to describe the activity of those called and commissioned by Jesus. The word group connoting service, namely, *diakoneō*, *diakonia* and *diakonos* appears thirty-four times in the proto-Paulines compared with twenty-nine times in the gospels and seventeen times in the deutero-Paulines; this vocabulary understandably refers to Christian ministry more often in the letters than in the gospels. Together with his rival Apollos, Paul designates himself as a *diakonos* through whom the Corinthians have believed (1 Cor 3:5); but the following verses (3:6–9) show that he does not attribute his personal success or that of Apollos to themselves but to God, "for we are God's fellow workers" (3:9: *theou synergoi*). In 2 Cor 11:23 he ironically claims to be a better servant than his rivals, the false apostles working in Corinth.

The understanding of Paul's missionary activity as a *diakonia*, that is, a service or ministry, is based primarily on his reflections in 2 Cor 2:14—6:10.[9] He begins by describing his Corinthian Christians as "a letter from Christ delivered by us" (2 Cor 3:3; RSV); the Greek verb used here is *diakonētheisa*; the Corinthian Christians by the quality of their lives bear witness to others that they have been formed by the Spirit of the living God through the ministry of Paul.[10] Eschewing all self-confidence Paul then attributes all his confidence to God alone "who has qualified us to be ministers (*diakonous*) of a new covenant, not in a written code but in the Spirit" (3:6).[11] Throughout this text Paul uses the first person plural when speaking of himself; he may include his apostolic associates, but it is much less likely that all Christians are intended except when they are explicitly included as in 3:18. In the following verses (3:7–18) he compares the glory of the ministry of the Spirit and of righteousness delivered by Christ with the glory of the ministry of death and condemnation delivered by Moses, using the word *diakonia* (RSV: dispensation) for both the old and new covenants.[12] It is the latter covenant or *diakonia*, namely, that delivered by Christ, which has been given to Paul by God (4:1). His ministry, therefore, is intimately related to the work of Christ and his Spirit. The subject matter of his preaching is not himself, but Christ. For what we preach is not ourselves, but Jesus Christ as Lord, with ourselves as your slaves (*doulous*; RSV: servants) for Jesus' sake" (4:5). When he says in 4:7 that "we have this treasure in earthen vessels, to show that the transcendent power belongs to God and not to us," the treasure he is talking about is his ministry.[13] He returns to the theme of his ministry in 5:18–19: "All this is from God, who through Christ reconciled us to himself and gave us the ministry of reconciliation (*tēn diakonian tēs katallagēs*); that is, God was in Christ reconciling the world to himself, not counting their trespasses against them, and entrusting to us the word (*ton logon*; RSV: message) of reconciliation." God is the reconciler, Christ is the means of reconciliation; Paul is the one who makes that reconciliation available to others. "So we are ambassadors (*presbeuomen*) for Christ, God making his appeal through us" (5:20a). Paul sees himself as the vicegerens of Christ, making Christ's own work present to others: "We beseech you on behalf of Christ, be reconciled to God" (5:20b). Christ himself speaks and acts in and through Paul, his ambassador.[14]

Like the rabbinic notion of the *shālîah* (apostle), the notion of ambassador in this text implies a disappearance of the person of Paul behind the person of Christ in such a way that Paul's ministry makes Christ himself present. The understanding of his ministry expressed in this text is not isolated in Paul, but is fundamental in all his apostolic activity. He sees his ministry as "working together" (*synergountes*) with God (and/or Christ) (6:1). "We put no obstacle in any one's way, so that no fault may be found with our ministry (*diakonia*), but as servants (*diakonoi*) of God we commend ourselves in every way" (6:3–4).[15]

Paul understands his ministry primarily as a service of God and of Christ. At the same time, however, it is a service of those whom he evangelizes. "I robbed other churches by accepting support from

them in order to serve you" (2 Cor 11:8: *pros tēn hymōn diakonian*);
it is a *diakonia* for the Gentiles (Rom 11:13).[16] This service of others
embraces not only the proclamation of the gospel to the Gentiles,
but also material assistance to the Jewish-Christian "saints" in Jerusalem.[17]

Paul as *Apostolos*

Paul nonetheless refers to himself more frequently as an "apostle of Jesus Christ."[18] The formula serves as a self-introduction in 1
and 2 Corinthians and equivalently in Galatians and Romans.[19]
Paul only refers to the twelve in the creedal formula of 1 Cor 15:5.
Except when using the term of himself or of isolated individuals (2
Cor 8:23; Phil 2:25; Rom 16:7), he refers to a group which is wider
than the twelve. In 1 Cor 15:3–7 "all the apostles" is a group that is
wider than the twelve but narrower than the five hundred.[20] This
group of apostles, in addition to being favored with an appearance
from the risen Christ, must also have received a mission from him.
If they were eyewitnesses to the public ministry of Jesus, they may
have been Luke's seventy (Luke 10:1) or those who qualified as
substitutes for Judas (Acts 1:21–26). According to Gal 1:17, 19 they
are associated with Jerusalem. There is no way of knowing how
many individuals were included in this group; they are nonetheless
to be distinguished from the false apostles and the superlative apostles of 2 Cor 11—12;[21] they more than likely included the twelve
and are related to the apostles of 1 Cor 12:28–29 who have first
place among the charismatics. It is not clear that all those who are
called "apostles" in the NT saw the risen Christ and received a
commission directly from him.[22] It is unlikely that Silvanus and
Timothy are to be included in the term *apostoloi* as it is used in 1
Thess 2:6, for it is almost certain that these two neither saw the
risen Christ nor received a mission directly from him;[23] Paul frequently uses the first person plural when speaking of himself.
James, Cephas and John enjoyed some special position in the Jerusalem church (Gal 2:9), but their relation to the wider group of
Jerusalem apostles is not clear from the text of Galatians. In 1 Cor
9:3–12 Paul defends his right to live by his apostolic work along
with Barnabas, the other apostles, the brethren of the Lord and
Cephas; in this whole section Paul is defending his status as an
apostle alongside the Jerusalem apostles; it is not clear under what
title Paul claims for Barnabas the same right to support.[24] The word
"apostle," therefore, is used by Paul of the emissaries of local

churches (2 Cor 8:23; Phil 2:25), of the Jerusalem apostles including the twelve with whom he claims equality, and of himself in a special sense.

In Galatians and 1 Corinthians Paul defends his independence and authority as an apostle against critics who considered him both inferior to and dependent upon the Jerusalem apostles, including Cephas and the twelve. He was not an eyewitness to the public ministry of Jesus, and his claim to having seen the risen Christ and received a mission from him was spurious for some, because it occurred after the ascension of Jesus which marked the end of the appearances for the Jerusalem apostles[25]; Ananias' vision (Acts 9:10–16) may have served to guarantee the authenticity of Paul's claim. Paul established his claim to be an apostle on an equal footing with the Jerusalem apostles on the basis of having seen the risen Lord (1 Cor 9:1) and of having received a mission from him. He expresses his own understanding of that experience in Gal 1:15–16a: "When he who had set me apart before I was born, and had called me through his grace, was pleased to reveal his Son to me (RSV; en emoi), in order that I might preach him among the Gentiles. . ." In 1 Cor 15:8–9 he added his own vision of the risen Christ to the initial and founding appearances. According to Gal 1:1 he was convinced that his apostleship was not from men or through men, but through Jesus Christ and God the Father. He meant that he was in no way dependent upon the Jerusalem apostles for his authority; the text may also imply that there were apostles whose claim was based on human authority alone. Paul's sense of apostleship was rooted solely in his personal meeting with the risen Christ and the interior conviction resulting from that experience. Paul, of course, is referring to the Damascus experience (Gal 1:15–17) which is presented on three different occasions in the Acts of the Apostles (9:1–19; 22:6–16; 26:12–18).[26]

Paul's encounter with the risen Christ on the road to Damascus was more than a conversion; it was a prophetic call, and the literary presentations of that call in the NT are modeled on the vocation narratives of the OT prophets. Paul's own account in Gal 1:15–16 uses the language of Jer 1:5. The element of vocation is also apparent in the three narratives of Acts (9:6, 15; 22:10, 14–15; 26:15–18; cf. 22:21). The gratuity of Jesus' call is confirmed in Paul's case by the complete reversal of his convictions. The revelation of the risen Christ on the road to Damascus established for Paul the truth of Christian claims for Jesus. On this basis he can affirm the independence of his apostolic call and of his understanding of the gospel.

This personal call by the risen Lord did not exclude the need for instruction in the Christian tradition by Ananias (Acts 9:17–19); Paul also considered it necessary to compare his preaching with the preaching of the Jerusalem apostles (Gal 1:18—2:10).[27] From these contacts, and doubtlessly from others which are not recorded, Paul would have acquired the knowledge of those traditional formulas and words of the Lord to which he refers in his letters.[28] The only concession which he would make with regard to his own apostolate was to acknowledge that its origins were abnormal (1 Cor 15:8–11). It was nonetheless the same apostolate as that of James, Cephas and John in Jerusalem (Gal 2:9–10), regardless of what others might think. What was distinctive of Paul's apostolate with reference to that of the Jerusalem apostles was its special, but not necessarily exclusive orientation to the Gentile mission. He not only refers frequently to his apostolate to the Gentiles,[29] but in the letter to the Galatians Paul works out the scriptural and the theological bases for the Gentile mission itself. This peculiar preoccupation for the universality of the gospel justifies his use of the expression "my gospel" or "our gospel."[30]

In the deutero-Pauline literature Paul is viewed as "the apostle" *par excellence*.[31] In the Acts of the Apostles he is the author's protagonist for carrying the gospel from Antioch to Rome (Acts 13—28), even though he does not fit the criteria established in Acts 1:21–22 for a place among the twelve apostles of Jesus. The manner in which Paul's apostolate was incorporated into the apostolate of the twelve and ultimately accepted in the church, against much opposition, is sufficient evidence that this ministry was not simply a culturally conditioned, human phenomenon theologized by subsequent reflection. From the beginning, it was a gratuitous call by Jesus without a priori conditions.

Paul's Understanding of His Apostolate

Paul's understanding of his ministry cannot be adequately understood simply by considering his use of the words *diakonos* and *apostolos*. After Damascus Paul's life was entirely absorbed by his apostolate and ministry. His literary activity was itself an exercise of that ministry; the letters were written as instruments of teaching, correction and encouragement; they were directed primarily to those communities where he had already preached the gospel and founded churches. The letters are the only archaeological remains of a career which profoundly influenced the early life of the Chris-

tian church. Hence these letters must be read carefully in their entirety to build up a picture of the way in which Paul conceives
himself as a servant and apostle of Jesus Christ. Much of what he
says about himself can be applied to Christian discipleship in general, but it is as an apostle that Paul writes. His understanding of his
ministry may be seen in the way he writes about his responsibility
both to the gospel and to his Christian communities. Sometimes
Paul has to create distinctive language to express his thought. At
other times he gives new content to the language used by civic and
religious leaders and by the philosophical teachers of his day.
These literary phenomena testify to the fact that Paul's understanding of his ministry is not derived primarily from the contemporary
culture but from his personal relationship with the risen Lord. In
theological terms Paul's understanding of his apostolate is a revealed understanding and is not derived either from his culture or
from the Jerusalem apostles.

Paul was called to his ministry by an act of divine grace which
brought about a total change in the orientation of his life. The appearance of the risen Jesus on the road to Damascus changed Paul
from an ardent persecutor of Jewish Christians to the zealous apostle of the Gentiles whom we meet in the letters. He refers to his
former experience as a persecutor of the early church in Gal 1:13–
14, 1 Cor 15:9 and Phil 3:6. He speaks of his divine call as a revelation of God's Son (Gal 1:15–16) and attributes it solely to the
grace of God (1 Cor 15:10). In Phil 3:4–14 he reflects upon the re-
orientation which that experience inaugurated in his life. It led to
the abandonment of his Pharisaic past and of the confidence which
he had placed in his obedience to the law as a means of salvation.
He describes it as "being seized by Christ Jesus" (Phil 3:12; RSV:
"because Christ Jesus has made me his own") and a pursuit of
Christ, not merely as an object of conceptual knowledge but as a
pattern of life and the only source of salvation. He declares in Phil
3:10–11 that he seeks an existential knowledge of Christ, of the
power of his resurrection and of participation in his sufferings with
a view to a future share in his resurrection.[32] It can be said, therefore, that Paul's ministry grew out of a sudden encounter with the
risen Christ and that a personal relationship with God and Christ
henceforth dominated his existence. Not only did Christ form Paul's
personal life (Gal 2:19–20; 6:14; Phil 1:21), but he was driven by an
inner necessity to pursue in his whole life the universal saving
purpose of Christ himself.[33] In this Paul may be compared to Jeremiah in whom the word of the Lord had become a burning fire

which he could not contain (Jer 20:9). This personal fascination with the risen Christ and with his saving purpose accounts for the paradoxes which are found in Paul's letters. On the one hand Paul displays unshakable confidence and pride in his mission and boastfully defends himself; on the other hand he is keenly aware of personal weakness and humbly effaces himself before the grandeur of his ministry. Two characteristics are prominent in Paul's understanding of his service and of his apostolate: (1) the integration of ministry with the work of God in Christ; (2) the personal self-effacement of the minister.

Paul's Ministry as Gift and Power

First of all, Paul sees himself as an object of divine mercy and his apostolate as a gift of God. He is keenly aware of the fact that because he formerly persecuted the church of God he is now unfit to be called an apostle (1 Cor 15:9). His call is an unmerited gift of God's mercy (1 Cor 15:10; 2 Cor 4:1). His ministry is a grace given to him by God (1 Cor 3:10);[34] this conviction on Paul's part was not simply subjective, because it was recognized by James, Cephas and John in the Jerusalem church (Gal 2:9). On the same occasion it was also recognized that the gift of Paul's ministry was ordered in a special way to the Gentiles; Paul refers again to his ministry among the Gentiles as a gift in Rom 15:15–16. He is also conscious of the fact that the same grace and mercy of God which called him accompanies him in his ministry (1 Cor 15:10) and gives him the right both to challenge others (Rom 12:3) and to give advice in matters not covered directly in the tradition of Jesus' words (1 Cor 7:25, 40).

The gospel with which Paul is entrusted, however, is not simply a message or a creed which he has received from Christ or from tradition and which he must pass on. The gospel is a transcendent power which is communicated to others through the life and work of the apostle. In his earliest letter Paul is conscious of the fact that his proclamation of the gospel is a communication of transcendent power: "For our gospel came to you not only in word, but also in power (dynamis) and in the Holy Spirit and with full conviction" (1 Thess 1:5). "And we also thank God constantly for this, that when you received the word of God which you heard from us, you accepted it not as the word of men but as what it really is, the word of God, which is at work in you believers" (1 Thess 2:13). Again in writing to the Corinthians, "my speech and my message were not in plausible words of wisdom, but in demonstration of the Spirit and power (*dynamis*), that your faith might not rest in the wisdom of men but in the power (*dynamis*) of God" (1 Cor 2:4–5). His preaching of the cross of Christ and of the wisdom of God is not in words "taught by human wisdom but taught by the Spirit" (1 Cor 2:13). He is a steward of the mysteries of God (1 Cor 4:1–2). His presence and his activity among the Corinthians is not mere talk, "for the kingdom of God does not consist in talk but in power" (*dynamis*; 1 Cor 4:20). As a messenger of the gospel, he is only a servant and fellow worker of God; he sees his task as a limited one, that of planting the seed; someone else waters, but God alone is responsible for its growth (1 Cor 3:5–9). The gospel itself is the power (*dynamis*) of God for salvation (Rom 1:16). God then is the primary agent in Paul's understanding of his ministry, but God exercises his power through the preaching and teaching of Paul.

Paul normally uses the Greek word *dynamis* for the power or authority he has received from God; on two occasions (2 Cor 10:8; 13:10) he uses *exousia*, the word more commonly used in the synoptic gospels for the power and authority of God that is operative in Jesus and which he confers upon the twelve and the seventy. Luke in his gospel uses both *dynamis* and *exousia* with reference both to Jesus (4:36) and the twelve (9:1). The same divine power which was operative in the ministry of Jesus and shared by Jesus with the twelve and the seventy is also at work in the ministry of Paul. As was pointed out earlier, real power is involved in the ministry, but the source of that power is God and it must be exercised after the pattern of Jesus, in humility and service.

Paul as the Instrument of God and of Christ

Human speech, of course, does not merely communicate information; it also reveals the person of the speaker and is often an exercise of power moving others to action. Yet there is something quite distinctive in Paul's understanding of the gospel as a communication of divine power and not simply of a human message, however exalted that message might be. Paul sees his preaching as a channel of the power of God and as an effective presentation of the work of God in Christ.

Paul's understanding of his *diakonia* as a way of making present God's work in Christ is most clearly expressed in 2 Cor 5:17–20. A new creation is being realized through the reconciling action of God through Christ. The prior initiative of God is essential to Paul's understanding of salvation.[35] This reconciling action of God and its effects have been revealed in the death and resurrection of Jesus. Those who believe in the risen Jesus as God's messiah are thereby reconciled to God through a spiritual union with the risen Christ[36] and have their sins forgiven. According to Paul this reconciling action of God through Christ is made present to others through his ministry.[37] He is not a reconciler in his own right, but he is the servant of a reconciliation already brought about by God through the death of Christ. He continues to make that reconciling action of God present through "the word of reconciliation" (ton logon tēs katallagēs) which he preaches. In 5:20 Paul then draws a conclusion (oun) about his ministry from these considerations. "So we are ambassadors for Christ, God making his appeal through us."[38] Paul does not use this figure of speech for his apostolate elsewhere in the authentic letters.[39] An ambassador acts for and as the vicegerens of the one who sends him. The personality of the envoy recedes before the person of the one in whose name he speaks or acts. The concept was well known "in the Greek-speaking part of the Roman empire for an official representative of Caesar (Latin:legatus)."[40] In the religious sphere Philo speaks of the logos as God's ambassador.[41] Without using the same language Epictetus describes the true Cynic as the messenger of Zeus to humanity.[42] Hence Paul can say that God speaks and acts through him, making the same appeal through his preaching as he made in the cross of Christ. The effectiveness of the cross as God's act of reconciliation continues in the preaching of the apostle: "We beseech you on behalf of Christ, be reconciled to God" (5:20b). Bornkamm's comment on this passage deserves quotation in full:

> The use of the solemn official term presbeuō is justified by the apostle (oun) on the ground that the divine act of reconciling the world in Christ entails also the institution of a ministry of reconciliation. . . . The preaching, then, is not just a later imparting of the news of the act of salvation; it is an essential part of it . . . the authority of the message rests on the fact that Christ Himself speaks in the word of His ambassador, or—and it amounts to the same thing for the apostle—that God Himself uses the apostle as a mouthpiece to utter His own admonition . . . in the word of the ambassador Christ Himself speaks . . . the apostle represents Christ. Hence it is inadequate to take the hyper Christou presbeuomen of 5:20 to mean "for the cause of Christ." This does not do justice to the special feature of the em-

bassy, i.e. the representation of Christ and the resultant authority of the message.[43]

Although Paul does not use the same language elsewhere in his letters, this understanding of his ministry is never far from his mind. In Gal 3:1 he speaks of his preaching to the Galatians as a public portrayal of Jesus Christ as the crucified one.[44] In 1 Corinthians he tells his readers how he made the cross of Christ the sole subject of his preaching.[45] More succinctly in 2 Cor 4:5 he writes, "For what we preach is not ourselves, but Jesus Christ as Lord, with ourselves as your slaves (doulous, RSV: servants) for Jesus' sake" (dia Iēsoun).

Paul the apostle does not have a program or agenda of his own. His sole purpose is to further the work of Christ, or rather it is Christ who continues to work in and through Paul. It is not merely an expression of enthusiastic rhetoric when Paul writes, "I feel a divine jealousy for you, for I betrothed you to Christ to present you as a pure bride to her one husband" (2 Cor 11:2). The action of God acquiring a people for himself through the cross and resurrection of Jesus continues in the work of the apostle. Later in 2 Corinthians Paul expresses his conviction that Christ is speaking in him (2 Cor 13:3; cf. 2:17; 12:19). In Rom 10:14-21 he extends this understanding of ministry to all preachers of the gospel. Writing to the Romans about the need of preachers, he writes, "So faith comes from what is heard, and what is heard comes by the preaching of Christ" (10:17 RSV; dia rhēmatos Christou; l.v.: dia rhēmatos theou).[46] It is always the word of God or the word of Christ which is heard in the authentic preachers of the gospel; and it has the same effect as the preaching of Jesus, namely, salvation or condemnation (2 Cor 2:15-16).

The language Paul uses in these texts suggests something more than the rabbinic notion of the shālîaḥ (apostle) or the Greco-Roman notion of the presbeutēs (ambassador). Such envoys operate by virtue of a legal fiction mutually recognized by the parties concerned; they are the representatives of those who sent them and remain dependent upon their superiors in all they say or do. On the other hand, they are not instruments through whom the superior really acts; the actions of the ambassador may be disowned by the sender. In Paul's understanding of his ministry, God and Christ are really present and active in his proclamation of the gospel. Such an understanding is not simply a legal fiction; it can only be called sacramental.[47]

God is the primary agent in Paul's work. God gave him the task of laying a foundation (1 Cor 3:10). With Timothy, he is engaged in the work of the Lord (1 Cor 16:10). Speaking of himself, Silvanus and Timothy he writes to the Corinthians, "But it is God who establishes (bebaiōn) us with you in (eis) Christ, and has anointed (chrisas; RSV: commissioned) us" (2 Cor 1:21).[48] God, too, is responsible for the success of Paul's ministry and the consequent communication of the knowledge of God and Christ throughout the world. "But thanks be to God who in Christ always leads us in triumph, and through us spreads the fragrance of the knowledge of him[49] everywhere" (2 Cor 2:14). God alone is the source of the apostle's confidence, for it is God who has empowered him[50] for his ministry (2 Cor 3:4–6). It is the power of Christ that is operative in him (2 Cor 12:9b) and he is capable of all things in the one who strengthens him (Phil 4:13).[51] Paul sees himself and his associates as the servants and fellow workers of God.[52] God is the principal agent; the apostle is his instrument, making present to others the action of God in Christ. Such an understanding gives a sacramental dimension to the proclamation of the gospel; it is also responsible for the personal self-effacement which is another characteristic of Paul's understanding of his ministry.

Paul's Self-Effacement

In 2 Cor 3:7–11 Paul explains how the ministry of the new covenant in the Spirit surpasses in splendor the old Mosaic covenant. Although Paul writes impersonally in this passage, it is easy to sense how proud Paul himself is of the ministry to which he has been called. In 2 Cor 5:20a he understands himself and his associates in ministry as instruments of God in Christ. Paradoxically, it is precisely this high theological estimation of his ministry which prompts Paul to be so self-effacing in his letters. In such a strong personality as Paul, one might suspect some rhetorical overkill, if it were not for the profound sense of unworthiness and of gratitude for the overpowering grace of God which is present everywhere in the letters. This self-effacement characterizes Paul's relationship to God and Christ as well as his relationship to others, both his converts and those he seeks to convert.

He sees himself, first of all, as a limited instrument of God's power and grace. He only plants, others water, but God is responsible for the growth (1 Cor 3:5–9). He is careful not to exaggerate his own importance in the work of ministry or to collect his own personal following, lest the primacy of Christ be obscured by the rivalry of the preachers (1 Cor 1:10–16). "For Christ did not send me to baptize but to preach the gospel, and not with eloquent wisdom, lest the cross of Christ be emptied of its power" (1 Cor 1:17). It is not certain that this insistence on the wisdom of God and the folly of the cross (1 Cor 1:17–25, 2:1–2) represents a new tactic on Paul's part after personal failure in Athens (Acts 17:22–34).[53] In any case, he now relies not on what he calls earthly wisdom but on the grace of God, holiness and godly sincerity (2 Cor 1:12). It is the power of Christ which is at work in him, not his native ability (2 Cor 12:9b). He also recognizes that he is not the only preacher of the gospel; normally, he refrains from preaching the gospel in communities that others have founded (Rom 15:20), although the letter to the Romans appears to be an exception to that rule.[54]

Christ is the subject of his preaching, not himself, because Christ, the revealer of God, has already taken possession of his own heart. "For what we preach is not ourselves, but Jesus Christ as Lord, with ourselves as your servants for Jesus' sake. For it is the God who said, 'Let light shine out of darkness,' who has shone in our hearts to give the light of the glory of God in the face of Christ" (2 Cor 4:5–6).[55] He realizes that he and any minister is inadequate for the task. "Who is sufficient for these things?" (2 Cor 2:16c). "Not that we are sufficient of ourselves to claim anything as coming from us; our sufficiency is from God" (2 Cor 3:5). As the aroma of Christ to God he has to accept the fact that some will be saved by his preaching, while others will be lost; this realization overwhelms him (2 Cor 2:15–16).[56]

Paul is also self-effacing before his converts so that his own person may not in any way be an obstacle to the gospel (2 Cor 6:3). "Here for the third time I am ready to come to you. And I will not be a burden, for I seek not what is yours but you . . . I will most gladly spend and be spent for your souls" (2 Cor 12:14–15a). In writing to the Philippians he is prepared to postpone the fulfillment of his own desire to die and to be with Christ for the benefit of the Christian community at Philippi (Phil 1:21–26). To put it colloquially, Paul is not "stuck on himself"; he is prepared to adapt his own behavior to the sensitivities, culture and needs of those whom he seeks to win for Christ. Paul reminds the Galatians that he has become like them for their sakes (Gal 4:12).[57] He is prepared to sacrifice his own rights and freedom for fear of offending others. With the Corinthians he does not press his right to receive material support from them, lest he put an obstacle in the way of the gospel of

Christ (1 Cor 9:3–18). With rhetorical flourish, he sums up his willingness to put himself out for the gospel: "For though I am free from
all men, I have made myself a slave to all that I might win the
more. . . . I have become all things to all men, that I might by all
means save some. I do it all for the sake of the gospel, that I may
share in its blessings" (1 Cor 9:19–23). In dealing with the issue of
idol meats at Corinth, he boldly calls others to the same practice of
self-effacement before the consciences of the weak: "Therefore, if
food is a cause of my brother's falling, I will never eat meat, lest I
cause my brother to fall" (1 Cor 8:13).

Realizing that the effectiveness of his ministry is dependent
upon God and not himself, Paul is content to appear weak, inferior
and even ineffectual so that any success he has will be attributed to
God and not to himself. Although the tone throughout is ironic,
Paul protests his own insignificance in order to shame and admonish the spiritually boastful Corinthians. ". . . For I think that God
has exhibited us apostles as last of all, like men sentenced to death,
because we have become a spectacle to the world, to angels and to
men. We are fools for Christ's sake . . . we have become, and are
now, as the refuse of the world, the offscouring of all things" (1 Cor
4:9–13). He is certainly sincere, even though rhetorical, in speaking
about his ministry in 2 Cor 4:7–12: "But we have this treasure in
earthen vessels, to show that the transcendent power belongs to
God and not to us. We are afflicted in every way, but not crushed;
perplexed, but not driven to despair; persecuted, but not forsaken;
struck down, but not destroyed; always carrying in the body the
death of Jesus, so that the life of Jesus may also be manifested in our
bodies. For while we live we are always being given up to death for
Jesus' sake, so that the life of Jesus may be manifested in our mortal
flesh. So death is at work in us, but life in you." In a series of
rhetorical paradoxes Paul confesses that he does not care what hap-
pens to him personally, provided the saving work of God is fur-
thered through his ministry (2 Cor 6:1–10). Reluctantly boasting of
his achievements in 2 Cor 11—12 to defend his apostolate, he nonetheless admits that his only valid boast is his own weakness (2 Cor
11:30). Through personal experience he has learned that God's work
is more apparent in frail instruments. "My grace is sufficient for
you, for my power is made perfect in weakness" (2 Cor 12:9). The
willingness to be associated with Christ in his weakness explains
Paul's protest in Gal 6:14. "But far be it from me to glory except in
the cross of our Lord Jesus Christ, by which the world has been
crucified to me, and I to the world." This disregard of self enables

him to accept imprisonment and even the rebukes of rival preachers, provided the cause of Christ is advanced (Phil 1:12–18). "Only
that, in every way, whether in pretense or in truth, Christ is proclaimed; and in that I rejoice" (Phil 1:18).

In so evaluating his ministry, Paul's thought is in harmony with
God's pattern of action throughout the OT since the time of the
exodus. God always acts with his people in such a way that men
and women cannot take the credit for what is achieved, but whatever is achieved is seen to be the work of God.[58] Just as the cross of
Christ is the power of God and the wisdom of God offered to Jews
who seek signs and Greeks who seek wisdom (1 Cor 1:24), God
chooses what is low and despised in the world "so that no human
being might boast in the presence of God" (1 Cor 1:29). Both Paul's
call and his conduct of the apostolate illustrate that fundamental
principle which is apparent in all God's dealings with his people.

Paul's Apostolic Consciousness

Even though Paul recognized that he was the limited instrument of God and of Christ, he was nonetheless a human instrument
and responded to his call with all his personal gifts and with a zeal
that was comparable to the zeal with which he had previously persecuted the Jewish Christians. He devoted himself to his converts
and acted as though he was personally responsible for their perseverance and progress in the Christian life. This personal concern is
evident in the very first letter (1 Thess 3:1–13). The personal involvement of the apostle in the fate of his communities is most
vividly illustrated in the emotional letter to the Galatians. Here Paul
is passionately disturbed for fear that his new converts may be sub-
jected to Jewish practices as a condition of salvation. "I am afraid I
have labored over you in vain" (Gal 4:11). The verb used here—
kopiaō—means "to work hard." It is this same sense of personal
responsibility and initiative which led him to forego his right to
support from the Corinthians (1 Cor 9:12–18), even though he may
have done so with a touch of personal conceit (1 Cor 9:17–18). He
realized too that he must discipline himself lest he fail to obtain the
goal which he so ardently desired for others (1 Cor 9:26–27). In
other words, Paul practiced what he preached!

In the same vein, Paul does not hesitate to propose himself as
an example for others, but only insofar as he reflects Christ in his
behavior. "Give no offense to Jews or Greeks or to the church of
God, just as I try to please all men in everything I do, not seeking

my own advantage, but that of many, that they may be saved. Be imitators of me, as I am of Christ" (1 Cor 10:32—11:1). The example of the apostle himself is a means of passing on the tradition.[59]

On the other hand, when he feels compelled to boast of his own achievements, and even of visions, in order to defend the validity of his own apostolate in 2 Cor 11—12, he repeatedly apologizes for something he would rather not do.[60] He is well aware of his own achievements and success, but resists the temptation to take credit for them, preferring to give all the credit to God and his overpowering grace. Nonetheless, the human frailty of Paul the man peeks through the exalted understanding of his ministry on a number of occasions. In 1 Cor 15 he has to correct a "Freudian slip" of self-conceit: "I worked harder than any of them, though it was not I, but the grace of God which is with me" (15:10). In 2 Cor 8:5 he is surprised at the generosity of the Macedonians in the matter of the collection and attributes it to the way they responded both to the Lord and to himself! Even though Paul's self-effacement dominates his understanding of his ministry, the human tendency to self-conceit which breaks through from time to time assures us that Paul too shares in the sinful condition of all humanity, in spite of the powerful action of God's grace within him.

a) Formed by Christ

In order to form Christ in others Paul has to let himself be formed by Christ. Christ is Paul's life (Gal 2:20; Phil 1:20–21). In all the letters there is no more personal confession of the primacy of Christ in his life than Phil 3:3–14.[61] He sees all his hardships, including imprisonment, as means of conforming himself to the suffering Jesus and of advancing the cause of the gospel of Christ.[62] "The gospel of Christ" is a favorite expression of his, appearing in all the authentic letters except Philemon.[63] If he proposes himself as a model for imitation, it is only to the extent that he has modeled his life after that of Jesus (1 Cor 10:33—11:1). In his exhortations he seeks to reflect the meekness and gentleness of Christ (2 Cor 10:1).

b) Forming Christ in Others

Formed by Christ, Paul devotes his life to forming Christ in others. He uses the imagery of father, mother, parent and nurse to describe his ministry. "For though you have countless guides in Christ, you do not have many fathers. For I became your father in Christ Jesus through the gospel" (1 Cor 4:15). ". . . like a father with his children, we exhorted each one of you and encouraged you and charged you to lead a life worthy of God, who calls you into his own kingdom and glory" (1 Thess 2:11–12). "I feel a divine jealousy for you, for I betrothed you to Christ to present you as a pure bride (RSV; *parthenon hagnēn*) to her husband" (2 Cor 11:2)[64] "My little children, with whom I am again in travail until Christ be formed in you" (Gal 4:19). ". . . I seek not what is yours but you; for children ought not to lay up for their parents, but parents for their children. I will most gladly spend and be spent for your souls. If I love you the more, am I to be loved the less?" (2 Cor 12:14–15). "But we were gentle among you, like a nurse taking care of her children" (1 Thess 2:7).

c) The Liturgical Quality of Paul's Ministry

Because of his pastoral care the Corinthians are described as "a letter from Christ," because they have been formed through Paul by the Spirit of the living God (2 Cor 3:2–3).[65] It is in the context of forming Christ in others that Paul uses cultic and priestly language for his ministry. The community at Corinth is described by Paul as the temple of God and Paul cares for that temple: "Do you not know that you are God's temple and that God's Spirit dwells in you? If any one destroys God's temple, God will destroy him. For God's temple is holy, and that temple you are" (1 Cor 3:16–17).[66] The community at Philippi is described as a sacrificial offering to God and Paul is ready to let his life be poured out as a libation upon that offering. "Even if I am to be poured as a libation upon the sacrificial offering of your faith (*epi tę thusią kai leitourgią tēs pisteōs hymōn*), I am glad and rejoice with you all" (Phil 2:17).[67] The ministry of charity (*hē diakonia tēs leitourgias tautēs*) to the saints in Jerusalem on the part of Gentile Christians is as so many thanksgiving sacrifices to God (2 Cor 9:12; cf. Rom 15:27).[68] The most significant text in this regard is Rom 15:15–17: "But on some points I have written to you very boldly by way of reminder, because of the grace given me by God to be a minister (*leitourgon*) of Christ Jesus to the Gentiles in the priestly service of the gospel of God (*hierourgounta to euaggelion tou theou*), so that the offering (*prosphora*) of the Gentiles may be acceptable (*euprosdektos*), sanctified by the Holy Spirit. In Christ Jesus, then, I have reason to be proud of my work for God." The language in this text is clearly cultic in origin, but it is not applied to any ritual sacrifices or even to the celebration of the eucharist. It is applied to the preaching and teaching ministry of

Paul; the ministry is ordered to forming the Gentiles by the Holy Spirit[69] so that they may offer themselves to God as an acceptable sacrifice (Rom 12:1). In this transferred sense Paul performs priestly service without in any way detracting from the unique priesthood of Christ.[70] This transferred use of cultic language by Paul builds upon the spiritualizing of temple cult which was already far advanced in some forms of Judaism, especially among the Essenes and the Pharisees.

d) The Promotion of Christ

As a minister of the gospel, the truth of Christ is Paul's sole concern. He himself speaks in Christ (2 Cor 2:17; 12:19) and he wants to make it clear that it is Christ who speaks in him (2 Cor 13:3). He knows that he would be ineffective if he were working against the truth; he can only work for the truth (2 Cor 13:8), and for Paul the truth is knowledge of God and Christ. "We destroy arguments and every proud obstacle to the knowledge of God, and take every thought captive to obey Christ, being ready to punish every disobedience, when your obedience is complete" (2 Cor 10:5–6).[71]

e) Motivated by Love

In his ministry Paul is motivated by the love of God revealed through Christ (2 Cor 5:14–15).[72] This love is a power within him leading him to expend himself on those whom Christ came to save. The letters are full of expressions of affection for his Christians, even when he feels compelled to deal firmly with them. "For I wrote you out of much affliction and anguish of heart and with many tears, not to cause you pain but to let you know the abundant love I have for you" (2 Cor 2:4). Most of the letters begin with expanded expressions of thanksgiving, prayer and affection for those whom he is addressing.[73] Though such expressions were formal parts of the ancient letter-form, Paul displays personal involvement with his communities through the way he expands such formal greetings.

Prayer for those he serves is an integral part of ministry for Paul; the language he uses suggests that it was a constant accompaniment of his apostolic activity.[74] He is also aware of his own need for support from the prayers of his Christian communities and does not hesitate to ask for it.[75] The significance that he assigns to the prayer of petition is another sign of his dependence on God in all aspects of his apostolate. Finally, he is even prepared to forego union with Christ in death in order to be of further service to the Philippians (Phil 1:24–26). The primacy of love in his own life must have inspired to some degree the hymn to *agapē*, which he calls "a still more excellent way" (1 Cor 12:31—13:13).

Paul is not satisfied with simply preaching the gospel. The love of Christ which motivates him inspires him to give his very self. "So, being affectionately desirous of you, we were ready to share with you not only the gospel of God but also our own selves, because you had become very dear to us" (1 Thess 2:8). A concrete verification of this gift of self is his practice of supporting himself by his own work.[76] Jesus had questioned Peter about the quality of his love before entrusting him with the care of his sheep (John 21:15–17); in a similar way Paul's personal devotion to his converts flows from his commitment to Christ.

f) Paul, the Apostle of the Universal Gospel

Paul is generally known as the apostle of the Gentiles. He is particularly conscious of his special call to this mission[77] and it is this mission which dominates his thought in the letters. Nonetheless, Paul was by birth and education a Jew. It would have been a failure on his part to honor the universality of the gospel if his special mission to the Gentiles resulted in disregard for his own Jewish people. He affirms this universality in Rom 15:8–9: "For I tell you that Christ became a servant to the circumcised to show God's truthfulness, in order to confirm the promises given to the patriarchs, and in order that the Gentiles might glorify God for his mercy." Paul's pattern of missionary preaching as reflected in the Acts of the Apostles—beginning with the Jews and God-fearers in the synagogues and going to the Gentiles only when the Jews refused to believe—is not directly evident from the letters; but Paul's apostolic interest in his own people is reflected particularly in Rom 9—11.

Introducing his reflections on the role of the Jews in God's plan of salvation, Paul gives expression to the deep personal sorrow and anguish that is in his heart and catalogues the historical privileges of the Jews (Rom 9:1–5). This same heartfelt anxiety is expressed again in Rom 10:1 and 11:1–2. There is no reason to doubt the sincerity of these expressions of personal involvement, even though God's fidelity to the Jewish people is also of theological importance for Paul; for if God has not been faithful in keeping his promises to the Jews, Paul would have no grounds for believing that the same God would be faithful to the Gentiles who have believed in Christ.

Throughout Rom 9—11 Paul ponders theologically the destiny of the Jewish people in the light of his own experience of the Gentile mission and of the Jewish scriptures. His resolution of the problem appears in Rom 11: ". . . at the present time there is a remnant chosen by grace (11:5) . . . through their trespass salvation has come to the Gentiles so as to make Israel jealous (11:11). . . . Inasmuch then as I am an apostle to the Gentiles, I magnify my ministry in order to make my fellow Jews jealous, and thus save some of them. For if their rejection means the reconciliation of the world, what will their acceptance mean but life from the dead? (11:13–15) . . . even the others, if they do not persist in their unbelief, will be grafted in, for God has the power to graft them in again (11:23) . . . a hardening has come upon part of Israel, until the full number of the Gentiles come in, and all Israel will be saved (11:25–26)." In Paul's thinking, God's fidelity to his promises has for the moment been guaranteed in "the remnant," that is, the Jewish Christians who have believed in Jesus as the Christ. At the same time, Paul has seen how in fact Jewish infidelity has been contributing to the spread of the gospel among the Gentiles; the spiritual riches of the Jewish tradition are now available to God-fearers and pagans through faith in Christ without the less acceptable burdens of circumcision, and of dietary and purity laws. Paul hopes that the success of the Gentile mission will be a prod which will someday result in the reintegration of unbelieving Jews into the existing remnant.

The very complexity and tortured character of this long development in Rom 9—11 is an indication of Paul's own commitment not simply to the Gentile mission but to his own Jewish people. Ultimately, however, it is absolute trust in a God who is faithful to his promises which has guided Paul to this resolution of what must have appeared to be a very confused pastoral situation.

g) *Apostolic Encouragement and Boldness*

A particular example of Paul's devoted love is the practice of encouragement which always accompanies his letters and which he considers to be very important for the building up of the church. He uses the verb *parakaleō* of his own ministry in all the letters except Galatians.[78] He refers to his preaching to the Thessalonians as a disinterested appeal (*paraklēsis*; 1 Thess 2:3–4). He values prophecy above tongues because this gift has the power to encourage and build up the church (1 Cor 14:1–6, 31). Encouragement for Paul is a necessary part of the Christian life; he not only encourages those to whom he writes but also recognizes his own need of encouragement and rejoices when encouragement comes his way from God or from his Christians (2 Cor 1:3–7; Phlm 7). God is the ultimate source of all encouragement (2 Cor 1:3; Rom 15:5; cf. Rom 12:1) and Paul sees himself as an instrument of that divine encouragement toward all in affliction.

The greatest encouragement of all is the knowledge of God's reconciling love through the death of Christ. God continues that encouraging appeal—"Be reconciled to God"—through the ministry of reconciliation he has given to Paul (2 Cor 5:18–20). This apostolic encouragement or *paraklēsis* is an appeal made to others to repent, to believe in Jesus Christ our Lord and to persevere in that faith and in the practice of Christian love even in the face of opposition, suffering and persecution. The appeal draws its passion from the love that God has showered upon men and women in Christ Jesus. It is a communication of the strength and power of God to those who believe in Christ. Such *paraklēsis* of others is part and parcel of Paul's ministry.[79]

Out of the encouragement Paul received from God flowed the trust with which he engaged in the apostolate. After praising God for the encouragement he has given him (2 Cor 1:3–7), Paul continues: "For we do not want you to be ignorant, brethren, of the affliction we experienced in Asia; for we were so utterly unbearably crushed that we despaired of life itself. Why, we felt that we had received the sentence of death; but that was to make us rely not on ourselves but on God who raises the dead; he delivered us from so deadly a peril, and he will deliver us; on him we have set our hope that he will deliver us again" (2 Cor 1:8–10). "Such is the confidence that we have through Christ toward God. Not that we are sufficient of ourselves to claim anything as coming from us; our sufficiency is from God, who has qualified us to be ministers of a new covenant . . . " (2 Cor 3:4–6). "So we do not lose heart. . . . For this slight momentary affliction is preparing for us an eternal weight of glory beyond all comparison, because we do not look to the things that are seen but to the things that are unseen; for the things that are seen are transient, but the things that are unseen are eternal" (2 Cor 4:16–18).

This trust is the source of his apostolic boldness or *parrhēsia*.[80] He is not ashamed of the gospel he preaches (Rom 1:16) or of the sufferings which come his way because of that preaching (Phil 1:12–20). The most eloquent expression of Paul's confidence is to be found in the rhetorical peroration of Rom 8:31–39; this burst of confidence flows from the experience of the apostle himself but is intended for the encouragement of all Christians: "For I am sure that neither death, nor life, nor angels, nor principalities, nor powers, nor height, nor depth, nor anything else in all creation, will be able to separate us from the love of God in Christ Jesus our Lord" (8:38–39).

h) The Experience of Opposition

The same trust and boldness is the source of his courage to preach the gospel against opposition. Opposition accompanied Paul's work throughout his life. In 1 Thess 2:14–16 he refers in passing to the opposition he had already experienced from the Jews; 1 Thess 2:2 touches on the opposition he faces from Gentiles at Philippi.[81] Judaizers were his opponents in the churches of Galatia and Philippi, and false apostles of uncertain origin in Corinth.[82]

Confident that he was doing God's work, he was not afraid of human opposition. He had to defend himself against accusations of all kinds, especially of preaching the gospel out of self-interest; the society of Paul's day was characterized by many popular preachers and philosophers who sought to persuade people and lead them astray by their sophistries. Paul has to protest the sincerity and disinterestedness of his own preaching (1 Thess 2:4–7); this self-defense is especially eloquent in 2 Corinthians: "For we are not, like so many, peddlers of God's word; but as men of sincerity, as commissioned by God, in the sight of God we speak in Christ" (2 Cor 2:17). "We have renounced disgraceful, underhanded ways; we refuse to practice cunning or to tamper with God's word, but by open statement of the truth we would commend ourselves to every man's conscience in the sight of God" (2 Cor 4:2). He is suspected of acting in a worldly fashion (2 Cor 10:2), but boldly asserts in Gal 1:10 that he is not seeking popularity, but only the will of God: "Am I now seeking the favor of men, or of God? Or am I trying to please men? If I were still pleasing men, I should not be a slave (*doulos*; RSV: servant) of Christ."

There is a paradox in this self-defense on Paul's part; he needs a good reputation in order to be heard, but he cannot appear to be self-serving. Only the interior conviction of the truth of his message, a conviction which he has by the gift of God, prevents this self-defense from appearing as arrogant self-justification.

i) Fidelity to the Tradition

Paul is a teacher of a message which he has not invented but which he has received from the revelation of the risen Christ on the road to Damascus and from the tradition of the early church. He is a steward of the mysteries of God (1 Cor 4:1–2). His task is not to develop a philosophy or a theology of his own, but to be faithful to the tradition he has received and to use that tradition to illumine every new situation which arises. The letters of Paul are examples of how he discharged his stewardship with trustworthiness. Concern for the truth and continuity in handing on the gospel already appear in his struggle with the Judaizers of Galatia (Gal 1:6–9). He is concerned with consistency in his teaching (1 Cor 4:17) and fidelity to the tradition he has received. "I commend you because you remember me in everything and maintain the traditions even as I have delivered them to you" (1 Cor 11:2). Even when his own arguments seem to fail him, the practice of the churches is a source of guidance (1 Cor 11:16). The eucharistic tradition is used in 1 Cor 11:17–34 to regulate disorderly conduct at the celebration of the Lord's supper. In 1 Cor 15 he has recourse to the traditional creed (15:3–5[7]) to deal with objections to the resurrection of the dead. With the Corinthians as with the Galatians Paul is afraid that they are too readily adopting a different gospel from the one he preached (2 Cor 11:4). In calling others to imitate him, Paul also sees his own life and example as an instrument of tradition.[83]

In Philippians 2 he uses a traditional hymn about the self-emptying of Christ (2:6–11) to foster Christian community among the Philippians (2:1–5). In this case, Paul shows his creativity by the way he uses a traditional christological text for a pastoral purpose; the example of Jesus as he is proclaimed in worship serves as a model for building up the local community in love. His exhortation to chastity in 1 Cor 6:12–20 is another example of the way Paul draws ethical and parenetic conclusions from a doctrinal tradition. The good news of God in Christ has practical consequences for the way Christians live; Paul is at pains to draw these consequences from the tradition he has received. Fidelity to tradition for Paul is not a mere repetition of received formulas, but a dynamic exploration of how the tradition throws light upon new situations as they arise.

Another way in which Paul demonstrates his fidelity to tradition is the formation he gives to his fellow workers, both male and female. They are not merely assistants to Paul, but extensions of his own apostolic ministry. According to 1 Cor 4:17 Timothy's task is to remind the Corinthians of Paul's own teaching. Titus is said to share the care for the Corinthians as Paul himself (2 Cor 8:16).[84] It is not always clear, when Paul uses first person plural pronouns, whether he is speaking only of himself or associating other apostolic workers with himself. If he is doing so, this manner of speech implies that Paul's understanding of ministry is meant to inspire others who were not apostles of the Jerusalem church like the twelve, nor favored with an appearance of the risen Christ as was Paul. In other words, fidelity to the tradition led Paul to form other apostolic ministers to extend and continue his work.

j) Paul's Use of His Apostolic Authority

The final point that needs to be made about Paul's understanding of his ministry is his confidence in his authority and his reluctance to impose that authority. In this way he exemplifies in his own life the instructions Jesus gave the twelve about the exercise of authority in Mark 10:42–45. In responding to the Corinthians on the question of marriage in 1 Cor 7, Paul does not have a word of the Lord to meet all the situations which arise. In advising the unmarried to remain celibate, Paul is confident that his opinion is trustworthy (7:25); in the same way, in advising against second marriages, he says, "I think that I have the Spirit of God" (7:40). In 1 Cor 9 he defends his right (exousia)[85] to be married and to receive material support from the Christians to whom he preaches, even though he has personally chosen not to use these rights for the sake of the gospel. On the other hand, he does not hesitate to see in the regulations he draws up for prayer meetings a command of the Lord and he insists firmly on their observance. "If any one thinks that he is a prophet, or spiritual, he should acknowledge that what I am writing to you is a command of the Lord. If any one does not recognize this, he is not recognized" (1 Cor 14:37–38).

Paul is sure enough of his own authority that he expects obedience from the Corinthians, provided the decision is related to the cause of Christ and is made with the help of Christ's Spirit. Paul's instructions for dealing with the incestuous man at Corinth illustrate this principle. "For though absent in body I am present in spirit, and as if present, I have already pronounced judgment *in the name of the Lord Jesus* on the man who has done such a thing. When you are assembled, and my spirit is present, with the power (*dynamis*) of our Lord Jesus, you are to deliver this man to Satan for the destruction of the flesh, that his spirit may be saved in the day of the Lord Jesus" (1 Cor 5:3–5). In 2 Cor 2:9 he says that he is writing to test the obedience of the Corinthians; but it is their obedience to the gospel that he is testing, not their obedience to his personal authority.[86] At the risk of boasting he undertakes to defend his apostolic authority (*exousia hēmōn*) in 2 Cor 10:7–18, but recognizes at the same time that this authority has its limits and that it must be exercised in dependence on Christ. He also knows how to distinguish what he says and does on his own authority from what he does in the Lord's name. In his lengthy boast against the false apostles at Corinth (2 Cor 11:5–29), he comments parenthetically, "What I am saying I say not with the Lord's authority (RSV; *kata kyrion*) but as a fool in this boastful confidence; since many boast of worldly things, I too will boast" (11:17). He does not claim any personal authority on the basis of his own merits, but only on the basis of what God and Christ work in him (2 Cor 11:30; 12:1–5); this includes the signs and wonders and mighty works (*dynameis*) which are the signs of an apostle (2 Cor 12:12). The same word *dynameis*, of course, is also used in the synoptic gospels for the miracles of Jesus. He is confident of possessing as a gift of God a real authority (*exousia*) for building up the church (2 Cor 13:10). In virtue of that gift he writes boldly even to a community he does not know personally (Rom 15:15). His confidence is rooted in the fact that he is not the purveyor of a personal message, but of the gospel of God, and that that gospel is not just a human philosophy but the very power (*dynamis*) of God (Rom 1:16). Paul is merely an instrument of that divine power, but nonetheless a free, human and responsible instrument.

Conscious of the authority which he possesses as a minister of the gospel, Paul is reluctant to use that authority unless it is strictly necessary for the truth of the gospel or the safeguarding of the Christian life in his communities. He is no doubt aware of the danger of imposing himself on others or of being seen by others as bearing a merely personal authority, rather than the authority of God. He also recognizes that the same God and Christ of whom he is the apostle are also at work in the Christians he serves; his work is but the catalyst for the work of God. "Not that we lord it over (*kyrieuomen*) your faith; we work with you for your joy, for you stand firm in your faith" (2 Cor 1:24).[87] He prefers to remind them of their own commitment to the Lord Jesus, to encourage and persuade them, even to cajole and shame them into an obedient response rather than to command them, even if he does so in the name of the Lord. The God Paul serves seeks a free response; so does his servant Paul. A good example of the way he solicits attention for his teaching may be seen in 2 Cor 7:2–4: "Open your hearts to us; we have wronged no one, we have corrupted no one, we have taken advantage of no one. I do not say this to condemn you, for I said before that you are in our hearts, to die together and to live together. I have great confidence in you; I have great pride in you; I am filled with comfort. With all our affliction, I am overjoyed." In the matter of the collection he refrains from commanding but appeals to their generosity (2 Cor 8:8) and gives practical advice on how to act in this same matter (2 Cor 8:10). Reluctant to be severe, he writes 2 Cor 10—13 to prepare his arrival (2 Cor 13:10). The little note to Philemon is a concrete example of the way Paul prefers to use his authority. He is well aware that Christ has given him the authority to command Philemon to free the slave Onesimus and to send him back to Paul (v 8); but he prefers to appeal (*parakaleō*) for love's sake (v 9). He sends Onesimus back to his owner so that Philemon might be perfectly free in responding to Paul's request. "I preferred to do nothing without your consent in order that your goodness might not be by compulsion but of your own free will" (v 14). There are other ways of soliciting a Christian response besides commanding. "Confident of your obedience, I write to you, knowing that you will do even more than I say" (v 21). Apostolic authority should be used to foster Christian freedom and not to secure conformity. In these examples, we see a very confident apostle trying to exercise his authority after the pattern laid down by Christ himself.

Conclusion

Although Paul was not an eyewitness to the public ministry of Jesus and received his call to the apostolate in an entirely unique and unexpected way, he exhibits in his understanding of ministry the same attitudes that we discovered in Jesus' instructions to the twelve and the seventy. His call was utterly gratuitous. His ministry was a making present the reconciliation which God revealed through the cross and resurrection of Christ. He lived in total dependence on God and his grace and gave freely of what had been given to him. He was conscious of possessing a real authority but exercised it cautiously, lest he himself get in the way of the word of God. He expected his fellow workers to view their ministry in the same way and provided for continuity in the preaching of the gospel and in the living of the Christian life. Paul is unique because of the nature of his call and his foundational role. While he did not initiate the mission to the Gentiles, he nonetheless extended it and gave it a solid, theological justification, thereby guaranteeing the universality of the gospel. He formed others in the same understanding of ministry and expected them to carry on the same work, for by the time he wrote 2 Cor 5 and Phil 1 he was aware that he would not live to see the coming of the Lord. The deutero-Paulines illustrate how his disciples responded to his expectations.

The Deutero-Paulines

Regardless of whether Paul was responsible or not for the writing of Colossians, Ephesians and the pastorals, an understanding of his apostolate lives on in this correspondence. At the same time there is also development beyond the explicit thought of Paul to meet new circumstances which arose in his communities after his death. In this way the authority of Paul was kept alive in his own churches and his understanding of the ministry was continued in others.[88]

a) Colossians

Paul's status as an apostle of Christ Jesus by the will of God is maintained throughout these letters (Col 1:1).[89] The prayers of the apostle extend to all who believe, even though they may not be his own converts (Col 1:9–12).[90] As an apostle he is a servant (diakonos) of the universal gospel and of the body of Christ, the church (Col 1:23–25).[91] His physical sufferings are seen in solidarity with those of Christ for the building up of the church (Col 1:24–25). He has received a gift from God in virtue of a divine plan (oikonomia) to bring the word of God to completion, a word that is otherwise called the mystery (mystērion; Col 1:25–26).[92] By seeking to present every human being (panta anthrōpon) perfect in Christ (Col 1:28), he does not allow the individual to be swallowed up in the collectivity. In continuity with the authentic Paulines all the apostle's work is the fruit of God's power working in him (Col 1:29).[93] Concern for tradition is still apparent (Col 2:6–7). Finally, the apostle asks for the prayers of those he serves and is constantly looking for an opportunity to preach the mystery of Christ (Col 4:3–4).[94]

b) Ephesians

In this letter Paul is described as a prisoner of Christ Jesus (Eph 3:1) as he described himself in Phlm 1, 9. His ministry is the gift of God's grace (Eph 3:2, 7) and the fruit of revelation (Eph 3:3). This revelation consists in the mystery of Christ (Eph 3:3–4) as the means of reconciliation between Jews and Gentiles and for the incorporation of the Gentiles into "the commonwealth of Israel" (Eph 2:12). This divine plan for universal reconciliation is the content of Paul's preaching and the mission of the church which is the body of Christ the head (Eph 2:13–22; 3:7–10; 4:11–16). Paul himself is presented as "the very least of all the saints" in such a way that the grandeur of his ministry to the Gentiles may appear more effectively as a gift of God (Eph 3:8).

In the authentic letters Paul proposed himself as an object of imitation because the example of Christ was visible in his life; in Ephesians Paul is no longer proposed as a direct object of imitation because he is no longer personally present as an example; the recipients of the letter are urged instead to be imitators of God "as beloved children" with Christ himself as their example (Eph 5:1–2). The personal element which is so characteristic of the authentic letters of Paul is totally absent from Ephesians; Paul himself belongs to the past, but his inspiration is still dynamic.

c) The Pastorals

The portrait of Paul the apostle is drawn in even stronger strokes in the pastorals. He is still presented as the apostle of Christ Jesus by God's decree.[95] The expanded introduction of the letter to Titus expresses Paul's understanding of his apostolate as a commission from God to make known the mystery of his love hidden since ages past. The instructions which Paul gives to Timothy and Titus, and through them to those whom they shall appoint, reflect the apostle's own understanding of ministry. For the author of the pastorals it is the ministry of Paul which is being continued in a new age. A principle is enunciated in 1 Tim 1:5 which certainly governed Paul's exercise of authority and is proposed here as the goal of all authority in the church: "The aim of our charge (para-ggelia) is love that issues from a pure heart and a good conscience and sincere faith." At this point in the study we are interested only in the way Paul's own apostolate is presented by the author of the pastorals. A subsequent chapter will examine the similarities between Paul's ministry and the ministries of Timothy, Titus, the presbyters and the deacons.

The text of 1 Tim 1:11–16 may be described as a literary portrait of Paul the apostle. He has been entrusted with "the good news of the glory of the blessed God" (1:11). His apostolate is a gift, an empowering by Christ Jesus for service (diakonia; 1:12). The gratuity of Paul's call to ministry is more apparent because of his former state as persecutor of Christ's church (1:13); he is personally the recipient of God's mercy in such an extraordinary way that others should be able to see in him an effective example of Christ's saving work for sinners (1:15–16).[96] Later he is described as a herald, an apostle and a teacher of the Gentiles (1 Tim 2:7; cf. 2 Tim 1:11). The universal import of the gospel is strongly affirmed in the request for prayers for all humankind including pagan rulers (1 Tim 2:1–2), and in the proclamation of the universal saving will of God our savior (1 Tim 2:3–6; 4:10).

The motivation which inspires the writing of the pastoral epistles is precisely continuity in ministry; Paul himself has given the individual Timothy a pastoral mission to the communities in the region of Ephesus and plans to meet him personally to provide further encouragement and instruction; in the meantime, however, he is writing "so that, if I am delayed, you may know how one ought to behave in the household of God, which is the church of the living God, the pillar and bulwark of truth" (1 Tim 3:14–15; cf. 4:13). Paul is presented as one who wants to see his own understanding of ministry continue in those he has formed.

Cultic language appears again in 2 Tim 4:6 where Paul views his life as a libation.[97] In 2 Tim 1:3 the cultic word latreuō is used for Paul's service of God in continuity with the worship of his Jewish ancestors. In the course of encouraging Timothy in his ministry, Paul implies that Timothy has received the same gifts from God himself: "For God did not give us a spirit of timidity but a spirit of power and love and self-control" (2 Tim 1:7). Paul is a prisoner (desmios) of the Lord (2 Tim 1:8), as he described himself in Phlm 1, 9. His commitment to the gospel is the occasion of personal suffering, but as always his confidence for the future rests in the power of God (2 Tim 1:12; 2:9–10; 4:6–8, 17–18). In excusing his accusers (2 Tim 4:16) Paul is the imitator of Christ (Luke 23:34) and Stephen (Acts 7:60). Timothy has been witness to Paul's own life; he should let that experience form his own (2 Tim 3:10–17). Finally, Paul expresses his hope that the tradition will be continued through Timothy (2 Tim 1:13–14; 3:14) and that Timothy in turn will commit the tradition to trustworthy individuals (2 Tim 2:1–2).

d) 2 Thessalonians

This brief consideration of the deutero-Paulines illustrates the way in which the apostolic authority of Paul lived on after his death and became a model for Timothy, Titus, the presbyters and the deacons. Pseudonymity, however, could be a dangerous way of prolonging Paul's authority. If 2 Thessalonians is deutero-Pauline, as many commentators think today,[98] it demonstrates how the Pauline tradition could be exposed to misrepresentation: apocalyptic enthusiasts are disturbing Pauline communities by insisting on the imminence of the *parousia* on Paul's authority; forged letters purporting to be from Paul are being circulated (2 Thess 2:1–2); the letter must be guaranteed by Paul's own handwriting (2 Thess 3:17; cf. Gal 6:11; 1 Cor 16:21; Phlm 19). It is also known from 2 Pet 3:15–16 that the teaching of Paul was being misrepresented in the early second century. The author of 2 Thessalonians considers himself obliged to insist on fidelity to the traditions received from Paul either orally or in writing (2:15). Although the historical Paul was reluctant to command, the author of 2 Thessalonians does not apologize for doing so in 3:4, 6, 10, 12, 14![99] The exhortations of 2 Thess 3 imply a Pauline moral tradition in which his own example of self-supporting work is a major element. Obedience to this tradition is imperative; the pattern of discipline used by Paul with the incestuous man at Corinth is applied (1 Cor 5:1–5; cf. Matt 18:15–17); nonetheless, reconciliation, not rejection, is still the purpose of the discipline (2 Thess 3:14–15). The sternness with which the author of 2 Thessalonians must deal with departures from the authentic Pauline tradition may be an indication that the apostolic age is passing and pseudonymity is no longer an adequate way of preserving the apostolic tradition.

IV

NEW TESTAMENT PROVISIONS FOR MINISTRY

Direct and articulated evidence in the NT for the understanding of ministry in the church is, practically speaking, limited to what is said in the gospels about the ministry of Jesus and his provision for the ministry of his disciples, and to what Paul has to say about his own ministry. The information provided by the NT literature for the organization of ministry in the continuing church is, at best, episodic and derivative. The primary interest of the NT authors is the spread of the gospel and the building up of local communities in the church. The organizational and juridical questions of a later age are not addressed in the NT; it is illusory to think that the exegesis of NT texts can provide direct answers to contemporary issues. The NT texts can, however, suggest certain theological attitudes which informed the thinking of the NT authors; these same theological attitudes should still inform contemporary thinking about ministry in the church. This chapter will explore the ways in which NT writers are solicitous about leadership and continuity in the local communities. From the discrete examination of the different NT books, it will be seen that, in spite of limited information and diverse terminology, a certain theological picture emerges about the meaning of leadership and ministry in Jesus' church.

The Role of the Twelve

The role of the twelve in the ministry of Jesus and in the early church was unique. They were the eyewitnesses of the public ministry of Jesus and of the resurrection and ascension. They played a symbolic role as "the tribal leaders" of the new Israel (Matt 19:28) and as the foundation stones of the new Jerusalem (Rev 21:14). They were the recipients of the primary revelation of God in Jesus Christ. Revelation is a form of communication; there can be no revelation without someone to receive it. Consequently, the twelve or others like them are essential to the historical revelation of God in Jesus of Nazareth. As recipients of this revelation, the twelve can have neither substitutes nor successors.

The twelve, however, were not simply the recipients of the revelation in Jesus. They were given a mission and authority (ex-ousia) by the earthly Jesus and by the risen Christ. This mission and authority were ordered to preaching the kingdom of God, to teaching all that Jesus had commanded, and to healing the sick, casting out demons, raising the dead, calling to repentance and communicating the forgiveness of sins and the gift of eternal life. These activities must continue until the full realization of the kingdom. The author of 2 Peter explains to his readers that the Lord's return is dependent upon the adequacy of the preaching of repentance: "The Lord is not slow about his promise as some count slowness, but is forbearing toward you, not wishing that any should perish, but that all should reach repentance" (3:9).

It is true, of course, that biblical criticism has challenged the historicity of Jesus' provision for a continuing ministry and his intention to establish a "church." Such intentions on Jesus' part are found to be in contradiction with his expectation of the kingdom of God within his own lifetime (Mark 9:1; 13:30; Matt 10:23). It must nevertheless be remembered that Jesus' eschatological preaching was in continuity with the eschatological preaching of the OT prophets. As such, it was lacking in temporal perspective; it used the concept of imminence as a rhetorical device to urge conversion; and, finally, its realization was dependent upon the response of the hearers.[1] In a very real sense the kingdom was realized in Jesus' own person through the resurrection and ascension; in the risen Jesus the ruling power of God was completely victorious in the head of a new human race. Consequently, provision for a ministry that would continue beyond the lifetime of the twelve cannot be a priori excluded from the intentions of Jesus, even though it only came to be realized later under the guidance of the Holy Spirit.

The mission of the seventy in Luke 10:1–16 is an indication that for this evangelist the mission and the authority given to the twelve in Luke 9:1–6 were not exclusively theirs. Luke does not tell us whether or how these seventy functioned after the resurrection of Jesus; they may have been the Jerusalem apostles referred to by Paul or, in the mind of Luke, they may have been types either of the presbyters or of itinerant evangelists. If the seventy are to be identified with the Jerusalem apostles of Paul's letters, they too would have been unique in having seen the risen Christ and received a mission directly from him. The synoptic gospels also testify to the existence of individuals who act in Jesus' name, but who are not connected with either the twelve or the seventy.[2] The community discourse in Matt 18 presupposes the existence of a structured community which claims close contact with Christ himself. None of these indications establish beyond all doubt that Jesus provided explicitly for a continuing ministry, either during his lifetime or before the ascension. They nonetheless do indicate that Christian communities in the latter half of the first century recognized a distinction between the role of the twelve as eyewitnesses and their function as preachers of the gospel; the same communities also claimed Jesus as the authority behind local arrangements for leadership and ministry.

The Role of Paul

Over ten years before the composition of the earliest gospel, Paul in his letters reflected upon the meaning of his own ministry and provided in some way for its continuation in his fellow workers, both male and female. Yet Paul's role in the foundation and spread of the Christian church was also unique. This uniqueness was based on the special revelation of the risen Christ on the road to Damascus. In this respect Paul too is unique and can have no successor. Nonetheless he was explicitly preoccupied throughout his lifetime with the continuity of the tradition for which he was responsible. He expected that his fellow workers in the apostolate would conduct themselves as he did and be motivated as he was. They were not favored with a revelation of the risen Christ as was Paul, but the spirit of Paul lived on in them as is apparent in the deutero-Paulines.

Post-Apostolic Ministry in the New Testament

The literature of the NT, for the most part, does not deal directly with the organization of ministry in the church. Only the pastorals speak directly about a continuing ministry in the church, but these letters are not juridical in character; 1 Timothy, which most closely approximates later church order documents, is a personal letter and an exhortation. Indirectly, however, the NT documents do reflect patterns of ministry and leadership as they existed at the time in the communities for which they were written. Yet no NT writing provides a sufficiently adequate picture of local administration upon which to base future developments. Even the letters of Ignatius of Antioch which offer the earliest (about 110 C.E.) and clearest picture of a three-tiered ministry—bishop, presbyters (elders) and deacons—were not written as church order documents.

No Christian community or denomination today can claim direct NT authority for its structures of ministry and leadership. All present arrangements are developments beyond NT times. Although the various Christian denominations do appeal to the NT to legitimize their structures of ministry, such appeals are selective and extrapolate from a very slender base of reliable information. Scholarly reconstructions of local organization in the NT churches interpret the silences of the texts in the light of later ecclesiologies and of modern sociological studies. No NT document offers a total picture of local organization, with the result that the silence of the text proves nothing about the existence or non-existence of any procedures for the selection and commissioning of community leaders. It cannot be presumed that the words used for local leaders in the NT are technical terms for offices; it is much too early to expect any standardization of titles throughout the churches of Palestine, Syria, Asia Minor, Greece and Rome.

There is likewise no clarity within the NT about the precise functions of those in leadership positions. Apparently Paul himself did not ordinarily baptize (1 Cor 1:13–17). Judas Barsabbas and Silas are called leading men (*andras hēgoumenous*) among the brethren (Acts 15:22) and prophets (Acts 15:32), but they were chosen by the apostles, the presbyters and the whole church of Jerusalem to accompany Paul and Barnabas to Antioch. Phoebe, the *diakonos* of the church at Cenchreae, may or may not have been a deaconess in the technical sense, but she is called the *prostatis* of many and of Paul himself. The word *prostatis* is usually rendered as "helper" or "patroness"; this language tells us nothing precise about her functions in the church at Cenchreae.[3] It is a case of *hysteron proteron* to infer them from the functions of ordained deaconesses which are only attested much later.

Both men and women were hosts and hostesses of house churches, but there is no information about what other functions they may have had besides those associated with hospitality; Paul is the one who both teaches and breaks bread in a house church in Troas (Acts 20:7, 11). The text of 1 Tim 5:17 implies that presiding and teaching were the most highly regarded functions of the presbyters, but not necessarily the function of all presbyters; the meaning of "presiding" is not clear.

The historian may legitimately use analogies from ancient and contemporary society to reconstruct the life of these early churches, but such reconstructions remain hypothetical at best, and do not provide a solid basis for juridical decisions in a church which professes to be in continuity with apostolic tradition. The lived practice of the churches is a stronger historical witness to apostolic tradition than the reconstructions of modern historians and exegetes which are based on NT documents alone. Unfortunately, the documents which have survived do not tell us all that we might like to know. The most that can be said with any kind of historical confidence is that there were in the NT churches individuals who exercised leadership roles and that among the functions of these leadership roles was that of perpetuating what had already been given by Christ to the apostles.

The continued existence and effectiveness of the church, like that of any other social group, requires the presence and activity of leaders, regardless of how these leaders may emerge from the group or of how they are installed and called to account by the group. There is therefore no good reason to doubt that factors of a social and cultural nature were also at play in the historical development of ministerial structures in the Christian church. On the other hand, there is an additional dimension to local leadership and ministry in the Christian church which cannot be reduced to the operation of existing social and cultural patterns. The Christian church has its origins in Jesus' mission from the Father. The power and the authority that Jesus received from the Father to preach, to teach and to heal he also communicated to the twelve and the seventy. Such power and authority is properly called "hierarchical," because it comes from God and is to be exercised in love and service after the model established by Jesus and in his name.[4] Paul too is very conscious of this divine power at work in his ministry, both as a source of his *parrhēsia* or boldness and as the guarantee of his success. Specialized ministry does not exist in the Christian church simply to supply the social needs of the group, as these needs may vary with cultural change. Ministry in the church is primarily ministry to the gospel of Jesus Christ and is the exercise of that power and authority of God which comes only from Jesus through the twelve and Paul.

The Twelve and the Seven

Very little can be learned from the NT about the local leadership in Christian communities and about post-apostolic ministry in the church. One NT narrative does, however, describe how the twelve communicated a share of their responsibility and authority to others during their own lifetime. That narrative is the appointment of the seven in Acts 6:1–6. The occasion for the appointment of the seven was a social need within the Jerusalem community which the twelve apparently could not handle by themselves. The reason given in the text was lack of time, but cultural factors were no doubt operative as well. The twelve were Hebrews, that is, Aramaic-speaking Jewish Christians; the problem concerned Hellenists, that is, Greek-speaking Jewish Christians; the Hellenist widows were being neglected in favor of the Hebrew widows by those responsible for distributing community charity. The work of the gospel was already being threatened by social and cultural patterns of behavior which were less than Christian. The twelve[5] took the initiative in seeking a solution, but involved the whole community by offering the solution to them for approval. The community was asked to pick out "seven men[6] of good reputation, full of the Spirit and of wisdom." Candidates with ordinary human and properly Christian qualities were sought. The community determined those best fitted to serve their present needs. There is no indication in Acts that they were particularly "charismatic" individuals, if by "charismatic" is meant someone who stood out from the rest by reason of enthusiastic or ecstatic behavior. They were simply outstanding Christians who were motivated by the Spirit of Jesus in their ordinary behavior. The text says that they were chosen (exelexanto), but the manner of election is not described; lots do not seem to have been involved as in the case of Matthias (Acts 1:26); the text also implies that the community agreed about the choice. Mere election by the community, however, does not appear to be enough. The community presented them to the twelve who appointed them (katastēsomen; 6:3) with prayer and the laying on of hands.[7]

The laying on of hands in the biblical and rabbinic tradition generally involved the communication of some kind of authority or blessing, as indicated by the context.[8] The rite of laying on of hands, in its biblical and Jewish context, symbolized more than a formal approval by the twelve of a choice already made by the community; it signified a transfer of power and authority. In this case, men (andras, v 3) are chosen for a task which on the face of it concerns only women. The sequel of the narrative in Acts, however, shows that the seven did more than distribute food to Greek-speaking Jewish Christian widows. They preached the gospel to Hellenists, Samaritans and Gentiles; they baptized, healed and worked signs and wonders; they explained the Jewish scriptures, a task usually associated with the ministry of teaching; they even offered themselves to death for their convictions. The first martyr was not one of the twelve, but one of the seven! In the narrative of Stephen's death Luke is at pains to show the parallelism between the crucifixion of Jesus and the martyrdom of Stephen. As a preacher of the gospel, as a worker of miracles, as a teacher of the scriptures and as a martyr Stephen continued the ministry of Jesus (Acts 6:8—8:1). Philip, one of the seven, preached, healed the sick and cast out demons, explained the scriptures and baptized (Acts 8:5–40).

The twelve did not share the fullness of their power and authority with the seven. When Philip evangelized Samaria, Peter and John were sent by the apostles in Jerusalem (Acts 8:14) to confirm Philip's mission and to lay hands on the new Christians so that they might receive the Holy Spirit (Acts 8:15–17). Simon Magus saw in this action of Peter and John the exercise of an authority (exousia) which he as a baptized Christian did not possess (Acts 8:13, 19)!

In the narrative of Acts 6, the twelve are not providing for the continuity of their ministry after their death, but they are providing for the pastoral needs of the community which they themselves are unable to satisfy. The twelve recognized the need and they initiated a procedure for meeting it, but they acted in concert with the whole community. By the laying on of hands they shared some of their power with the seven who had already been chosen by the community. The ministry of the seven was certainly broader than the distribution of charity; they also preached, healed, baptized and taught but under the supervision of the twelve. The sources are insufficient to define their ministry further. The seven may very easily have exercised a ministry among the Hellenists which was almost identical with that of the twelve among the Hebrews; they are the ones who were scattered after the death of Stephen and who carried the gospel to Samaria and beyond. Nevertheless, Luke's narrative shows the twelve providing for the ministerial needs of the community as these needs arise and sharing some of their God-given power and responsibility with others by the laying on of hands. This model is important for the future of ordained ministry in the church.

The Pauline Communities

The letters of Paul were written well before the gospels and the Acts of the Apostles. These letters are all addressed to local communities, not to community leaders;[9] they deal with community problems, but they do not directly address issues of community organization. They nonetheless do reflect in a variety of ways the presence of leaders within the local communities without being explicit about their functions or the way in which they were chosen and recognized.

In the first place, Paul makes frequent mention of his fellow workers, both male and female, who assist him in his apostolic ministry. He recognizes that they are devoting themselves to their ministries with the same devotion and motivation as he himself, but he does not tell us enough about their activities to allow a full description of their functions. Did they baptize? Did they preside at the Lord's supper? Did they preach? Did they teach? What services were discharged by all those whom Paul commends in Rom 16, especially Phoebe, the *diakonos* of Cenchreae and the apostles Andronicus and Junia(s)? Since Paul does not consider baptism to be one of his normal functions (1 Cor 1:13–17),[10] his fellow workers probably baptized. In the only NT narrative which reflects the actual celebration of the eucharist (Acts 20:7–12), it is Paul who both teaches and breaks bread.[11] Epaphras appears to have evangelized Colossae on Paul's behalf (Col 1:7), Prisca and Aquila, a Jewish Christian couple from Rome whom Paul met in Corinth and who traveled with him to Ephesus, completed the instruction of Apollos who nonetheless had already been teaching on his own (Acts 18:24–28). Of twenty-eight individuals whom Paul greets in Rom 16, eight or nine are women; of the women he says that they "worked hard" (*kopiaō*; vv 6, 12), but he does not tell us what they did. The NT documents simply do not provide answers to these questions. The exegete is certainly not justified in limiting their functions to those mentioned in the letters. At the same time, however, attempts to extrapolate from this silence can produce nothing more than conjectures in the absence of reliable evidence from non-biblical sources.

Secondly, the presence of some form of local leadership is attested in practically all the letters, though there is no uniformity in the terminology used. In 1 Thessalonians, the earliest of the Pauline letters and the first piece of Christian literature to have survived, the existence of a local leadership is acknowledged. "But we beseech you, brethren, to respect those who labor among you (*eidenai tous kopiōntas en hymin*) and are over you in the Lord (*proïsta-menous hymin en kyriō*)[12] and admonish you (*nouthetountas hy-mas*), and esteem (*hēgeisthai*) them very highly in love because of their work" (1 Thess 5:12–13). Without being more specific, these verbs describe important roles for certain individuals in the community on behalf of others. The very next verse, however, suggests that at least some of these functions were not exclusively theirs. "And we exhort you, brethren, admonish (*noutheteite*) the idle, encourage the faint-hearted, help the weak, be patient with them all" (1 Thess 5:14).[13] On the one hand, everyone in the community is responsible for the services which build up the body of Christ, but on the other hand, some of these necessary services are formally guaranteed by certain individuals. The goals of both leadership and membership are the same; cooperation must exist between them, but distinct responsibilities devolve upon some members for the good of the whole community.

Paul does not see local leaders as stifling the work of the Spirit, but already, at this early date, he sees the necessity for discernment in identifying the Spirit's work. "Do not quench the Spirit, do not despise prophesying, but test everything, hold fast what is good, abstain from every form of evil" (5:19–22). These words are addressed to the community as a whole, not to leaders in particular. Discernment is the work of the whole community; in 1 Thessalonians no specific role is assigned to the local leaders in the process of discernment; later in 1 Cor 12:10 Paul will speak of a gift of discernment of spirits as a God-given service within the community.

The problem of discerning the Spirit arose quickly in Paul's own apostolic career over the issues raised by the Judaizers. The danger of deforming the gospel did not arise only after the death of the apostles or with the rise of gnosticism. Paul himself has to fight to protect the truth and freedom of the gospel; he does not passively leave the outcome to the Holy Spirit; the tone of Galatians is sufficient evidence of Paul's active and passionate involvement. The letter is addressed to the Galatian community in general without any reference to leaders in the community. Nonetheless, the exhortation of Gal 6:6 presupposes the existence of teachers in the community. "Let him who is taught the word (*ho katēchoumenos ton logon*) share all good things with him who teaches (*tō katē-chounti*)." This exhortation may reflect a common maxim derived from philosophical schools where common life was fostered;[14] the formulation used here by Paul may be his adaptation of the slogan to the communication of the gospel message (ton logon).

The Corinthian church has sometimes been advanced as an early Christian community guided solely by the Spirit and by those possessed of charismatic gifts without any institutionalized offices.[15] Yet 1 Corinthians was written precisely because of the lack of order, unity and harmony within the Corinthian community. Paul does not address leaders directly but he does acknowledge the need for local leaders strong enough to act when necessary. This is clear in the matter of incest (1 Cor 5:1–5, 9–13) and again with respect to lawsuits among Christians (1 Cor 6:1–8). In the latter case Paul instructs the community to appoint someone to act as judge (6:5). If such matters are to be judged within the community and according to gospel standards, some individuals must function as leaders and be respected for their judgments. In 1 Cor 16:15–16 Paul asks that such respect[16] be shown toward the household of Stephanas and even appeals for submission to such fellow workers and laborers. "Now, brethren, I appeal to you, respect the household of Stephanas, because they are the first converts in Achaia, and they have devoted themselves to the service (diakonian) of the saints; submit[17] to such men and to every fellow worker and laborer." Throughout this letter Paul exercises authority as an apostle, but he does not appeal to the personal authority of an office; rather he bases his instructions upon the imperatives of the gospel and upon the understanding of Christian unity in the body of Christ; he is constantly appealing to the existential reality of the Christian's union with the risen Lord for a solution to the problems which divide the community; his exercise of authority at Corinth is not based on personal prerogatives but on the nature of the Christian's calling: Be what you are!

At the same time, however, Paul encourages full scope to the exercise of a variety of Spirit-inspired charisms, ministries or activities within the local community of Corinth.[18] He insists, however, that these individual gifts not be used for personal aggrandizement, but for the building up of the community (1 Cor 12:7–11, 28; 14:3–5, 12, 26). These charisms are not simply natural qualifications which are then evaluated theologically as gifts of the Spirit. Nor are they all exercised in an ecstatic or enthusiastic state. It may have been easy to recognize the extraordinary character of the faith that moves mountains, the working of miracles, tongues and the interpretation of tongues. The same extraordinary character may not have been so obvious with the gifts of intelligible speech such as wisdom, knowledge, teaching and prophecy, nor with the gifts of the discernment of spirits, helping and administration (ky-bernēseis), nor in some cases of healing if the art of medicine was also involved. These gifts were seen by the Corinthians as endowments of the Holy Spirit and had become a source of spiritual rivalry in the community. Even though some of the gifts may have enhanced natural qualifications, they were understood by those who possessed them as related to the gospel; but in their disordered use they were dividing the community. For example, a naturally generous person may be inspired by conversion to special zeal for the poor in the community, but in practice that person may become a source of contention in the community because of the demands which he or she may place upon others who do not share the same enthusiasm. Such zeal is indeed a manifestation of the Spirit in the service of the gospel, but its exercise may lack the patience and gentleness of Christ.

It is important not to identify the so-called "charismatics" of Corinth with "the charismatic person" as described by the early twentieth century sociologist Max Weber. For Weber (1922) a charismatic person is an innovative personality who disrupts traditional patterns of social structure and claims an authority that is legitimated by the direct experience of divine grace or of a transcendent power. Weber would also call a person of extraordinary insight "charismatic."[19] The NT uses the word charisma only for gifts bestowed by God;[20] its use is not limited to extraordinary and transitory manifestations of transcendent power or insight. Salvation itself and eternal life are charismata of Christ and of God (Rom 5:15, 16; 6:23); the privileges and promises of God to Israel are charismata (Rom 11:29); marriage and celibacy as permanent states of the Christian life are charismata of God (1 Cor 7:7); deliverance from an unbearable affliction in answer to prayer is called a charisma (2 Cor 1:8–11; RSV: blessing); the mutual encouragement of Christians one for the other is also a charisma (Rom 1:11–12); on the basis of 1 Cor 12:31—13:13 the word charismata may include the common gifts of faith, hope and especially love; according to 1 Cor 14:1, love and prophecy are the gifts to be preferred;[21] in the pastorals Timothy's own ministry is understood as a permanent charisma which is in him by the laying on of hands; as a permanent gift it can lie dormant, but be stirred into new life (1 Tim 4:14; 2 Tim 1:6).[22] Among such gifted persons Paul assigns first, second and third rank to the apostles, the prophets and the teachers who were responsible for the initial foundation of Christian communities (1 Cor 12:28).[23]

This usage is not identical with Weber's understanding of *charisma* and allows for permanent states and offices in the community to be recognized as gifts of the Holy Spirit. The dichotomy of charism and office has no foundation in the NT.[24] The exhortation in 2 Tim 1:6 to "rekindle the gift of God that is within you through the laying on of my hands" implies, however, that what is given by the Spirit and is meant to build up the body of Christ may degenerate into a purely bureaucratic function.

The various lists of charisms which appear in the NT[25] are not identical nor is any list exhaustive. A variety of gifts may be possessed by the same individual; Paul himself claims to enjoy charisms of both intelligible speech and tongues (1 Cor 14:18–19). There is, however, no foundation in the NT literature for reserving the exercise of all the charisms to one individual in the community, such as the residential bishop or the local priest. The presumption conveyed by the context in every case is that a variety of gifts would be exercised by a variety of gifted persons in any local community. The Second Vatican Council (1962–1965) sought to reestablish this NT pattern for the local church.[26] At this long remove, however, it is impossible to recover an exact description of the way each of these gifted persons functioned in the local churches of the first century. Nor is there any need either to preserve all the charisms listed in the NT or to limit charisms in the church to those mentioned in the NT; there may be new gifts for new situations.

Rivalry for local leadership was a major issue when Paul wrote 2 Corinthians, but no precise pattern of local leadership can be discerned from the letter. The "superlative apostles" seem to be itinerant missionaries rather than resident leaders.[27] Philippians as usual is addressed to the whole community, "to all the saints who are in Christ Jesus at Philippi" (1:1), but Paul then adds *syn episkopois kai diakonois*.

Translation here depends on whether these terms are used in the technical sense of the later church offices of bishop and deacon, or whether they are still being used in a general and functional sense of overseers and servants. Only here in the authentic Pauline letters does the word *episkopos* occur; the word *diakonos* is certainly used in a technical sense in 1 Tim 3:8–13, but the meaning of *diakonos* in Phil 1:1 and Rom 16:1 depends on the extent to which later church structures are already present in the communities founded by Paul. More commonly in the NT the word *diakonos* is generic and refers to any service or ministry from that of Christ himself to that of the least Christian. Barring the convenient evasion of considering the phrase as a later gloss,[28] those described as *episkopoi kai diakonoi* in Phil 1:1 might very easily be identified with the individuals described in 1 Thess 5:12–13.

If, however, the terms are used technically in Phil 1:1 for the local leaders at Philippi, then there is a real continuity in church order between the communities founded by Paul and the churches of the pastorals. The words *episkopos* and *diakonos* appear in 1 Timothy and Titus as local leaders. In Philippians the same words must connote some form of local leadership which Paul does not see as hostile to the work of the Spirit. In the same letter Paul refers to several fellow workers, including Clement and two women, Euodia and Syntyche, who seem to be having some sort of disagreement (4:2–3).

There are no references to local leaders in the church at Rome, but in the list of charisms (Rom 12:6–8) the word *proïstamenos*, which had already been used for local leaders in 1 Thess 5:12, reappears. In Rom 12:8 the RSV translates "he who gives aid, with zeal"; though lexically correct and possible, there is no reason why *proïstamenos* should not be rendered the same way in both texts; thus Rom 12:8 would read "he who is in charge, with zeal."[29] Reference has already been made to the fellow workers, male and female, whom Paul greets in Rom 16 as well as to the special problems related to Phoebe, the *diakonos* of Cenchreae (Rom 16:1–2), and to the *apostoloi*, Andronicus and Junia(s).[30] Philemon may be considered to have exercised some form of local leadership in the church which met in his house (v 2), but once again no further information is available concerning the actual functions of these domestic hosts and hostesses in the early communities. This personal note to Philemon adds nothing to what has already been seen with reference to local leadership in the churches addressed by Paul in the other authentic letters.

Other New Testament Writings

References are also made to local leadership in the other NT letters, in Acts and in the Revelation to John. Since the dating of these writings is uncertain, it is impossible to treat them in a strictly chronological order. The sequence followed here is arbitrary and implies nothing with regard to the development of church organization.

a) Hebrews

A new word for local authorities, hēgoumenoi,[31] is introduced by the author of Hebrews. The root verb, hēgeomai, means "to lead." The same word is used in a saying of Jesus with reference to leadership: "Let the leader (ho hēgoumenos) become as one who serves" (Luke 22:26). The word appears in Heb 13 in two different contexts. In Heb 13:7 it refers to leaders of the past who spoke the word of God to the community and are now being offered as examples: "Remember your leaders, those who spoke to you the word of God (hoitines elalēsan hymin ton logon tou theou); consider the outcome of their life and imitate their faith." The other text (Heb 13:17) calls for obedience to present leaders: "Obey (peithesthe) your leaders and submit (hypeikete) to them, for they are keeping watch over your souls (psychōn), as men (RSV; masculine plural pronoun, autoi) who will have to give an account. Let them do this joyfully and not sadly, for that would be of no advantage to you." The letter ends with an invitation to greet all your leaders and all the saints (Heb 13:24).[32] The authority of leadership here is based on the theological character of their service; the chief services mentioned are speaking the word of God to the community and keeping watch (agrypnousin) over their souls; these services might otherwise be described as the work of an overseer, an episkopos; they are also parallel to those of presbyteroi in 1 Tim 5:17.

b) 1 Peter

1 Peter is generally considered to be pseudonymous and of uncertain date.[33] If the letter antedates the Acts of the Apostles and the pastorals, the pseudonymous author would then be the first to introduce the word presbyteros into the vocabulary of local leadership.

What is more interesting for the purpose of this study is the way the author connects the work of the presbyteros very closely with the ministry of Christ and of Peter. Early in the letter he designates Christ as "the shepherd and guardian (poimena kai episkopon) of your souls" (1 Pet 2:25). The word translated "guardian" by the RSV is the same word, episkopos, that is used in Phil 1:1 and in the pastorals, and later rendered as "bishop." Christ then is the primary shepherd and bishop. Later in 1 Peter Christ is again designated as "the chief shepherd" (archipoimēn) of the presbyter-shepherds whom the author is addressing (1 Pet 5:4). In 1 Pet 5:1 Peter is presented as a sympresbyteros of the other presbyters; in other words, the presbyters are considered to be exercising functions which Peter also exercises. The exhortation of 1 Pet 5:1–4, like the instruction of Christ in Mark 10:42–45, deals with the exercise of authority in the church: "So I exhort the elders (*presbyterous*) among you, a fellow elder (*sympresbyteros*) and a witness of the sufferings of Christ as well as a partaker in the glory that is to be revealed. Tend the flock of God that is in your charge (*poimanate to en hymin poimnion tou theou*; a variant reading adds *episko-pountes*,[34] 'overseeing'), not by constraint but willingly (as God would have you),[35] not for shameful gain but eagerly, not as domineering (*katakyrieuontes*)[36] over those in your charge but being examples to the flock. And when the chief shepherd is manifested you will obtain the unfading crown of glory."

Three things are to be noticed in this text: (1) the flock belongs to God; (2) the vocabulary of shepherding and overseeing is closely associated with the presbyters; (3) the function of presbyters in the community is closely associated with the ministry of Christ and of Peter. Similar associations are also found in Paul's discourse to the presbyters of the church of Ephesus in Acts 20. Moreover, Peter is presented here as handing on to other church leaders Jesus' own instructions to the twelve on the exercise of authority.

c) The Acts of the Apostles

In the Acts of the Apostles it is always difficult to distinguish Luke's literary and theological contribution from his sources. In narrating the history of the first decades of the church, he may also be using language and ideas which belong to the church of the 80s rather than to the past. Continuity between the ministry of Jesus and the church of his own day is certainly one of Luke's principal theological themes.[37]

For Luke the twelve apostles are the necessary link between the historical Jesus and the post-resurrection church. This is clear from the conditions required by Peter in a substitute for Judas: "So one of the men (*andrōn*) who have accompanied us during all the time that the Lord Jesus went in and out among us, beginning from the baptism of John until the day when he was taken up from us—one of these men (*toutōn*) must become with us a witness to his resurrection" (Acts 1:21–22).

In the first twelve chapters of Acts the twelve are in charge in Jerusalem and exercise supervision personally or through emissaries over the new communities in Samaria, Judea and as far as Antioch. The twelve initiate a solution for the problem of the Hellenist widows and appoint the seven with prayer and the laying on of hands (Acts 6:1–6).[38] Peter and John are sent by the apostles in Jerusalem to give their approval to the new community in Samaria and to lay hands on them that they may receive the Holy Spirit (Acts 8:14–25). Peter journeys among the new communities of Judea, Galilee and Samaria (Acts 9:31–32); he visits Lydda and Joppa (Acts 9:32–43). From Joppa he is summoned to Caesarea Maritima by a vision and by messengers from Cornelius (Acts 10:1–48); he must nonetheless explain to the Jerusalem church his reasons for receiving uncircumcised Gentiles (Acts 11:1–18). When Gentiles are first converted in Antioch, the church of Jerusalem sends Barnabas to Antioch to check out this new development and to establish communion (Acts 11:19–24). The twelve apostles do not appear again in Acts except at the Jerusalem council in Acts 15.

The community at Antioch in these early days appears to have been ruled by prophets and teachers (Acts 13:1–3); after being moved by the Holy Spirit they send out Barnabas and Saul, with prayer, fasting and the laying on of hands. Barnabas had already received a commission to Antioch from the Jerusalem church (Acts 11:22) and Saul had received his commission from the risen Christ. This laying on of hands in Acts 13 can only be a commissioning by the leaders of the church of Antioch for a specific mission;[39] this mission may explain Luke's unusual use of the term "apostle" for Barnabas and Saul in Acts 14:4, 14.[40]

Presbyters appear in the Jerusalem church in Acts 11:30; 15:1–29; 16:4 and 21:18–26. The reference to presbyters in Acts 11:30 may be out of chronological order, since the famine foretold by Agabus in Acts 11:28 probably refers to the one which occurred in Palestine in the late 40s.[41] James, the brother of the Lord but not one of the twelve, speaks for the presbyters of the Jerusalem church in Acts 15 and 21. These presbyters appear to have succeeded the twelve apostles as leaders in the church at Jerusalem.

The apostles and the presbyters appear together in Acts 15, and in Acts 16:4 their common action at the Jerusalem council is again referred to. It is well known that the composition of Acts 15 constitutes a complex literary problem.[42] If Luke has combined two distinct events in this one chapter, it may be his way of demonstrating his thesis of continuity between Peter and the twelve, on the one hand, and James and the presbyters, on the other. The twelve do not appear after Acts 15; prior to Acts 15 the presbyters appear only in Acts 11:30 and James in Acts 12:17; in Acts 15 the two groups appear together and act in concert.[43] For Luke the work of James and the presbyters continues the work of Peter and the twelve and this work is under the guidance of the Holy Spirit.

Similarly, in Acts 14:23 and 20:17–35 Luke connects the presbyters of the churches of Asia Minor with Paul. Most commentators consider these references to Paul and presbyters to be anachronistic because presbyters appear nowhere in the authentic Pauline letters.[44] According to Acts 14:23 Barnabas and Paul, on their first missionary journey out of Antioch, appointed presbyters in the churches of Lystra, Iconium and Pisidian Antioch. "And when they had appointed[45] elders (presbyterous) for them in every church with prayer and fasting, they committed them to the Lord in whom they believed."

Later, on his final journey to Jerusalem, Paul's ship stops at the port of Miletus in Asia Minor. From there Paul calls the presbyters from Ephesus and delivers a touching farewell discourse (20:17–35). In the course of the discourse he addresses the presbyters in these words: "Take heed to yourselves and to all the flock (panti tǭ poimniǭ), in which the Holy Spirit has made you guardians (etheto episkopous), to feed (poimainein) the church of God which he obtained with the blood of his own Son" (Acts 20:28).[46] The language of shepherding and overseeing is applied here to the presbyters of Ephesus as in 1 Peter 5. Their appointment is also attributed directly to the Holy Spirit, even though they were probably appointed in the same way as the presbyters of Lystra, Iconium and Pisidian Antioch. Luke does not tell his readers how these presbyters were chosen or installed, and there is no mention here of the laying on of hands as in Acts 6:6 and 13:3.

It has been shown that Paul recognized the role of local leadership in practically all his letters. He never called these leaders presbyteroi, but he did call them episkopoi kai diakonoi (Phil 1:1). It cannot, therefore, be said that Paul did not provide local leadership for his communities as Acts 14:23 indicates. These local leaders in the Pauline churches may not have been called "presbyters" until later, but Paul would certainly agree with the way their responsibility is described in Acts 20:28. Thus Luke also demonstrates continuity between Paul and what he knows as presbyteral structure in the churches of Asia Minor.

d) Ephesians

In the epistle to the Ephesians the universal church is presented as the body of Christ who is its head. It is also presented as
a building growing toward the fullness of Christ (Eph 2:19–22). The
apostles and prophets of the past are the foundation stones of that
building (Eph 2:20; cf. 3:5). Christ is described as the chief corner-
stone holding the foundation together, or as the keystone, that is,
the peak of the arch which not only holds the arch together but is
also the goal toward which the whole building grows—a temple of
God in which the Spirit dwells.

For the author of Ephesians the church is radically one, but that
basic unity needs to be constantly fostered: ". . . eager to maintain
the unity of the Spirit in the bond of peace. There is one body and
one Spirit, just as you are called to one hope that belongs to your
call, one Lord, one faith, one baptism, one God and Father of us all,
who is above all and through all and in all" (Eph 4:3–6). In this one
church everyone has received a special gift from Christ. "But grace
(hē charis) was given to each of us according to the measure of
Christ's gift" (kata to metron tēs dōreas tou Christou; Eph 4:7). The
author then lists some of these gifts, obviously limiting himself to
the most important ones: "And his gifts were that some should be
apostles, some prophets, some evangelists, some pastors and teachers,[47] for the equipment of the saints, for the work of ministry (eis
ergon diakonias), for building up the body of Christ,[48] until we all
attain to the unity of faith and of the knowledge of the Son of God,
to mature manhood (eis andra teleion) to the measure of the stature
of the fullness of Christ . . ." (Eph 4:11–13).

In this text of Ephesians, the gifts listed in 4:11 are understood
not as transitory manifestations of the Spirit but as the provision of
Christ the head for his body the church. The gifts mentioned are all
related to the proclamation of the gospel and the pastoral care of the
community. In the light of Eph 2:20 (cf. 3:5), the apostles and the
prophets belong to the past as the foundation stones of the present
structure of the church.[49] The evangelists are most likely the itinerant preachers of the author's own day. In the Greek text, pastors
and teachers are mentioned together under one article, suggesting
either that pastoral guidance and instruction in the meaning of the
gospel are similar charisms (cf. Mark 6:34) or that the two functions
were performed by the same individuals. Pastors and teachers must
have been the resident leaders of the author's day.

If the apostles and prophets were constitutive of the church's foundation in the past, the evangelists, pastors and teachers are equally constitutive for the present. The church cannot do without the charisms of preaching, teaching, and pastoral care; such charisms are permanent provisions of the risen Christ for his church. The text of Eph 4:1–11 represents a stage in the development of the church's inner life when the functions of preaching, teaching and pastoral leadership are recognized as permanent gifts of the exalted Christ for the building up of his body. This understanding of ecclesial office is theological, not juridical; the authority of the office rests on its relationship to the gospel, not on the juridical status of the officeholder. The charisms of the Spirit which Paul saw to be of primary importance in 1 Cor 12:28, namely, apostles, prophets and teachers, are now seen as constitutive provisions of Christ the head for his body, the church.[50]

e) James

Presbyters appear as healers in James 5:14–15: "Is any among you sick? Let him call for the elders of the church, and let them pray over him, anointing him with oil in the name of the Lord; and the prayer of faith will save the sick man, and the Lord will raise him up; and if he has committed sins, he will be forgiven."[51] Presbyters, as leaders in the local community, have a healing and reconciling role to play by virtue of their office and not in virtue of another charism. The anointing with oil is done in the name of the Lord and with prayer; it is the healing power of Jesus which is at work in the action of the presbyters; the prayer of faith is recognition of dependence upon the life-giving power of God revealed in Jesus. The association of physical healing and forgiveness recalls the healing of the paralytic in Mark 2:1–12; the anointing with oil reflects the ministry of healing for which Christ empowered the twelve in Mark 6:7–13; the requirement of prayer is also pointed out to the disciples by Jesus in Mark 9:28–29.

f) The Johannine Letters

The author of 2 and 3 John identifies himself as "the presbyter" (ho presbyteros; 2 John 1; 3 John 1). The same individual is most likely the author of 1 John as well. The designation of "presbyter" or "elder" in this case is not to be understood in the same sense as the presbyters of 1 Peter, Acts and the pastorals. This presbyter considers himself to be an authoritative interpreter of the Johannine tradition; in the light of Papias' use of the term *presbyteros*, the author of the Johannine letters is probably a disciple of the eyewitness who stands behind the Johannine tradition.[52]

The presbyter is faced with a growing problem among the Christians for whom he considers himself responsible; some have seceded from the community (1 John 2:18–19). He objects to their understanding of the gospel as it affects the person of Christ, the sinlessness of the Christian and mutual charity.[53] He is confident of his own interpretation of the tradition and tries in 1 John to reassure those who thus far have remained faithful to him as their teacher. In the first part of the letter he reminds the Christians that they all have received the Spirit and so are able to discern the truth themselves (1 John 2:26–27; 3:19–24); in so doing he reflects the teaching of Jesus in the fourth gospel on the role of the Paraclete in the life of the disciples. Later, however, he acknowledges the need for a discernment of spirits (1 John 4:1–6; cf. 1 Thess 5:19–22). The criterion of the truth which he offers is confession of the true humanity of Jesus Christ: "Every spirit which confesses that Jesus Christ has come in the flesh is of God, and every spirit which does not confess Jesus is not of God" (1 John 4:2–3).

In 2 and 3 John the presbyter is concerned about the recognition of his own authority. In each of these letters he is writing to other communities as if he has some responsibility for them. In one community, however, he is encountering opposition in the person of Diotrephes: "I have written something to the church; but Diotrephes, who likes to put himself first, does not acknowledge my authority (RSV; *ouk epidechetai hēmas*). So if I come, I will bring up what he is doing, prating against me with evil words. And not content with that, he refuses himself to welcome the brethren, and also stops those who want to welcome them and puts them out of the church" (3 John 9–10). The exact status of Diotrephes and his relationship to the presbyter is far from clear. He may be the leader of a local community on the verge of severing communion with the presbyter; it is more likely that he is the host of a house church who has begun to treat all traveling missionaries with suspicion, even those of the presbyter (cf. 2 John 10–11); in the eyes of the presbyter he is responsible for dividing the community, if not leading it into schism or heresy.[54]

Problems of doctrinal integrity and personal jurisdiction seem to be surfacing at roughly the same time in communities of the Johannine tradition. R.E. Brown has argued with some cogency[55] that as the problems reflected in 1, 2 and 3 John began to arise, part of the community drew closer to the Petrine tradition which had a more clearly defined and external teaching authority. This move, Brown suggests, is reflected in the appendix to the gospel, John 21, where the authority of Peter is recognized without jeopardy to the position held by the disciple whom Jesus loved as the original teacher of the community.[56] Those who did not follow this move would have drifted into gnosticism. The evidence is not clear enough to establish Brown's thesis beyond doubt, but his suggestions are a reasonable interpretation of the evidence.

g) Revelation

The author of Revelation (or the Apocalypse) identifies himself as someone named John who has been exiled to Patmos for his preaching of the gospel (Rev 1:9). He is a Christian prophet, but he cannot be identified with either the author of the fourth gospel or the presbyter of the Johannine letters.[57] In this prophetic and apocalyptic book, the twelve apostles have a symbolic role as the foundation stones of the new Jerusalem (Rev 21:14). Local leaders are not mentioned in the book unless, as some commentators have suggested, "the angels of the seven churches" in Rev 1:20 are to be understood as symbols for local bishops. They receive the letters which John the prophet writes on behalf of the triumphant Christ to the churches of Asia Minor (Rev 2—3) and are addressed by Christ as responsible for the Christian life of the communities. More commonly, the angels are interpreted as the heavenly guardians of the earthly communities.[58] If perchance local bishops are meant, they are considered to be responsible for the fidelity of the local community to the gospel and for its correction; they are answerable to Christ himself. Traditionally, too, the angel symbolizes protection and guidance; in the letters of Revelation, the angels also mediate Christ's own words to the churches. It is more likely, however, that the local church is addressed as a collectivity in the person of its heavenly protector.

Presbyters also appear in Revelation in the form of the twenty-four elders around the throne of God. The symbolism of these presbyters is widely disputed. They have been identified as the angels in charge of the world, the heavenly representatives of the twelve tribes of Israel and the twelve apostles of the Lamb (cf. Rev 21:12, 14), the twenty-four courses of priests (1 Chr 24) or Levites (1 Chr 25), or the reunited kingdoms of Israel and Judah (cf. Ez 37:15–23), each with twelve administrative districts. Feuillet's extensive study of the question concludes that they are the saints of the OT dressed as kings and priests.[59] If Feuillet is correct, the twenty-four presbyters of Revelation represent the OT people of God and are not relevant for the study of ministry in the NT.

h) The Pastorals

The letters of Timothy and Titus, if deutero-Pauline as most commentators would agree today,[60] may well be the latest witnesses in the NT to the existence and the significance of local leaders in the early churches. These letters appear first of all as exhortations to Timothy and Titus and encourage them to fidelity in their respective ministries. As such, they reflect concern for carrying on what Paul himself was doing. The advice given in 1 Tim 1:3 is similar to Paul's apostolic anxiety in Galatians: "Charge certain persons not to teach any different doctrine." The fostering of love is the purpose of all apostolic authority (1 Tim 1:5; cf. 1 Cor 12:31— 13:13). The threat of the Judaizers may be detected in 1 Tim 1:7. The pastorals contain both pastoral advice to Timothy and Titus, and instructions for providing local leaders in the churches. Nowhere is Timothy or Titus called *presbyteros* or *episkopos*, but as fellow workers and emissaries of Paul they appear to enjoy some form of general authority over a large number of local communities in the region of Ephesus and in Crete.[61] It may be legitimately presumed that the understanding of the ministry of Timothy and Titus which is proposed as Pauline in these letters would also apply to those whom they install as leaders in the local churches.

In speaking of Timothy's ministry Paul is presented as saying that it came to him as a gift of God (1 Tim 4:14; 2 Tim 1:6) accompanied by prophetic utterances (1 Tim 1:18; 4:14) and the laying on of hands (1 Tim 4:14; 2 Tim 1:6). In 1 Tim 4:14 the *charisma* of his ministry is attributed to prophecy accompanied by the laying on of hands (*dia prophēteias meta epitheseōs tōn cheirōn tou presbyteriou*); in 2 Tim 1:6 the gift of God (*to charisma tou theou*) is attributed simply to the laying on of Paul's hands (*dia epitheseōs tōn cheirōn mou*). The prophetic utterances were some form of inspired indication that Timothy was suitable for service in the church; according to 1 Tim 1:18, this souvenir of his inspired calling should be a source of strength in the ministry.[62] According to 2 Tim 1:6 it was Paul who laid hands on Timothy, installing him in his ministry; according to 1 Tim 4:14 Paul would have been included in a college of presbyters who together would have installed Timothy in his ministry.[63] In either case there is a transmission of power or authority from Paul and/or the presbyters to Timothy which is distinct from his prophetic call. This gift of God, which comes to Timothy by prophetic call and the laying on of hands, is a permanent possession which can nonetheless be neglected or lie dormant. "Do not neglect the gift which you have, which was given you by prophetic utterance when the elders laid their hands upon you" (1 Tim 4:14).

In the exhortations of 2 Tim 1:6–7 Paul associates Timothy's ministry with his own as a gift of God. "Hence I remind you to rekindle the gift of God that is within you through the laying on of my hands; for God did not give us a spirit of timidity but a spirit of power (dynameōs) and love and self-control." He calls Timothy to fidelity and integrity in his ministry (1 Tim 1:19) and counsels him not to be ashamed of the gospel, as Paul himself was not ashamed (Rom 1:16), nor to be disheartened by suffering; for his ministry is sustained by the power of God (kata dynamin theou) as was Paul's (2 Tim 1:8).

The task of teaching is strongly emphasized in the pastorals,[64] as it was a prominent activity in Paul's ministry; the authentic letters may all be understood as teaching. There must also be continuity between Timothy's teaching and that of Paul. "Follow the pattern of the sound words which you have heard from me, in the faith and love which are in Christ Jesus" (2 Tim 1:13). Continuity in the purity of the gospel must be maintained until the coming of Christ (1 Tim 6:14, 20). The message of the truth is a gift of the Holy Spirit to Timothy as it was to Paul (2 Tim 1:14). He is called to function in his ministry as Paul functioned in his. "Preach the word, be urgent in season and out of season, convince, rebuke, and exhort, be unfailing in patience and in teaching. . . . As for you, always be steady, endure suffering, do the work of an evangelist, fulfill your ministry" (diakonian; 2 Tim 4:2, 5).

Timothy is called a servant of Christ Jesus (diakonos Christou Iesou; 1 Tim 4:6) and a slave of the Lord (doulos kyriou; 2 Tim 2:24), just as Paul designated himself. Timothy is also called an evangelist (2 Tim 4:5; cf. Eph 4:11; Acts 21:8), a term Paul never used of himself; on the other hand, he is not called an apostle; only Paul is "the apostle."

There is no doubt that the pastorals are much more concerned with the purity of doctrine and the defense of the faith than were the authentic letters of Paul.[65] It is the responsibility of the minister of Christ to protect the faithful from all deformations of the gospel and from useless speculations. Hope in the living God and the salvation he offers to all men and women must be kept alive in the face of the more immediate allurements of lesser views of human fulfillment (1 Tim 4:10). This preoccupation need not be seen as surprising nor deforming, for the initial eyewitnesses are now gone. With the delay of the *parousia*, initial enthusiasm has necessarily waned and, as the author of Hebrews suggests (12:1), the attraction of sin has reasserted itself. If Paul had to defend the truth of the gospel during his lifetime, such dangers are bound to increase after the first generation has disappeared. This preoccupation with "sound doctrine" which is detected in the pastorals may be a legitimate argument against Pauline authenticity, but it is also a necessary adjustment to the death of the eyewitnesses and a wise provision for fidelity to the gospel of Jesus Christ. Although it is no longer possible to recreate the historical circumstances which gave rise to these letters, we must nonetheless allow that they address real problems in the post-Pauline era. The better attested phenomenon of second century gnosticism indicates that such precautions were not unwarranted.

Paul's emissary has an authority similar to that of Paul to speak, to encourage and to correct (Titus 2:15).[66] Disciplinary action is also provided for (1 Tim 1:19–20; Titus 3:10–11), as Paul himself counseled in 1 Cor 5:1–5.[67] The need for encouragement, a major element in Paul's own preaching and ministry, is also emphasized in the pastorals.[68] Teaching must also be reinforced by personal example (1 Tim 4:12, 15; Titus 2:7–8), as Paul was at pains to do in his own ministry. Timothy is encouraged to be a man of God in his own life, because personal holiness contributes to the effectiveness of the ministry and guarantees the salvation of the minister.[69]

The pastorals are not only exhortations addressed to Timothy and Titus for their own ministry; they are also instructions to Timothy and Titus to provide for local leadership in the churches for which they are responsible. The *presbyteroi-episkopoi* are the leaders of the local churches. Although there is no unanimity among commentators concerning the relationship of *presbyteroi* to *episkopoi* in the pastorals, the evidence suggests that local leadership was provided by a college of presbyters, some of whom functioned as overseers (*episkopoi*; cf. 1 Tim 5:17–18). The fact that the personal noun *episkopos* appears only in the singular in the pastorals (1 Tim 3:2; Titus 1:7) is not sufficient evidence to affirm that monarchical bishops were already in place in these communities; the use of the singular may be simply generic;[70] all the presbyters of the church of Ephesus are called *episkopoi* in Acts 20:28 and the leaders of the Philippian church are called *episkopoi kai diakonoi* (Phil 1:1).

Men are encouraged to seek a leadership role in the local community. "If any one aspires to the office of a bishop (*episkopē*), he desires a noble task" (1 Tim 3:1).[71] It has been pointed out that the qualities sought in an *episkopos* are those that might be sought in any civil leader and that consequently the church is now providing for its own leadership in a purely secular way (1 Tim 3:2–7; Titus 1:5–9).[72] The qualities of hospitality (*philoxenon*; cf. 1 Tim 3:2; Titus 1:8) and teaching ability (*didaktikon*; cf. 1 Tim 3:2)[73] are nonetheless specifically related to the building up of a Christian community. Teaching is considered to be the most eminent function of the presbyters (1 Tim 5:17) and is related to "presiding" (*proïstēmi*). It is not particularly surprising that a successful home life should be seen as a testing ground for either public or church service.[74] The warning against recent converts is simply a warning against appointing the immature, even though the danger is expressed in theological terms: ". . . he may . . . fall into the condemnation of the devil" (1 Tim 3:6). A good reputation with the public is important for the spread of the gospel, just as it is important for successful public service.

It is true that this sounds like a prosaic, almost calculating approach to providing the local church with good leadership, but it may also be a way of discerning the Spirit. The age of the eyewitnesses and of the apostolic founders of churches is now past. Human prudence is certainly at work, but with a view to assuring continuity with the apostolic past. There is no reason why the Holy Spirit might not direct this work of human prudence and respect socio-cultural patterns for the emergence of leaders in the local community. At the same time, however, such a process of "natural selection" does not preclude the integration of these emerging leaders into a form of ministry which has preceded them and which has been responsible for the very existence of the Christian community in which they appear. Nor does this process of selection preclude an empowerment by their predecessors in ministry which is not from the people, but from God and Christ as was Paul's apostolate and that of the twelve. The *presbyteroi-episkopoi* described in 1 Tim 3:2–7 are said to be installed by the laying on of Timothy's hands (1 Tim 5:22). Timothy's own ministry was described as a gift of God communicated to him by prophecy and the laying on of Paul's hands and those of the presbyterate. The role of prophecy need not exclude the use of human prudence; on the other hand, in such cases human prudence must be docile to the Holy Spirit and guided by gospel values.

The pastorals do not explicitly involve the community in the selection of presbyters, but neither do they exclude it. It is possible to recognize in the pastorals a pattern that is similar to that described in Acts 6:1–6: Timothy takes the initiative in seeking from the community presbyters who are endowed with the human and Christian qualities suited to proclaiming the word of God and shepherding a Christian community; selection by the community, which is explicitly mentioned in Acts, is not excluded in the pastorals; empowerment follows through the laying on of hands by those who already possess the particular charism of ministry that is being handed on. At this stage in the development of Christian ministry, there is no evidence for the juridical definition of functions and offices; continuity in preaching, teaching and reconciling governs the instructions given to Timothy and Titus for the selection and commissioning of presbyteroi-episkopoi and diakonoi. The same warning about not quenching the Spirit, but testing it (1 Thess 5:19–22), applies here as well. The guidance of the Spirit does not exclude, but even invites the exercise of ordinary human prudence enlightened by faith and the values of the gospel of Jesus. If Acts 6:1–6 reflects historical fact, then the process for the selection of presbyters in the pastorals is parallel with what the twelve themselves have already initiated.

The vocabulary used by Luke in the narrative of Acts 6:1–6 reflects the narrative of Num 27:15–23 in which Moses empowered Joshua to succeed him as leader of God's people by the laying on of hands.[75] It was Moses who possessed an abundance of the spirit and God distributed some of it to the seventy elders (Num 11:16–29). In Num 27 Moses took the initiative in asking the Lord for someone to lead the people as he himself had done. "Moses said to the Lord, 'Let the Lord, the God of the spirits of all flesh, appoint (RSV; MT: yipqod; LXX: episkepsasthō) a man over the congregation, who shall go out before them and come in before them, who shall lead them out and bring them in; that the congregation of the Lord may not be as sheep which have no shepherd' " (Num 27:15–17). Joshua as one of Moses' chosen men (Num 11:28) already enjoyed a gift of the spirit but he was destined by God for an additional gift. "And the Lord said to Moses, 'Take Joshua the son of Nun, a man in whom is the spirit, and lay your hand (LXX: "hands" as in Num 27:23 and Deut 34:9) upon him. . . . You shall invest him with some of your authority, that all the congregation of the people of Israel may obey' " (Num 27:18, 20). Unlike Moses, however, who spoke with God face to face, Joshua and the people he leads must seek the word of the Lord from Eleazar the priest (Num 27:21). Finally, Joshua is commissioned through the laying on of Moses' hands in the presence of Eleazar the priest and the whole congregation (Num 27:22–23).

A later comment on this text shows how it was understood: "And Joshua the son of Nun was full of the spirit of wisdom, for Moses had laid his hands upon him; so the people of Israel obeyed him, and did as the Lord had commanded Moses" (Deut 34:9).[76] The spirit by which Joshua ruled depended on Moses laying hands on him.

This biblical pattern of Moses and Joshua clearly indicates that the empowerment of Joshua is from God through Moses and not from the people; it also implies that Joshua's leadership of the people is directed by the word of God and that the obedience of the people is to the word of God mediated through the priest and Joshua. By using this pattern for the narrative of Acts 6:1–6, Luke is affirming that the share of authority given by the twelve to the seven is also from above, from God through Christ and the twelve, even though the selection of the seven has been made by the whole community.

If the narrative of Acts 6:1–6, on the other hand, is a theological construction of Luke, it would mean that second and third generation Christians recognize that there is continuity between the authority of Christ and the twelve, on the one hand, and their local leaders or presbyters on the other. Their authority is the authority of God mediated through Christ and the twelve by the laying on of hands. The selection of candidates for leadership may follow normal socio-cultural processes, processes which inevitably change with time and needs. The Holy Spirit can and does work through these ordinary human channels, but their functioning must be governed by the peculiar goals of the church and the promotion of the cause of Jesus. If the founding events are not kept in mind, the continuing institution may lose sight of its original purpose or fall victim to bureaucratic routine and secular models of exercising authority.[77]

Qualifications similar to those of the episkopos were also required of the deacons, both male and female; hospitality and teaching ability are not mentioned in their regard.[78] On the other hand, commitment to the gospel is explicitly mentioned with respect to the male deacons (1 Tim 3:9). The comments of Paul in 1 Tim 3:14–15 imply that the previous instructions about *episkopoi* and *diakonoi* are designed to guarantee continuity between the ministry of Paul and that of Timothy and of those whom he commissions. The truth which the church of the living God must sustain and defend is precisely the mystery of Christ "who was manifested in the flesh, vindicated in the Spirit, seen by angels, preached among the nations, believed on in the world, taken up in glory" (1 Tim 3:16). This same line of tradition is affirmed in the instructions to Timothy in 2 Tim 2:2: ". . . what you have heard from me before many witnesses entrust to faithful men (*pistois anthrōpois*) who will be able to teach others also."

Summary

From this examination of texts it is clear that the earliest NT literature does not tell us how local leaders emerged in the churches. On the other hand, there is no evidence for a local community without leadership of some kind. There is some evidence that leaders were recognized on the basis of generous service to the community. The Thessalonians are urged to respect their leaders, love them and hold them in high regard because of their work on behalf of the community (1 Thess 5:12–13).[79] Paul also expects the unruly Corinthians to respect and submit to the household of Stephanas and to everyone who assists them and labors hard (*ko-piaō*) for the community. Their devotion to the saints commands this recognition (1 Cor 16:15–16).[80] Most, if not all, of Paul's fellow workers, both male and female, may have been co-opted simply on the basis of generous service inspired by the gospel and by attachment to Paul.

There is no NT evidence for the formal recognition of local leaders nor is there any theology of leadership except for the initial apostles. On the other hand, there is in 1 Corinthians, Romans, 1 Peter and Ephesians a recognition that all services or ministries within the local community are gifts of God, of Christ or of the Spirit. These texts affirm a special provision by God for the specifically theological purpose of building up the body of Christ; it is not simply a question of organizing natural gifts. No one has any right to claim any of these gifts as his or her own, and their recognition is subject to the judgment of the whole community.[81] This judgment is realized in the community through the action of the Holy Spirit in the baptized who recognize the work of the same Spirit in

those who have received authentic charisms. Such discernment presupposes docility to the Spirit and to the gospel in those who pass
judgment; it is not simply a matter of personal opinion nor of counting votes.

More is involved here than a post-factum theologizing of ordinary socio-cultural phenomena. The divine initiative which motivated the revelation of the saving love of God in Jesus Christ is also
at work in providing the body of Christ with the services it needs
to bring the kingdom to fulfillment. Apostles, prophets and teachers
occupied preeminent positions in these early days (1 Cor 12:28;
Acts 13:1; Eph 2:20; 3:5). It is not clear that these individuals were
always itinerant; some prophets and teachers were resident at Antioch (Acts 13:1). The living presence of the twelve and of Paul may
have made any further precisions unnecessary. As the original apostles and prophets began to die, the preeminent functions of preaching, teaching and healing were seen to be necessary for the continuity of Christ's mission and for the growth of the kingdom of God.
The primacy of preaching and teaching is evident from Eph 4:11.

Healing is a work of local presbyters (James 5:13–15) and includes forgiveness of sins when necessary. The work of reconciliation which is synonymous with the gospel itself (2 Cor 5:18–20; cf.
Luke 24:47) is the primary and necessary healing; physical healing
may sometimes accompany the forgiveness of sins, as Mark 2:1–12
shows, either as a constitutive element or as a confirmatory sign (cf.
Mark 16:17–18, 20). These are the commissions and the powers
which Christ gave to the twelve and the seventy during his public
ministry and renewed for the eleven and their companions after the
resurrection. In the Acts of the Apostles the twelve, Stephen, Philip
and Paul are all engaged in these three activities of preaching,
teaching and healing. Paul instructs the presbyters of Ephesus to
carry on the same ministry which he had exercised among them.

The NT offers very little information about what has come to be
called the sacramental ministry in the Roman Catholic and other
episcopal churches. The risen Jesus instructs the eleven to baptize
(Matt 28:19) and baptism follows upon the preaching and/or teaching of Peter, Philip, Ananias and Paul in Acts.[82] Only Philip, however, is said to have personally baptized (Acts 8:38). The Greek verb
baptizō is used clearly of Christian baptism thirty-three times in the
NT, but only eleven times in the active voice. Peter, Paul and Ananias may be presupposed to have baptized, but this is not explicitly stated. In fact, in Acts 10:48 Peter instructs others to baptize
Cornelius and his household. Paul, of course, affirms explicitly that

"Christ did not send me to baptize but to preach the gospel" (1 Cor 1:17); he nonetheless admits to having baptized a few (1 Cor 1:14–16).

In the same way, the ordinary leader of the eucharist is not identified in the NT. Understanding the breaking of bread to be the celebration of the Lord's supper, this action accompanies the teaching of the apostles in the life of the early Christian community in Jerusalem (Acts 2:42, 46). Paul is explicitly said to have broken bread with the community of Troas, but after teaching them all night (Acts 20:7, 11). Paul is also reported to have broken bread and shared it with the crew while adrift at sea (Acts 27:35), but this is less likely to have been the eucharist; it is not accompanied by any preaching of the gospel and there is no evidence that the 276 on the ship (Acts 27:37) were all Christians. While the breaking of bread may not always be a reference to the eucharist in the NT, Paul does say explicitly that the celebration of the Lord's supper is a proclamation of the death of the Lord: "For as often as you eat this bread and drink the cup, you (plural) proclaim (*kataggellate*) the Lord's death until he comes" (1 Cor 11:26). The celebration of the eucharist then is a community proclamation of the death of the Lord and so is a form of preaching. Whoever presides at such community gatherings (cf. 1 Thess 5:12; Rom 12:8; 1 Tim 5:17; Heb 13:15–17) would no doubt be the "presider" at the eucharist, even though it is an act of the whole community. According to 1 Tim 5:17, it is the presbyters who preside, but the data is much too vague to be of juridical significance.

The forgiveness of sins belongs to the proclamation of the gospel (Luke 24:47; John 20:21–23) and characterizes the life of the Christian community (Matt 18:12–35), but the NT furnishes no information about the juridical form of the ministry of forgiveness. The twelve, the seven, Paul and Barnabas all exercise the ministry of healing in the name of Jesus.[83] Miracles are a sign of a true apostle (2 Cor 12:12), but also a special charism of the Spirit distinct from the charism of an apostle (1 Cor 12:9–10, 28–30). Finally, the presbyters of the local community by reason of their office anoint with oil, exercising a ministry of healing and forgiveness (James 5:14–15); but in the very next verse the author encourages all members of the community to confess their sins to one another and to pray for each other's healing (James 5:16; cf. 1 John 5:14–18).

This data suggests that what is now called the ministry of the sacraments was not separated from the ministry of preaching, teaching and healing, but was seen to be part and parcel of that ministry.

The action of the sacraments was itself a word of preaching, in keeping with the semitic mentality which did not separate word and event and for which the spoken word was itself a dynamic event.[84]

This subordination of sacramental actions to the preaching of the word explains the structure of John 6. In this chapter Jesus is presented as "the bread of life" which has come down from heaven to give eternal life to all who believe in him. Jesus is first of all "bread of life" in his own person and is to be received by faith before he is "bread of life" to be consumed in the eucharist. The first part of the discourse (John 6:32–51ab) deals with the reception of Jesus by faith; in the second part of the discourse (John 6:51c–58) Jesus speaks of the necessity of eating his flesh and drinking his blood in the eucharist. Although the two parts of the discourse may have been composed at different times, by placing them together in John 6 the evangelist wants to convey the idea that the reception of the body and blood of Jesus in the eucharist presupposes that one has already received Jesus by faith.[85] Word and sacrament are really inseparable.

After the death of Paul and the apostles and prophets of the first generation, there is evidence in the NT for a formalizing of leadership roles and for an explicit attempt to attach local *presbyteroi* and/or *episkopoi* to the first generation apostles of Jesus Christ. This evidence appears in Acts and in the pastorals. The twelve apostles of Jesus and the presbyters of the Jerusalem church are closely associated by Luke in Acts 15. The twelve are in charge in Jerusalem throughout Acts 1—12, except for an anachronistic reference to presbyters in 11:30, and they disappear after chap. 15 except for a retrospective reference in 16:4. In the latter part of Acts local leadership in the Jerusalem church belongs to James the brother of the Lord and the presbyters about him (Acts 21:17–18). It has been suggested that just as Luke's concept of an apostle (Acts 1:21–22) was his way of demonstrating continuity between Jesus and the post-Easter church, so too his composition of Acts 15 may have been his way of demonstrating continuity between the twelve apostles and the presbyters.

Presbyters also appear in the Pauline churches in Acts, even though the use of this terminology is probably anachronistic. It is not at all unlikely that Barnabas and Paul provided for local leadership, as indicated in Acts 14:23, even though these local leaders may not have been called presbyters from the beginning in the Pauline churches (cf. Phil 1:1). According to Acts 14:23 God's guidance was invoked by prayer and fasting (cf. Acts 13:2–3), but involvement on the part of the community is not mentioned here as in Acts 6:1–6.

The presbyters of Ephesus (Acts 20:17) were probably appointed in the same way as those of Lystra, Iconium and Pisidian Antioch (Acts 14:23). Their functions in the local community are given a high theological value in Acts 20:28: "Take heed to yourselves and to all the flock (*panti tǭ poimniǭ*) in which the Holy Spirit has made you guardians (*etheto episkopous*) to feed (*poimainein*) the church of God which he obtained with the blood of his own Son." Here the concepts of shepherding and overseeing are closely associated with the office of presbyter as in 1 Peter 5:1–4. Regardless of the human and historical manner of their designation, they are also seen to have been appointed by the Holy Spirit. The context of Acts 20 presupposes the approaching death of Paul. His apostolic authority and responsibility, given him by a gratuitous gift of God on the road to Damascus, are now seen to be exercised by the presbyters he appointed. Nonetheless, Paul's initial provision for local leaders was motivated by his apostolic concern for the growth of the body of Christ in the local community and so must be recognized also as the work of the Holy Spirit, regardless of the human and cultural factors that may have been at work in Paul's selection.

In other words, the peculiar necessity of continuing the ministry of Christ directed the operation of selecting leaders without necessarily violating socio-cultural patterns. On the other hand, this same necessity gave to those so selected a responsibility and an authority with respect to the gospel and in the service of the community of faith which was more than a simple commission from the local church.

According to the pastorals Timothy and Titus must correct and rebuke; the same responsibility devolves upon the presbyters; this function would be impossible if their authority came from the community. The author of 1 Clement, who probably wrote after the pastorals, argues against the removal of the *episkopoi kai diakonoi* of the Corinthian church in spite of the dissensions in the community. In the pastorals Timothy and Titus are instructed to continue this selection process begun by Barnabas and Paul. Although the community is explicitly involved in the choice of the seven in Acts 6:1–6, no explicit role is mentioned for the community in the appointment of presbyters either in Acts or in the pastorals; silence does not necessarily exclude such a role! In fact, the place of prophecy in the commissioning of Timothy (1 Tim 1:18; 4:14) may imply a role for the community. Finally, the instruction of Jesus to the twelve on the exercise of authority in Mark 10:42–45 is repeated in Peter's name in 1 Pet 5:1–4.

Conclusion

In Acts, Ephesians and the pastorals the divine appointment of certain local leaders is explicitly recognized. This recognition places these leadership roles in direct continuity with the Pauline and Petrine notion of charismatic gifts. Moreover, Acts and the pastorals speak as well of the laying on of hands as a rite for the commissioning of certain individuals for church service. According to 1 Tim 4:14 and 2 Tim 1:6 the rite was used for the commissioning of Timothy by Paul and a group of presbyters. Timothy is to use the same rite for the appointment of the presbyters he has selected (1 Tim 5:22). In Acts the rite is used by the twelve for the installation of the seven and by the prophets and teachers of Antioch for the mission of Barnabas and Paul. In Acts 6 the twelve commission the seven by this rite and share some of their power with them. In Acts 13, if Barnabas and Paul already had apostolic authority by reason of their call, the rite cannot mean anything more than a commissioning and a blessing on the part of the local community; in this sense Barnabas and Paul can be called "apostles" in Acts 14:4, 14, that is, they are apostles sent out by the church of Antioch (cf. Phil 2:25). In the pastorals the rite is a sign of a certain continuity between Paul and the other presbyters associated with him in the commissioning of Timothy and between Timothy and the presbyters he appoints.

If Acts 6:1–6 records historical facts from the early days of the church, the use of the laying on of hands for the commissioning of presbyters would be a development from the action of the twelve in commissioning the seven. If, on the other hand, Acts 6:1–6 is a piece of Lucan theology, it affirms that the power and the authority given by Jesus to the twelve may be shared with others as community needs may suggest and that the rite of the laying on of hands which is a sign of that sharing is patterned after the same rite which Moses used for passing to Joshua some of the authority which God had given to him over his people (Num 27:15–23; Deut 34:9).

In 1 Clement continuity in ministry is expressed by the fact that the apostles appointed (kathistanon) the episkopoi kai diakonoi (42.4; cf. 44.2–3), but the laying on of hands is not mentioned. The use of the same verb, kathistēmi, in Acts 6:3 for the appointment of the seven by the twelve, and in 1 Clement 42.4 and 44.2–3 for the appointment of the *episkopoi kai diakonoi* by the twelve, suggests that the author of 1 Clement may have had Acts 6 in mind, even though he does not explicitly mention the laying on of hands. This silence is insignificant unless one is treating these texts as strictly juridical. What is theologically significant to the author of 1 Clement is the continuity in ministry from Jesus to the twelve and from the twelve to the *episkopoi kai diakonoi*, not the juridical and sacramental acts by which that continuity is publicly expressed.

CONCLUSIONS

The Limitations of the Study

The organization of ministries in the early church was already an historical fact prior to the canonization of the NT. The three-tiered ministry of bishop, presbyters and deacons was already in place in Antioch and in certain communities of Asia Minor about 110 C.E. when Ignatius of Antioch wrote his letters.[1] By the beginning of the third century, the bishop is clearly the central figure in local ministry throughout the church.[2] The question of a NT canon was still in flux at the end of the second century and the beginning of the third, even though it may be taken for granted on the authority of Irenaeus and the Muratorian Fragment that the four gospels, the Acts of the Apostles, thirteen letters of Paul, 1 John and 1 Peter were already recognized as canonical scripture. The developments in the local organization of the ministry, therefore, took place historically without the benefit of a canon of NT scripture. Certain books which were later recognized as canonical may have influenced developments in certain areas of the church, but the major influence must have been a combination of the oral preaching of the gospel reaching back to the time of the apostles and socio-cultural factors in the local communities. An exclusive influence cannot, on strictly historical grounds, be assigned to one factor or the other;[3] both operated together in a symbiotic relationship which produced the situation that prevailed at the beginning of the third century.

The canonization of the NT did not, as the history shows, disturb patterns of ministry already developed in the church. By receiving as canonical certain pieces of literature which did not reflect prevailing patterns of local organization, the church acknowledged that such structures were not dependent on the NT scriptures for their legitimacy. That legitimacy must have been founded on the continued action of the risen Christ and of the Holy Spirit in the church, as recognized by the author of the letter to the

119

Ephesians and by the author of the Acts of the Apostles. Consequently, the attempt to justify later developments in the organization of church ministry either juridically or theologically on the basis of the NT alone must be considered historically anachronistic.

Since the NT only reflects patterns of local ministry indirectly, this literature cannot serve as a juridical basis for later developments. The reconstructions of historians who argue from silence are equally precarious because the argument from silence may be used to support contrary positions. Hence, it is my contention in this study that the NT cannot function either as an historical or as a juridical norm for the legitimacy of what historically are later developments in ecclesial ministry. For this reason, I have tried to let the NT texts speak for themselves and say no more than can be established on the basis of sound, exegetical and historical arguments.

At first sight, the results of this study may appear meager or unduly minimal for the understanding of ministry in the church today. I am convinced, however, that the literature of the NT, taken as a whole, does offer important theological insights into the significance of church ministry. I also consider it important that these insights be kept in mind in all the developments of ministry which are necessarily demanded by historical and socio-cultural factors throughout the history of the church; these insights will serve as valuable criteria in discerning authentic from non-authentic tradition. In the Acts of the Apostles Luke was at pains to show how the Holy Spirit was at work in the spread of the gospel and in the growth and development of the early church. The same narrative of Acts also shows that the early church knew conflict not only with outsiders who did not yet believe, but also with believers who had not yet understood the full implications of the gospel or who, through human weakness, failed to live according to the demands of the gospel. Everything that happened spontaneously in the community was not the work of the Holy Spirit. The action of the Holy Spirit had to be discerned through a process which involved conflict, the clash of personalities and opinions, consultation with the community, and ultimately a judgment by those who occupied leadership positions. In such a process agreement is achieved when those who hold conflicting positions humbly seek the truth of the gospel together in the light of the risen Christ and in docility to the Spirit of Jesus. The agreement or consensus which results is not the triumph of one side over the other, but the work of the same Holy Spirit acting in believers for whom the will of God is more important than their own point of view, no matter how dearly held, or their private good. The narrative of Acts 15 is a succinct account of this process at work in the church before there was any such thing as NT scriptures.

All developments in the history of the church are obviously not the work of the Holy Spirit. Everything that is labeled traditional is not by that very fact in legitimate continuity with the authentic tradition of the gospel of Jesus Christ and therefore normative. The Holy Spirit is still at work in the church but all that appears historically is not the work of the Spirit. The church must always be engaged in discerning the Spirit if it is to remain faithful to apostolic tradition and to the gospel of Jesus Christ. Thorough historical studies of the tradition are necessary if this discernment is to be made in a responsible way.

Fortunately, the cultivation of history in the last two centuries has contributed and continues to contribute to this process. Among such historical studies must also be included the critical study of NT literature. Without exhausting the significance of the NT for the life of the church in its worship, prayer and theology, critical biblical scholarship has sought to attain a better understanding of the meaning of the biblical texts at the time they were written. Such an historical understanding of the text is a safeguard against misusing texts for purposes for which they were never intended, even though it be admitted that these same texts may take on added meaning when read in the light of the whole of scripture and of the life of the church. As a literary witness to the preaching and teaching of the apostles about Jesus and to the founding events of the church, the canonical NT has become an essential criterion in the process of discernment in a church which professes to be apostolic. At the same time, however, everything that appears in the NT does not carry the same critical weight in forming a judgment concerning authentic apostolic tradition. The work of critical biblical scholarship is thus an important contribution to any discerning process in the life of the church, but biblical scholarship alone is incapable of making definitive judgments for the resolution of contemporary problems within the church.

Keeping these limitations in mind, I would like to reflect theologically on what the historical witness of the NT contributes to the understanding of ministry in the church today. This modest contribution needs to be completed by other historical, anthropological, sociological and theological studies. Such interdisciplinary study is necessary if we are to deal responsibly and adequately with the problems that face the church's ministry today. Yet we must always remember that it is the gospel of Jesus Christ that we are called to serve and that the literature of the NT is the primary historical witness to that gospel.

The Theological Significance of the Study

The primary analogue of all ministry in the church is the ministry which Jesus himself received from the Father for the salvation of the world. Jesus of Nazareth was sent by God to proclaim the good news of the kingdom and to make God and his love for all humankind known in the world. Jesus fulfilled this mission from the Father by preaching, teaching and healing, but also by submitting to the rejection, suffering and death which his personal fidelity to the will of God entailed. He trusted in the power of God to vindicate him and that trust was realized in the resurrection and in the new life which the risen Jesus continues to enjoy in the presence of God.

The good news of the kingdom proclaimed by Jesus is not a new doctrine about God, nor is it simply a new and more radical understanding of the will of God. The good news of the kingdom is a new initiative of divine power in the history of humankind; it is also the definitive manifestation of divine power in the history of humankind because God's initiative in Jesus brought Jesus himself, as the first member of a new human race, to the fullness of eternal life in the resurrection of the dead. The historical particularity of the ministry of Jesus and of its definitive revelatory significance is at the same time the heart and the scandal of Christian faith.

Jesus proclaimed the good news of the kingdom by his preaching, teaching and healing, but also by his life. Although we are inclined to treat preaching and teaching as merely exercises in verbal communication, the gospel writers view the preaching and teaching of Jesus as manifestations of power and authority; they also integrate his healing activity with the proclamation of the goods news of the kingdom. The good news of the kingdom is the power of God at work in Jesus to overcome evil in all its forms, including human sinfulness and death, and so the healings and exorcisms are proclamations of the kingdom and teachings with authority. Only in virtue of this power is Jesus' radical understanding of the will of God realizable in human lives. The parables of the kingdom are word pictures of what human life is like when God is in charge. Preaching, teaching and healing are not three ministries which are easily separable in theory or in practice, but they are integral parts of the one ministry of Jesus on behalf of the gospel of the kingdom. Jesus' own life is an integral part of that proclamation of the kingdom, so that ministry cannot be considered a professional activity or a job which is somehow distinct from the life of the minister. In the language of later theology, Jesus is the definitive "sacrament" of the life-giving power of God and of his love in the world. The gospel is not primarily doctrine or morality; the gospel is primarily power.

Although Jesus called all his disciples to follow him and to serve him in each other, especially in the poor and the needy, he gave power and authority to certain disciples freely chosen from among the others to assist him in his own ministry and to continue it after his death and resurrection. The twelve were chosen from a larger group of disciples and given "power and authority" to do the very things that Jesus was already doing, namely, to preach, to heal and, after the resurrection, to teach, but their teaching was circumscribed by what Jesus himself had taught. The power and authority which Jesus gave to the twelve was a share in the power and authority which he himself had from God. It was power and authority which involved responsibility for others; they were instructed to make disciples of all nations. While this power and authority was comparable to civil power and authority, it was not to be exercised according to any prevailing civil models; it was to be exercised in service after the example of Jesus who gave his life "as a ransom for many." As symbols for the twelve tribes of Israel, the twelve were to be the leaders and the foundation stones of a new people of God. Jesus was well aware of their proneness to fail, but he promised to be with them until the end of time and to ratify all decisions which were made in his name in the community of which they were the leaders.

According to Luke, Jesus also gave the same power to preach and to heal to the larger group of the seventy. The exact significance of this additional commissioning is not clear, but it seems safe to say that Luke recognized that some aspects of the ministry of the twelve had to continue in the church beyond their death. The power and authority of the twelve and the seventy, while constituting a specialized ministry within the community of Jesus' disciples, is not independent of the power and authority exercised by Jesus in his own ministry and which was a power and authority received from God. By guaranteeing to remain with his disciples and to ratify their decisions, Jesus implies that the authority of the twelve and the seventy is to be exercised in a sacramental mode, that is, it is not power and authority which they possess in their own right, but it is the power and authority of God which was given to Jesus and which operates through them as through an instrument. Another indication of the sacramental character of this authority may be seen in the way Jesus instructs the twelve to exercise it according to his own example (Mark 10:42–45).

Paul's letters are the only evidence we have of the way apostolic ministry was understood in the first generation of Jesus' disciples. Paul understood his ministry as a gift from God which he in no way deserved. It was a call and a mission to preach the good news of Jesus, dead and risen, primarily to the Gentiles, but also to build up the community of those who believed. He recognized that he had received power and authority from God for this purpose, but was careful to exercise that power and authority only in the name of Christ and for the sake of the gospel. He preferred to persuade rather than to command, but he did not hesitate to make decisions and to give advice which he expected to be recognized as the work of the Spirit and to be carried out as commands of the Lord.

Paul was nonetheless self-effacing in the exercise of his ministry, because he recognized that he was the weak and frail instrument of God and of Christ, whose power was more evident in the human weakness of the minister. Paul did not preach in his own name nor did he preach himself; rather God and Christ spoke through him as through an instrument. The apostle's preaching made present the reconciling action of God in Christ. This understanding of ministry is more than an ambassadorial function based on a legal fiction; it is a mysterious action of God and Christ in and through the activity of Paul which makes the grace and power of Christ present to others; such an understanding is sacramental, even though this theological concept of sacrament does not appear as such in the NT.

Paul saw his ministry primarily in terms of spreading the good news of God's reconciling love in Christ to all who were willing to listen, both Jews and Gentiles, and of forming the community of believers as a living offering to God in union with Christ. Preaching the gospel was more important for Paul than baptizing; he does not speak at all about celebrating the eucharist himself, although he understands the celebration of the Lord's supper as a proclamation of the death of the Lord in anticipation of his *parousia*. In this transferred sense we can speak of Paul's ministry as priestly. In the new covenant the true sacrifice offered to God is the gift of self and its purpose is to attain union with God. This true sacrifice has been realized once for all in the death and resurrection of Jesus, so that there is no longer any need of a ritual sacrifice of the levitical variety in the Christian dispensation.[4] The eucharist makes present in an exemplary way the unique sacrifice of Jesus in his death and resurrection and the Christian community unites its own living sacrifice (Rom 12:1) to that of Christ as an offering to God and as an expression of its desire to be united with God in Christ.

When Paul uses cultic language in Rom 15:16 to speak of his ministry, he is referring to his work of preaching and teaching, whereby he forms the Christian community to offer themselves to God as a living sacrifice in the conduct of their daily lives. There is no historical or exegetical reason to think that Paul has the celebration of the eucharist in mind in this text.[5] The ministry of the apostle may be considered priestly, not because he presides at a ritual sacrifice, albeit a sacramental one, but because by his preaching and teaching he forms a Christian community to offer themselves daily as a living sacrifice to God through Christ.[6] In this transferred or analogical sense cultic language is appropriately applied to Christian ministry, because according to the letter to the Hebrews the goal toward which all ritual sacrifice of the OT pointed has been achieved in the death and resurrection of Jesus; Jesus offered himself, not an animal sacrifice, and as man he really attained to union with God. The work of ministry is primarily concerned with forming others to make that same gift of self and to attain that same union with God, not merely as individuals but as the people of God.

For these reasons the ministry of the sacraments is subordinate to the ministry of the word, and the Second Vatican Council was correct to affirm in *Presbyterorum Ordinis* 4 that "it is the first task of presbyters (*Presbyteri . . . primum habent officium*) as co-workers of the bishops to preach the gospel of God to all." By taking this position the council returns to a NT understanding of specialized ministry and reverses, at least in principle, a theological understanding of ordained ministry which is at least seven hundred years old. In the Supplement to the *Summa Theologica* St. Thomas Aquinas wrote, "A priest has two acts: one is the principal, namely to consecrate the body of Christ; the other is secondary, namely to prepare God's people for the reception of the sacrament."[7] Our study of the NT evidence demands a complete inversion of this position taken by St. Thomas in the thirteenth century. The Second Vatican Council took a first step in reversing this theology and so brought the understanding of ordained ministry in the Roman Catholic Church closer to that of the reformers who insisted on the primacy of the ministry of the word.[8] Because of the weight of Aquinas' authority and of the tradition inspired by him, it will be some time before this initiative of the council and its full significance transform the thinking of Roman Catholics and the formation of candidates for ordained ministry.

The NT does not offer a consistent picture of how a specialized ministry developed in early Christian communities. The prerogatives and functions of local leaders are never spelled out in detail. The pastoral epistles are as close as the NT comes to a church order document, but even here the information they provide is far from complete. It is clear, however, from Acts, 1 Peter, James and the pastorals that the elders (presbyteroi) in each local community are responsible for preaching, teaching and healing and for protecting the community from misrepresentations of the gospel. They have the role of overseeing the life of the community, but apart from James, the brother of the Lord, there is no evidence in the NT that one of the local presbyters was recognized as the principal overseer or bishop. The role of deacons (diakonoi) in the sense of an established ministry is barely mentioned.

Paul and 1 Peter recognize a variety of charisms at work in the community, but priority is given to those associated with the communication of the gospel and the leadership of the community, that is, apostles, prophets, evangelists, teachers and shepherds (Eph 4:11; cf. 1 Cor 12:28). Presbyters do not appear in any of these lists of charisms, but their functions are clearly related to preserving continuity with the twelve and Paul in Acts, with Christ and Peter in 1 Peter, and with Paul in the pastorals. In Acts the twelve share some of their authority with the seven by the laying on of hands; in the pastorals Timothy and the presbyters are appointed and receive the charism of their ministry by the laying on of hands of those who exercised such ministry before them.

Such fragmentary evidence is not sufficient to reconstruct the shape of local leadership in the early church, but it is sufficient to indicate some form of continuity between what the twelve and Paul did and what emerged in the second century. The functions of preaching, teaching, and healing, in the widest sense of that word, remained essential in the life of the church. The presbyters were the local leaders and seem to have functioned as a college even after the single bishop (episkopos) emerged.[9] In 1 Clement local leaders, variously called episkopoi kai diakonoi and presbyteroi, are considered to have been appointed by the apostles and to continue their work.[10] In the Didache the *episkopoi kai diakonoi* of the local church carry on the work of the itinerant prophets and teachers. Continuity in the preaching of the gospel is of primary importance in both the NT and the apostolic fathers, even though there is no consistency in the terminology used for local leaders and even though the laying on of hands appears only in Acts 6 and in the pastorals as a rite for handing on the authority of a specialized ministry. What later emerged as ordained ministry in the church thus has its roots in Jesus' ministry of preaching, teaching and healing, in the ministry of the twelve, the seventy, and Paul, and in their provisions for continuity in handing on what they had received from Christ for the building up of the community of his disciples.

Presbyteral leadership in early Christian communities may easily have derived from the role of elders in Jewish communities and in other communities in the pagan Hellenistic world.[11] In Acts 20:17–35 it is clear that the presbyters are considered to have been appointed by the Holy Spirit as overseers (*episkopoi*) in the local church and are charged with Paul's responsibility for the gospel as he himself approaches death. Only in the pastorals do we hear of their appointment by the laying on of hands of those who are elders before them. According to Acts 14:23 Paul and Barnabas appoint local leaders who here are called *presbyteroi*. In Phil 1:1 Paul himself calls the local leaders *episkopoi kai diakonoi*. Prophecy was involved in the selection of Barnabas and Saul for their mission from the church of Antioch (Acts 13:2–3) and for the designation of Timothy for his responsibilities in the Pauline churches of the region of Ephesus (1 Tim 1:18; 4:14).

These isolated scraps of information do not paint a total picture of how local presbyters came to be recognized as assuming the apostolic responsibility of the twelve, of the seventy and of Paul for the gospel. They do suggest, however, that the first preachers of the gospel were guided by the Spirit to adapt an existing model of local government to provide for the continuity of the tradition.[12] The reference to Timothy's youth in 1 Tim 4:12 suggests that age was not necessarily a requirement for such responsibilities. All this data points to but does not prove that a traditional structure of local leadership was taken over but freely adapted under the guidance of the Spirit for the charismatic work of proclaiming the gospel. We may have here a symbiosis of natural processes with the action of the Spirit which cannot be reduced to a fully satisfactory and rational explanation. As J.L. McKenzie has affirmed in another con-

text, to seek a more comprehensible understanding of the process
may be to introduce a dangerous rationalism into the mystery of the
Spirit's guidance of the church.[13] A presbyteral structure of local
leadership did emerge and it was seen to be the work of the Spirit.
Those who exercised the presbyteral ministry were understood to
possess a permanent gift from God, a gift which nonetheless could
be misused or lie dormant. There is also evidence that this presbyteral structure operated collegially even after the emergence of a
single local bishop, but of this development the NT is silent or at
best ambiguous.

It is historically certain that the structures of church government have developed beyond the time of the original apostles and
the composition of the NT. These developments have been influenced by socio-cultural patterns, historical circumstances and sociological laws. To deny this would be to deny the incarnational
and sacramental nature of the church. All these developments,
however, have not been motivated by the desire to promote the
gospel of Jesus Christ. A better understanding of the christological
dimension of ministry in the NT will help to discern in the tradition
the work of "the spirit" from the work of "the flesh" and will also
direct renewal so that Jesus' own ministry of preaching, teaching
and healing will continue to remain effectively and sacramentally
present to his disciples and to the world. To make the ministry of
Jesus sacramentally present in the church and in the world is the
task of specialized ministry and the purpose of the power and authority given to those who are called to that ministry by God and by
Christ.

All disciples of Jesus, however, are called to be witnesses to
him and to the Father's love in the entire conduct of their lives, not
only among themselves but in their relationships with the non-
believing world. This mission and ministry is not a mission and
ministry of select individuals from among the baptized; it is the
mission and ministry of the church collectively as the body of
Christ. The lived reality of the church as a communion of brothers
and sisters in Christ is the sacramental sign of God's love in the
world. The mission and ministry of all the baptized is to promote
the reality of this communion reaching out to embrace all nations.
Specialized ministry is the sacramental sign of Christ's own ministry of preaching, teaching, proclaiming the kingdom of God, calling to discipleship, healing and reconciling, and building up the
body by its teaching. These activities belong in a generic way to all
the baptized in the body of Christ in the existential reality of their

daily lives. Specialized ministry is the sacramental sign of the effective presence of Christ the good shepherd to his body, the church. It is not a question of excluding the baptized from proclaiming the gospel, from exercising a ministry of healing and reconciling in their mutual relationships, or from building up the community by their example and teaching. This is indeed the *res sacramenti*. It is rather a question of providing in the church an effective sign of the continued presence of Christ the head to his body, the church. The NT does not give any directions for the juridical distribution of functions within the community. Modifications may always be made in the distribution of functions in the course of time, but it is the argument of this study that ordained ministry in the church is theologically the sacramental sign of Christ's own ministry and cannot be dissolved into the general ministry of all the baptized.

The Pastoral Significance of the Study

If it is correct to say that ordained ministry is the sacramental sign of Christ's own ministry, it follows that those who are called to this ministry should reflect the cause and the example of Christ in all their activity. In the Roman Catholic Church there has been a tendency, in practice at least, to limit the sacramental dimension of ministry to the *ex opere operato* action of the sacraments. The ordained presbyter or bishop acts in the name of Christ when he baptizes, presides at the eucharist, absolves from sins, and anoints the sick and the dying. The efficacy of these sacramental actions depends only on the intention of the minister to do what the church does. It was no doubt important, at the time of the Donatist controversy, to insist on this understanding of the sacraments so that the church would not be deprived of these visible signs of the presence and action of Christ, her bridegroom and head, because of the personal weakness of ordained ministers. Sacraments, however, are not mere rituals; they are at the same time proclamations of the word; the ritual must consequently be accompanied by a ministry of the word which recalls the preaching, teaching and healing action of Christ and his power; in this way there is elicited in those who receive the sacraments that faith without which it is impossible to please God and without which the sacraments are not fruitful in those who receive them. The new rituals for the sacraments which include a reading of the scriptures and a homily are evidence of the church's recognition that the ministry of the word is an integral part of the ministry of the sacraments. These two ministries cannot be separated without reducing ordained ministers to executors of quasi-magical rites. The proclamation of the word which accompanies the ministry of the sacraments is also sacramental; the presbyter or bishop does not speak in his own name; the authority of his preaching is rooted in the word of God, and only to the extent that his preaching and teaching appear as word of God do they command the obedience of the faithful. As part of the total sacramental action, such preaching and teaching is also an effective channel of God's grace, for the word of God is power.

The specialized ministry of the ordained is not limited, however, to liturgical or sacramental actions even when these are enriched by a proper proclamation of the word. Jesus moved among the people preaching the kingdom of God, teaching not only in the synagogues, but by the lakeside, on the mountain, in the plain, and in the temple of Jerusalem. He did not function as a priest according to the ritual of the OT or of the temple in Jerusalem. He associated with toll-gatherers and public sinners and those excluded from the community by ritual impurity. His presence among the disdained of society was the manifestation of God's love and forgiveness. He challenged the rich and the powerful; he unmasked the hypocrisy of the self-righteous. He understood the real meaning of law and liberated men and women from unnecessary, man-made burdens. The power of God was active through him to heal and to forgive; by his ministry to the sick and possessed he made the power of God against evil visible to his society. He offered hope to those who lived without hope and welcomed all to table-fellowship with himself and his disciples. In the name of his Father he sought to create in Israel a community of reconciliation and of forgiveness in which no one would be turned away. He also took time out from his active ministry to commune with his Father in prayer. It was this Jesus who chose the twelve and the seventy from among his disciples and empowered them to carry on this work of preaching, teaching and healing in his name and to bring to fulfillment the kingdom of God. The letters of Paul show us how one of his chosen ministers understood and exercised this specialized ministry.

Paul expected his co-workers to share his understanding of ministry. The author of the pastorals expected the ministry of Paul to continue in Timothy and Titus and in the presbyters whom they would appoint. Liturgical actions were not the primary activity of Paul or of his co-workers. Preaching the gospel of Christ and building up the community of Christians by their teaching were the primary activities of Paul and of his co-workers. They could have claimed material support from the communities in which they labored, but Paul and Barnabas at least supported themselves by their work in order to promote the gospel of Christ. The example of Paul suggests that there may be great flexibility in the lifestyle of ordained ministers, provided that preoccupation with spreading the gospel and the formation of the body of Christ among all peoples dominates the life of the minister.

Apart from the example of Christ himself, Paul is the only first generation apostle to provide the church an example of specialized ministry. He was flexible in the way he adapted his ministry to different situations in the course of his life, but his ministry was not a job or a profession which he moved in and out of at will. His ministry was his answer to a call and he considered himself under an interior necessity to preach the gospel (1 Cor 9:16–17). He was confident of his authority, but was self-effacing before the power of God that operated through him as through an instrument. He preferred to persuade rather than to command, but his exercise of authority was motivated by the gospel of Christ and not by the prerogative of office. God and Christ spoke through him, calling men and women to be reconciled to God and to each other. He was devoted to his people, constantly putting himself out for them and always remembering them in his prayers; love of Christ and of his communities filled Paul's human need for love. The example of Paul justifies great flexibility in the way specialized ministry may be exercised in the church, but it also offers a rich, theological understanding of what it means to be a specialized minister in the church. In rethinking the roles of bishops and presbyters in the church, the ministry of Jesus and of Paul must be constantly kept in mind. It is not a question of mechanically imitating any example from the past, but of letting the ministry of Jesus and of Paul be the major theological criterion for discerning what is fitting for specialized ministry in a different set of circumstances. The good news of God's power and love and the building up of the eschatological people of God are the goals of all ministry, both general and specialized, because they are the goals of Jesus.

There is no foundation in the NT for the clericalization or the sacralization of ordained ministers, separating them from the people of God and assigning them a more exalted position in society. Jesus and Paul lived among the people they served. The clerical state developed in the church under the influence of OT patterns of cultic priesthood and of the stratification of Roman society from the end of the second century and the beginning of the third.[14] Radical surgery will be necessary if patterns of specialized ministry are to become more evangelical.

The language of priesthood has also become deeply ingrained in popular and theological thinking about ordained ministry in the church. As the epistle to the Hebrews demonstrates, Jesus by his death and resurrection gives an entirely new meaning to priesthood and thereby abrogates all earlier priesthoods. Only Jesus is called a *hiereus* in the NT and only in the epistle to the Hebrews.[15] Jesus has achieved what all ritual priesthood seeks—union with God by the offering of himself. All Christians are called to join themselves with Christ in that self-offering and in that sense are a royal priesthood by reason of their baptism. The words *hierateuma* and *hiereis* are used of Christians in general in the NT, but in this transferred sense. Baptized Christians are not priests individually, but collectively are a priestly people offering themselves to God in and through Christ. According to 1 Pet 2:5–6 all Christians are living stones around the living stone which is Christ and as such form a house built by the Spirit, offering spiritual sacrifices acceptable to God through Jesus Christ; this reality makes the church as a whole into a holy priesthood (*hierateuma*). In the Christian church, what was said of Israel in Ex 19:5–6 is realized in a new and transformed way, because of the death and resurrection of Jesus. "But you are a chosen race, a royal priesthood, a holy nation, God's own people" (1 Pet 2:9).

In the same sense the risen Christ makes all believers kings and priests, as he is king and priest, according to Rev 1:6; 5:10; 20:6; it is not clear, however, whether these texts of Revelation refer to the present state of the baptized or to their eschatological state in the new Jerusalem.[16] The priestly worship of the Christian people is not expressed in cultic ritual, but in the gift of their lives (Rom 12:1) and the praise of their lips (Heb 13:15; 1 Pet 2:9; Col 3:16; Eph 5:19–20). This is the worship "in spirit and in truth" about which Jesus spoke to the Samaritan woman in John 4:20–24; it is not attached to any temple or to any cultic ritual. Jesus foretold the destruction of the Jewish temple in Jerusalem and its cult because in his own death and resurrection he achieved for the whole human race what all previous priesthoods and cultic rituals sought to obtain for their adherents without ever really attaining it. Jesus also rejected the Pharisaic purity laws as human traditions, even though the Pharisees sought by these laws to have all the people live by the same code of purity that was required of the temple priests. To reintroduce such cultic rituals and purity laws in the life of the church would be a form of Judaizing. The epistle to the Hebrews may have been directed against just such a tendency.

Paul can speak of his ministry as priestly or cultic because by his preaching of the gospel he forms the Christian community to offer themselves to God as living sacrifices through Jesus Christ who himself leads them to union with God. The eucharist is the supreme sacramental expression of the reality of the Christian life, but it should not in any way be considered a cultic sacrifice after the manner of OT and pagan rituals; it is the reality toward which all such rituals and cult tend. As long as we insist on speaking of priesthood in a univocal way and fail to understand the term analogically in the light of Christ's transformation of all priesthood, the continued use of this language will create confusion and misunderstanding.

Beginning with 1 Clement and Ignatius, there was a tendency to parallel leadership roles in the Christian community with the priests and Levites of the OT.[17] The NT and the Didache both speak of the eucharist in sacrificial and cultic language. These are examples of the way in which the early church used the OT to understand the new reality introduced by the risen Christ. Jesus did not institute a new ritual, but expressed in his own life and death the sacrificial obedience that humankind owes to the creator. The eucharist is a sacramental sign of the only true sacrifice, Jesus' gift of himself to the Father on the cross, but it is not a ritual sacrifice in any OT sense.

By the fourth century, however, *episkopoi* and *presbyteroi* were understood to be *sacerdotes*, because they presided at the sacramental representation of Christ's sacrificial death. Jewish and pagan concepts of cultic priesthood were transferred to the elders of the Christian community, whose principal responsibility was preaching the gospel, instructing the people and forming the community. The original designation of these leaders as *presbyteroi* in Greek and *presbyteri* in Latin had also taken on the meaning of *hiereis* in Greek and of *sacerdotes* in Latin. By the middle ages the function of the presbyters was so focused almost exclusively on offering the eucharistic sacrifice that the translation of the Latin *presbyter* into Old English as *préost* or *prest*, from which "priest" developed, was understood in the cultic sense of *sacerdos*, whose Old English equivalent *sacerd* rapidly fell into disuse.[18] This development was paralleled in most western European languages; only Spanish has retained the original word *presbítero* alongside the word *sacerdote*. This semantic development will make it very difficult to recover the

proper NT notion of the presbyter as the leader of the Christian
community.

The history of the Second Vatican Council's *Decree on the Ministry and Life of Presbyters* is evidence of the council's effort to
move away from a sacerdotal understanding of ordained ministry
toward a more presbyteral understanding, but English translations
of the council documents still render *presbyter* as "priest."[19] The
emphasis throughout the decree in on the role of presbyters as
preachers of the gospel and leaders of God's people in collaboration
with the bishops; only in article 5 on their sacramental ministry are
they said to be *participes Sacerdotii Christi speciali ratione* and to
exercise *suum sacerdotale munus* in the celebration of the eucharist. They are sometimes called *sacerdotes*, but not in their own
right. The continued use of the word "priest" to translate *presbyter*
in this decree fails to appreciate the effort of the council fathers to
refocus the theology of ordained ministry and will only delay the
influence of the council's thinking on Catholic people in general
and on the ordained in particular.

The ministry of the presbyter is priestly in a transferred sense
inasmuch as he acts in the person of Christ the priest and forms the
people of God for the priestly sacrifice of their lives in union with
Christ. A. Vanhoye has also discussed the relationship of the ordained to the unique priesthood of Christ and the general priesthood of all the baptized in the light of the epistle to the Hebrews
and the references to the priesthood of all believers in 1 Peter and
in Revelation.[20] He insists on the totally new character of Christ's
priesthood with reference to OT priesthood, pointing out that by his
death and resurrection Christ as man really attains the goal of all
ritual sacrifice. All Christians by reason of their baptism are called
to unite the sacrifice of their lives with this new and supremely real
sacrifice of Christ. By the witness of their daily living and their
praise of God the church as a whole exercises the priesthood of
Christ toward God and for the world. Vanhoye distinguishes the
ascending and descending mediation of the priest and then understands the priestly character of all the baptized in terms of the ascending dimension of priestly mediation, that is, the access of humankind to God; in this sense all Christians, including the
ordained, are priests with Christ by their baptism. With respect to
the descending mediation of priesthood whereby the priest brings
divine gifts to humankind, only Christ is the new mediator of God's
word and of his grace. By extrapolating from the role of the *hēgoumenoi* in Heb 13 as those who speak the word of God to the

Christian people and supposedly lead them in the sacrifice of praise and in doing good (Heb 13:7, 15–17), Vanhoye is able to recognize an instrumental priesthood in ordained ministers inasmuch as they act in Christ's name to communicate the word of God and the grace of God by their ministry of word and sacrament. Vanhoye may be stretching some NT texts beyond their historical meaning, but in my opinion he suggests a fruitful line of theological thinking about the priestly character of the people of God and of the ordained.

Specialized Ministry and the Ordination of Women

The primary purpose of this study has been to explore the christological dimension of ministry in the NT. There are many other aspects of ministry that must be considered before responsible decisions can be made for the effective renewal of ministry, both general and specialized, in the church today. Many studies have already been published and the literature in this field is now very extensive. The foregoing examination of the NT data demonstrates in my opinion the priority which the NT gives to the integrated ministry of preaching, teaching and healing and the way in which the ministry of the twelve, the seventy and Paul is presented not merely as a continuation of what Jesus himself began, but as a means of making present the continuing ministry of the risen Christ in the church and for the world. Although the NT does not use this language, the sacramental understanding of ordained ministry has its roots in the NT understanding of the mission Jesus gave to the twelve, the seventy and Paul and which Acts, 1 Peter and the pastorals see continued in the presbyters upon whom hands have been laid by those who discharged this ministry before them.

This study has not addressed the question of the ordination of women to the ministry of presbyters in the church today, nor does the data of the NT address this question. Women were certainly co-workers of Paul in his ministry; they prophesied and prayed in public gatherings of the church, and they exercised leadership roles of some kind, but the documentation is insufficient to determine the functions they fulfilled; certain widows were recognized by the churches of the pastorals as providing a service of prayer and charity for the community. There is, however, no evidence that they exercised the ministry of presbyters. A man was chosen to replace Judas among the twelve and seven men were chosen by the church in Jerusalem, ostensibly to provide a service to neglected widows, even though they shared other ministerial functions with the twelve, but under their supervision. As far as our sources permit us to affirm, these at least are historical facts. The culture of the time no doubt demanded that men be chosen for these roles, even though there were outstanding women in the Greco-Roman world who defied these normal patterns. Cultures change, and in the more developed parts of our world women are normally filling roles once reserved exclusively to men. It is therefore perfectly normal to ask whether historical facts of the past must still dictate the action of the church today.

On the other hand, the Christian church is not simply identical with other social and political groups. It is the people of God and the body of Christ, formed by his ministry, death and resurrection and nurtured by the gift of his Spirit. There is no doubt that this understanding of the church is a matter of faith in the definitive revelation of God in Jesus Christ, but it is equally certain that the christological dimension is essential to the understanding of the church. Essential, too, to faith's understanding of the church is the sacramental dimension. Jesus of Nazareth, dead and risen, is the effective sign of God's presence to the world. In Jesus Christ the invisible God has become visible, and in Jesus Christ the destiny of all humankind is revealed in history. The church, as the body of Christ, is the visible sign of the continued presence of the risen Christ in the world and has the ministry of acknowledging publicly and of making visible the rule of Christ in the world, and of cooperating with Christ the head in extending that rule in the world until all things are brought under his feet. Christ has also established within his body specialized ministers to make his presence and his ministry sacramentally visible both to the church and to the world. The general ministry of the baptized and the specialized ministry of the ordained are data of revelation in the Christian church on the basis of tradition and of the NT. This distinction between general and specialized ministry is not only traditional in the Roman Catholic, Orthodox and Anglican churches, but is widely shared by the major Protestant denominations, even though the latter generally do not include ordination among the sacraments, and reject the juridical aspect of apostolic succession in ministry and the priestly character of ordained ministry. The specialized ministry of the ordained cannot be easily dissolved into the general ministry of all the baptized without betraying the Christian faith's understanding of the church as given in the tradition and in the NT. If this tradition is truly a matter of faith, it is also the work of the Spirit of Jesus.

The question of the ordination of women to the ministry of presbyters can only be responsibly and adequately addressed within the context of this sacramental understanding of the church and of ordained ministry. The church's reality and *praxis* are rooted essentially in the revelation of God in Jesus Christ. This revelation was historically communicated to the apostles, so that apostolic *praxis* is somehow normative for the continuing life of the church. The church is both christological and apostolic and the Spirit operates in the church according to what the Spirit receives from Christ. The discernment of this apostolic norm is the constant task of a community of faith which exists only because of its faithful commitment to that revelation once communicated by Christ to the apostles.

A serious task of discernment faces the universal church in this matter of the ordination of women; the unity of the body of Christ is at stake in its resolution. If the practice of ordaining only men is not apostolically normative, then fidelity to the gospel of Jesus Christ demands that the equality of men and women in the body of Christ established in principle by baptism (Gal 3:28) be recognized as well in the specialized ministry of the church. If, on the contrary, that practice is apostolically normative, it is important that a more adequate and irenic theology and *praxis* of ordained ministry be developed so that the practice of ordaining only men and the way they exercise their ministry may cease to appear as a violation of that equality of men and women to which baptism into Christ has called us.

On the basis of the foregoing study, it seems to me that it is precisely the christological dimension of ordained ministry which has conditioned the church's practice of ordaining only men. Obviously, not everything that has happened in the history of the church is apostolically normative. What is apostolically normative has also been tarnished and obscured in practice by human sinfulness. Historical particularity, however, is part and parcel of the scandal of the Christian faith. To eliminate it entirely by philosophical and rational arguments, and arguments based on the history of culture would destroy it as the faith once revealed by Christ to the apostles. Sacraments are effective signs of this historical particularity, and they lose their value as signs once their visibility is obscured by excessive rationalizing or by gnostic mystification. Theologically, the practice of ordaining only men is rooted in the historical fact of the maleness of Christ whose personal ministry is symbolized by the ministry of the ordained. In the synoptics, in

John, in Paul, in Ephesians, and in Revelation Jesus in his public ministry and in his glorified state is the bridegroom of his community of disciples, the church.[21] The validity of this sacramental theology is at stake in the question of the ordination of women.

If I have been correct in identifying the christological dimension of ordained ministry as the reason for the church's practice of ordaining only men, then a discernment must be made concerning the validity of this tradition. The tradition may be neutral, that is, due to the inertia of custom: we have always done it this way. If this is true, then the practice can and should be changed where and as local conditions warrant it. The tradition may also be the consequence of a patriarchalism which is totally conditioned by the culture and which reflects a sinful domination of males which is contrary to the gospel. In this case, every effort must be made to change that tradition as soon as possible in order to remain faithful to the gospel. Finally, the tradition may be rooted in the will of Christ himself, acting in the church through his Spirit; the significance of the tradition would then be the effective symbolization of the presence of Christ's own ministry in the church. In these circumstances ordained ministry must be recognized as a mystery of faith, and those who by the gratuity of God's call exercise this ministry in the church must be more Christ-like in the way they exercise their ministry and foster that equality which Christ himself showed in his dealing with women and men alike.

NOTES

Introduction

1. Edward Schillebeeckx, *Ministry, Leadership in the Community of Jesus Christ* (New York: Crossroad, 1981) 2.

2. Schillebeeckx, *Ministry* 5–6.

3. Schillebeeckx, *Ministry* 3.

4. Schillebeeckx, *Ministry* 5.

5. Cf. also 1 Cor 6:15–17; 10:14, 16–17; B. Ahern, "The Christian's Union with the Body of Christ in Cor, Gal, and Rom," *CBQ* 23 (1961) 199–209.

6. Eph 1:22–23; 4:11–13; cf. Col 1:24.

7. W. Kasper, "Ministry in the Church: Taking Issue with Edward Schillebeeckx," *Communio* 10 (1983) 185–95.

8. A. Vanhoye, "The Ministry in the Church. Reflections on a Recent Publication, I—Data of the New Testament," *Clergy Review* 68 (1983) 155–164; the original French article appeared in *NRT* 104 (1982) 722–38.

9. In a later book in response to his critics, *The Church with a Human Face. A New and Expanded Theology of Ministry* (New York: Crossroad, 1985), Schillebeeckx generalizes about these criticisms, singling out W. Kasper, A. Vanhoye, P. Grelot and the Roman Congregation for the Doctrine of the Faith. Understanding some of their anxieties, Schillebeeckx nonetheless finds some of their criticisms incomprehensible and "usually related to small points of detail" (Preface xi). Schillebeeckx considers the criticism of P. Grelot, W. Kasper and above all A. Vanhoye to be unfair (270). In the book itself he addresses explicitly only the criticisms of Grelot. For Grelot's criticism, cf. Pierre Grelot, *Eglise et ministère. Pour un dialogue critique avec Edward Schillebeeckx* («Théologies»; Paris: Cerf, 1983). I continue to regard the criticisms of Kasper, Vanhoye and Grelot to be substantive and serious.

10. A. Cunningham, SSCM, "The Holy Order of a Sacred Ministry," *Chicago Studies* 22 (1983) 269–81.

11. Cf. J. Barr, "The Bible as a Document of Believing Communities," in his *The Scope and Authority of the Bible* (Philadelphia: Westminster, 1981) 111–33; W. Marxsen, *The New Testament as the Church's Book?* (Philadelphia: Fortress, 1971); B.S. Childs, *The New Testament as Canon: An Introduction* (Philadelphia: Fortress, 1985) 14: "The multi-layered quality of the Gospels and many of the epistles has further demonstrated the active participation of the community for whom the literature had a variety of functions." Childs would see the tradition being shaped by the texts which were canonized at a later date. Such influence may be granted but it would have remained local and exhortative, not universal and juridical.

12. E.g., H. Von Campenhausen, *Ecclesiastical Authority and Spiritual Power in the Church of the First Three Centuries* (Stanford, CA: Stanford University, 1969); E. Schweizer, *Church Order in the New Testament* (SBT 32; London: SCM, 1961).

13. Cf. Vanhoye, *Clergy Review* 68 (1983) 160: "What will be presented will be, not the witness of the New Testament about ministry, but a reconstitution of 'the story of the New Testament communities' . . . The perspective is appreciably different. No one will dispute the results of the historical research, but it is important, precisely, to respect whatever belongs specifically to it. It is natural in research to give attention to points that are obscure and to work hard to bring light to bear upon them. To reconstitute the history of the Christian communities, one must not be satisfied with what the texts explicitly supply, for their contribution is full of gaps. Hence an effort must be made to go beyond the texts, by means of all kinds of analyses, comparisons, conjectures and deductions. The results of such work will evidently only afford a limited degree of probability, varying with every case. Researchers are fully aware of this. In the last analysis, even from the point of view of historical truth, we cannot put on the same footing the overall descriptions which they attempt to produce and the witness provided by the ancient texts. The latter are documents, the bearing of which we are simply concerned to estimate; the former are hypothetical constructions, always open to revision on the basis of a fresh study of the documents. What holds good for the study of history, is still more valid for biblical theology: the latter is based on the witness of the texts in expressing the faith of the primitive Church and a rule of faith for the present-day Church. It can only confer secondary importance on the constructions of historians, whose function is restricted to sug-

gesting a complementary light in which to see the reading of the texts, without ever attempting to replace them."

14. Cf. Childs, *The New Testament as Canon* 3–53, esp. 42–43: "In spite of the constant emphasis on the diversity within the New Testament by modern scholars, historically by the end of the second century, if not before, the gospels were being read holistically as a unity within the circumference proscribed by a rule-of-faith . . ."

15. Cf. G.P. Fogarty, *American Catholic Biblical Scholarship. A History from the Early Republic to Vatican II* (San Francisco: Harper & Row, 1989).

16. Cf. J.A. Fitzmyer, "The Biblical Commission's Instruction on the Historical Truth of the Gospels," TS 25 (1964) 386–408. The substance of this instruction was incorporated into the Dogmatic Constitution on Divine Revelation (*Dei Verbum*) of the Second Vatican Council; cf. A.P. Flannery (ed.), *Documents of Vatican II* (Grand Rapids: Eerdmans, 1975) 761.

Chapter I

1. Normally speaking, synoptic parallels will not be cited except in those cases where a different meaning or different nuance is conveyed by the parallel text.

2. Repentance is the first response to the preaching of the kingdom of God called for by John the Baptist (Matt 3:2; Mark 1:4; Luke 3:3, 8) and by Jesus (Matt 4:17; Mark 1:14–15). It is also the first response required by the preaching of the early Church (Acts 2:38; 3:19; 17:30; 20:21; 26:20; Luke 24:47). Repentance is also a gift of God (Acts 5:31; 11:18). It is more than a change of heart; it is a movement, a return of the whole person to God; in the LXX the Greek verbs *epistrephō* and *apostrephō* render the Hebrew *shûb* (cf. Acts 3:19; 9:35; 11:21; 14:15; 15:19; 26:20; Matt 18:3); in later OT texts, *metanoeō* appears for *shûb*. Cf. E. Würthwein–J. Behm, "*metanoeō, metanoia*," TDNT 4.975–1008; D.L. Gelpi, *Charism and Sacrament: A Theology of Christian Conversion* (New York: Paulist, 1976); S. Hoppel-J.J. Walter, *Conversion and Discipleship. A Christian Foundation for Ethics and Doctrine* (Philadelphia: Fortress, 1986).

3. The text of Matt 10:40–41 is a fuller form of Luke 10:16. Luke derived his form of the saying from "Q", while Matthew may have drawn upon a fuller form from "M". Cf. J.A. Fitzmyer, *The Gospel according to Luke (X–XXIV)* (AB 28A; Garden City, N.Y.: Double-

day, 1985) 856–57; R. Bultmann, *The History of the Synoptic Tradition* (New York: Harper & Row, 1963) 143.

4. Only in the gospel according to Matthew does Jesus affirm the priority of Israel in such strong language; cf. also 10:5–6.

5. Jesus' parable presupposes the OT allusion to Israel as God's vineyard in Is 5:1–7 and to Israel as a vine in Ps 80:8.

6. The verb *apostellō* is used in all these synoptic texts, except in Luke 20:12, 13 where *pempō* is found. Cf. n. 37 below.

7. The verb *exēlthon* here could refer to his withdrawal for prayer, but the context suggests a stronger meaning. The preposition in compound verbs cannot always be pressed in Hellenistic Greek. In the parallel passage Luke rendered Mark's *exēlthon* as *apestalēn* (4:43), a divine passive of the verb *apostellō*.

8. The parallel in Luke 5:32 adds the words "to repentance" to the Markan text.

9. The text of Matt 11:19 (= Luke 7:34) uses the verb "to come" but without the same sense of urgency in the context; Jesus' way of life is contrasted with that of John the Baptist. Both, of course, had a mission from God.

10. The same formula *dei* is used in the parallel texts of Matt 16:21 and Luke 9:22. Cf. W. Grundmann, "*dei, deon esti,*" *TDNT* 2.21–25.

11. An almost identical summary appears in Matt 9:35; in 11:1–6 "the deeds of Jesus" are described in terms of healing, preaching and teaching. "Blessed is he who takes no offense at me" (11:6) implies Jesus' role as teacher from God.

12. The verb *euaggelizomai*, "to bring good news," is peculiar to Luke in the gospel and in the Acts of the Apostles where it appears ten and fifteen times respectively. Elsewhere in the gospels it only appears at Matt 11:5. Cf. G. Friedrich, "*euaggelizomai, euaggelion* etc.," *TDNT* 2.707–37.

13. "The Lord" in Luke 5:17 refers to God, not to Jesus. The embarrassment of the copyists is seen in the variants. Cf. J.A. Fitzmyer, *The Gospel according to Luke (I–IX)* (AB28; Garden City, N.Y.: Doubleday, 1981), 582. H. Schürmann, *Das Lukasevangelium* (HTKNT 3.1; Freiburg: Herder, 1969) 281.

14. The word appears in Mark 6:2 = Matt 13:54; Matt 13:58; Mark 6:14 = Matt 14:2; Matt 11:20–23 = Luke 10:13; Luke 19:37; Acts 2:22; the singular is used for a miracle of Jesus in Mark 6:5; both the singular and plural are used for miracles performed by the disciples of Jesus in his name (Mark 9:39; Matt 7:22); cf. also Acts 8:13; 19:11.

15. On the exegetical problems of this passage, cf. R.T. Mead,

"The Healing of the Paralytic—A Unit?" *JBL* 80 (1961) 348–54; J. Dewey, "The Literary Structure of the Controversy Stories in Mark 2:1—3:6," *JBL* 92 (1973) 394–401; C.P. Ceroke, "Is Mark 2:10 a Saying of Jesus?" *CBQ* 22 (1960) 369–90; C.S. Mann, *Mark* (AB 27; Garden City, N.Y.: Doubleday, 1986) 221–28; R. Pesch, *Das Markusevangelium* (HTKNT 2.1; Freiburg: Herder, 1976) 151–62 (with bibliography); Fitzmyer, *Luke* 576–86 on Luke 5:17–26; C.C. Caragounis, *The Son of Man* (WUNT 38; Tübingen: Mohr, 1986) 179–90.

16. Sinners should be understood as people of proven dishonesty or engaged in degrading occupations, and not simply those who failed to observe Pharisaic ritual law. Toll collectors in Galilee at the time of Jesus were considered to be simply dishonest and not collaborators with the Gentiles. Cf. J.R. Donahue, "Tax Collectors and Sinners. An Attempt at Identification," *CBQ* 33 (1971) 39–61, esp. 48–49, 54–61.

17. Mark 5:34 = Matt 9:22 = Luke 8:48; Mark 10:52 = Luke 18:42; Luke 7:50; 17:19.

18. Mark 3:4 = Luke 6:9; Mark 5:23 (the verb *zaō*, "to live," is added here); 5:28 = Matt 9:21; Mark 6:56 = Matt 14:36; Mark 15:30–31 = Matt 27:40–42 = Luke 23:35–37; Matt 27:49; Luke 23:39; Matt 8:25; 14:30; Luke 8:36, 50.

19. Luke 7:50; Matt 1:21; on arriving in the house of Zacchaeus, the chief toll collector, Jesus declares, "Today salvation (*sōteria*) has come to this house" (Luke 19:9).

20. Mark 8:35 = Matt 16:25 = Luke 9:24; Mark 10:26 = Matt 19:25 = Luke 18:26; Mark 13:13 = Matt 24:13; Mark 13:20 = Matt 24:22; Luke 8:12; 13:23; 19:10.

21. The verb *didaskō*, "to teach," appears with respect to Jesus fifteen times in Mark, nine times in Matthew and thirteen times in Luke; correspondingly, the verb *kēryssō*, "to proclaim," appears five times in Mark, four times in Matthew and twice in Luke outside the citation of Is 61:1–2. The abstract noun *didachē* is used of Jesus' teaching five times in Mark, twice in Matthew and only once in Luke. Cf. K.H. Rengstorf, "*didaskō, didaskalos* etc.," *TDNT* 2.135–65.

22. *Didaskalos* appears twelve times in Mark, ten times in Matthew and fourteen times in Luke. Luke uses an equivalent term, *epistatēs*, six times. "Rabbi" appears four times each in Mark and Matthew only.

23. Cf. Josephus, *Ant.*, 15.11.5 § 417 and the inscription discovered in 1871 by M. Clermont-Ganneau.

24. Although most commentators understand *tauta* as the cleans-

ing of the temple, it is possible to understand it of Jesus' whole career, especially if the narrative was originally independent of the present context. V. Taylor (*The Gospel according to Mark* [London: Macmillan, 1955] 470) cites Swete and Plummer in favor of the wider reference.

25. *Tōn pisteuontōn eis eme*; the parallel in Mark 9:42 (*eis eme*) is not textually certain; Jesus is also the object of the verb "to believe" in Matt 27:42, but the exact phrasing is not textually certain (*ep'auton, ep'autǭ* or *autǭ*).

26. Mark 2:5 = Luke 5:20 = Matt 9:2; Mark 5:34 = Matt 9:22 = Luke 8:48; Mark 5:36 = Luke 8:50; Mark 9:23–24; Luke 7:9 = Matt 8:10; 9:29; Mark 10:52 = Luke 18:42; Matt 15:28; 17:20 = Luke 17:6; Matt 8:13; Luke 7:50; Matt 21:21–22 = Mark 11:22–24.

27. Cf. Matt 7:24–27; Luke 4:22; 24:44.

28. The parallel text in Luke 6:46 reads, "Why do you call me 'Lord, Lord,' and not do what I tell you?"

29. Cf. John P. Meier, *The Vision of Matthew. Christ, Church and Morality in the First Gospel* (New York: Paulist, 1979) 222–64.

30. Cf. Gordon J. Hamilton, "The First Commandment: A Theological Reflection," *New Blackfriars* 69 (1988) 174–81.

31. Mark 1:35; 6:46 = Matt 14:23; Matt 11:25–27 = Luke 10:21–22; Mark 14:26–31 = Matt 26:36–46 = Luke 22:39–46; additionally in Luke 3:21; 5:16; 6:12; 9:18, 28–29; 11:1.

32. *Exousia* connotes the ability to perform an action without hindrance, as distinct from an intrinsic ability (*dynamis*). It also connotes a possibility granted by a superior authority such as the king or the state. In the LXX and Jewish literature it is used of God's absolute power and authority and for a right or permission given by God or the law. In the NT it generally connotes the power or authority of God exercised in nature or the spiritual world, e.g. by Satan, and for religious and civil government. According to W. Foerster, the *exousia* of Jesus and of the apostles is like "the invisible power of God whose Word is creative power." Derivatively it connotes a freedom given to the community, but always from God. Even the *exousia* of the antichrist is given by God and controlled by God. Cf. *TDNT* 2.560–75.

33. Cf. the parable in Luke 12:35–38; also Matt 23:8–12; Mark 9:35; Luke 9:48.

34. The phrase was coined by R. Bultmann to distinguish the preaching of Jesus from the preaching of the early church; cf. his *Theology of the New Testament* (London: SCM, 1965) 1.33: "The proclaimer became the proclaimed."

35. John the Baptist is also said to have been sent by God; in John 1:6; 3:28 *apostellō* is the verb used; *pempō* in 1:33.

36. 3:17, 34; 5:36, 38; 6:29, 57; 7:29; 8:42; 10:36; 17:3, 8, 18, 21, 23, 25; 20:21 for a total of sixteen times.

37. 4:34; 5:23, 24, 30, 37; 6:38, 39, 44; 7:16, 18, 28, 33; 8:16, 18, 26, 29; 9:4; 12:44, 45, 49; 13:20; 14:24; 15:21; 16:5 for a total of twenty-four times. John 20:21 has the finite form of both verbs. K.H. Rengstorf ("*apostellō* [*pempō*]," *TDNT* 397–406) admits that the two verbs are used almost indifferently in John, although earlier in the same article he argued that *pempō* emphasized the act of sending, while *apostellō* connoted commissioning and implied responsibility on the part of the one sent.

38. In Heb 3:1 Jesus himself is called the *apostolos* and high priest of our confession.

39. 4:34, 5:30; 7:16–18; 9:4, but especially 6:38–40; 12:49–50; 14:31.

40. In another sense his coming provokes judgment; cf. 9:39.

41. The first verb in 8:42 (*exēlthon*) refers to Jesus coming into the world; the second verb (*hēkō*) is taken over from the religious language of the time and refers to the saving appearance of a deity, or a human claim to be of saving importance. Cf. R. Schnackenburg, *Das Johannesevangelium* (HTKNT 4.2; Freiburg: Herder, 1971) 286; R.E. Brown, *The Gospel according to John I–XII* (AB 29; Garden City, N.Y.: Doubleday, 1966) 357; less definitively C.K. Barrett (*The Gospel according to St. John*, 2nd edition [Philadelphia: Westminster, 1978] 348).

42. John 17:3 is a gloss of the evangelist or of the final editor of the gospel. Cf. R. Schnackenburg, *Das Johannesevangelium.* Dritte Auflage (HTKNT 4.3; Freiburg: Herder, 1979) 195 (an editorial gloss); R.E. Brown, *The Gospel according to John XIII–XXI* (AB 29A; Garden City, N.Y.: Doubleday, 1970) 741 (a gloss of the final editor probably drawn from the liturgy of the Johannine church); B. Lindars, *The Gospel of John* (London: Oliphants, 1972) 519–20 (a parenthetical gloss, but the work of the evangelist); Barrett, *Gospel* 503.

43. Cf. John 4:34; 5:30; 6:38; 8:29; 14:31.

44. This dependence is expressed in texts such as John 3:34–35; 4:34; 5:19–20, 30, 36; 7:16; 8:26; 12:49; 14:24; 17:4. Equality with the Father appears in texts such as 5:18, 21; 8:58; 10:30, 33, 38; 14:8–11.

45. The formula appears six times outside the Johannine writings, but only in Matt 18:6 in the synoptics; Mark 9:42 and Matt 27:42 are textually uncertain.

46. Cf. also John 14:9.

47. The only exceptions are John 3:12; 4:48 and perhaps 20:8. The "heavenly things" (*epourania*) of 3:12 concern the new revelation Jesus has come to bring over and above the revelation of the Hebrew scriptures; cf. J.T. Forestell, *The Word of the Cross* (AnBib 57; Rome: Biblical Institute, 1974) 42–43. John 4:48 refers to an inadequate faith based on signs; the implied object could be Jesus or his word (cf. 4:50). In John 20:8 the implied object could be Jesus or the resurrection.

48. John 5:24; 12:44; 14:1; the characteristic Johannine formula, *pisteuō eis*, is used in 12:44 and 14:1; in 5:24 the verb is followed by a dative; cf. n. 51 below.

49. Cf. John 6:69; 8:24; 11:27, 42; 13:19; 14:10–11; 16:27, 30; 17:8, 21; 20:31. 4:21 may be an exception, but it concerns the eschatological moment of the new worship of God introduced by Jesus.

50. On Luke 10:16 and Matt 10:40, cf. n. 3 above.

51. The dative case used here connotes accepting what God says; it is not the full faith of personal commitment as expressed by the formula *pisteuō eis*.

52. J.P. Meier (*Vision of Matthew* 82–83) argues for understanding "the Son" in Matt 11:27 and Mark 13:32 in terms of "the Son of man." "The Son" also appears absolutely in relation to "the Father" in Mark 13:32 (= Matt 24:36) and in the baptismal formula of Matt 28:19.

53. In some cases, some manuscripts have a variant reading, "my Father."

54. John 3:35; 5:20, 21, 22, 23, 26; 14:13.

55. John 8:19, 28, 38, 49, 54; 10:18, 25, 29, 37; 14:20, 21; 15:15, 23, 24.

56. Cf. also John 14:10–11.

57. Cf. Ex 33:20, 23; Jgs 13:22; Deut 4:12.

58. Cf. Gen 32:30; Ex 33:18—34:8; Jgs 13:21–23; 1 Kgs 19:9–13; Is 6:5; Ez 1:28.

59. John 1:18; 6:46a; cf. also 1 John 4:12.

60. On the Paraclete, cf. e.g. J.T. Forestell "Jesus and the Paraclete in the Gospel of John," in *Word and Spirit. Essays in honour of David Michael Stanley on his 60th Birthday* (ed. J. Plevnik; Willowdale: Regis College Press, 1975) 151–97 with bibliography; Schnackenburg, *Johannesevangelium* 3.156–73; Brown, *Gospel* 1135–1144.

Chapter II

1. Various expressions are used for the crowds: e.g., *ochlos*: Matt forty-four times; Mark thirty-eight times; Luke forty-one times; John twenty times; *polu plēthos*: Mark 3:7–8; *plēthos* governing a genitive: Luke 6:17; 8:37; 23:27; *polloi*: Matt 12:15; *ho laos*: Luke 7:1; *pas ho laos*: Luke 7:29; *pantes*: Luke 9:23.

2. E.g., Mark 1:21–22; 2:4, 13; 3:7–10; 4:1; 5:21, 24; 6:32–33; 7:36–37; 8:1; 11:8–10; 12:37; Matt 8:1; 15:29–31; 22:33; Luke 4:42; 5:1, 15; 7:9, 11; 11:14; 12:1; 13:17; 14:25; 18:43; 19:3, 48; 21:38; John 6:2, 24–25; 12:17–18.

3. E.g., Mark 10:48; Luke 11:29; John 7:43; 9:16; 10:19.

4. E.g., Mark 8:34: "the multitudes with his disciples"; 10:46: "his disciples and a great multitude"; Matt 23:1: "the crowds and the disciples"; Luke 6:17: "a great crowd of his disciples and a great multitude of people"; 7:11: "his disciples and a great crowd"; 20:45: "in the hearing of all the people he said to his disciples."

5. Cf. R.E. Brown, *The Community of the Beloved Disciple* (New York: Paulist, 1979) 74: "I suggest that here John refers to Jewish Christians who are no longer to be considered true believers because they do not share John's view of the eucharist"; also p. 157 and his *John* 297.

6. Cf. Fitzmyer, *Luke* 1520: "Since Luke has never recounted the flight of the disciples (contrast Mark 14:50; Matt 26:56), some of them at least must be presumed to be included in the 'acquaintances' "; also p. 1447 on 2 :47–53.

7. One of the two is identified as Andrew, Simon Peter's brother. The other has been variously identified with John, the son of Zebedee, "the disciple whom Jesus loved," or Philip who is usually associated with Andrew in the gospel (1:44; 6:5–9; 12:21–22). There is no way of deciding this question. Cf. Brown, *John* 73–74; Schnackenburg, *Das Johannesevangelium* (HTKNT 4.1; Freiburg: Herder, 1965) 308.

8. Mark 1:16–20 = Matt 4:18–22; Luke 5:1–11; John 1:35–51; Mark 2:13–14 = Luke 5:27–28 = Matt 9:9.

9. Cf. Lamar Williamson, Jr., *Mark* (Interpretation. A Bible Commentary for Teaching and Preaching; Atlanta: John Knox, 1983) 106–07.

10. Cf. E.P. Sanders, *Jesus and Judaism* (Philadelphia: Fortress, 1985) 252–55; M. Hengel, *The Charismatic Leader and His Followers* (New York: Crossroad, 1981); cf. also Luke 14:28–32.

11. Cf. Schuyler Brown, *Apostasy and Perseverance in the The-*

ology of Luke (AnBib 36; Rome: Biblical Institute Press, 1969) 99–107, 122.

12. The paradigmatic character of the narrative for the Christian disciple is reinforced when it is recognized that Peter appears to have retained his home (Mark 1:29) and boat (Mark 3:9; 4:1) after following Jesus, and according to 1 Cor 9:5 traveled with a wife (sister). Cf. Mann, *Mark* 403; Fitzmyer, *Luke* 1205.

13. E.g., Mark 2:15; 3:7; 5:24; 10:32; 11:9; 14:54; Matt 4:25; 8:1, 10; 9:19, 27; 12:15; 14:13; 19:2; 20:29; Luke 22:39; 23:27; John 1:38, 40; 6:2; 11:31; 18:15; 20:6; 21:20.

14. E.g., Mark 1:18, 20; 2:14; 8:34; 10:21, 28; Matt 4:22; 8:19, 22; 9:9; 10:38; 19:28; Luke 5:11; 9:59, 61; John 1:43; 8:12; 10:4, 5, 27; 12:26; 21:19, 20, 22. Cf. G. Kittel, "*akoloutheō*," *TDNT* 1.210–16, esp. 213–15.

15. Mark 10:52; 15:41; Matt 8:23; John 1:37; 13:36–37.

16. The word appears sixty-six times in Matthew, sixty of which refer to the disciples of Jesus; forty times in Mark for the disciples of Jesus; twenty-six times in Luke; seventy-one times in John including Joseph of Arimathea, the secret disciple (19:38); twenty-eight times in Acts. Reference is also made to disciples of John the Baptist and of the Pharisees; in Matt 10:24–25 the word is used proverbially. The corresponding verb only appears in Matt 13:52; 27:57; 28:19 and Acts 14:21. Cf. K.H. Rengstorf, "*manthanō* etc.," *TDNT* 4.390–461, esp. 441–59.

17. The historicity of Jesus' choice of the twelve and that of their mission prior to Easter have both been questioned. Most recently, cf. H.O. Guenther, *The Footprints of Jesus' Twelve in Early Christian Traditions. A Study in the Meaning of Religious Symbolism* (American University Studies, Series 7: Theology and Religion 7; New York: P. Lang, 1985). Sanders (*Jesus and Judaism* 101–06) argues on the contrary that the choice of the twelve and their association with Jesus in his own ministry reflects the intentions of Jesus. Fitzmyer, *Luke* 752–53, 843, sees no reason to doubt that Jesus associated disciples with his mission during his lifetime. Since the early church saw itself so clearly as the new Israel and its mission as a continuation of the mission of Jesus, it may remain impossible to find a totally satisfactory answer to these questions of historicity.

18. Mark ten times; Matthew three times; Luke six times; John four times; Acts once.

19. Matt 10:1; 11:1; 20:17; 26:20; in the last two texts the presence of *mathētēs* is uncertain.

20. Except for Acts 14:4, 14 only the twelve are called "apostles" in Luke-Acts; six times in the gospel; twenty-six times in Acts; the word appears once in Matt 10:2 and once or twice in Mark (6:30 and as a variant reading in 3:14).

21. The whole discourse, as it now appears in Matt 10:5–42, is addressed exclusively to the twelve (10:5). The material in vv 5–14 is parallel to Mark 6:7–13 and the added material can easily apply to the mission of the twelve. Vv 15–16 are derived from "Q" and used by Luke with reference to the seventy (10:12, 3). With the exception of vv 23 and 40, the sayings collected by Matthew in 10:17–42 concern the post-resurrection mission and discipleship in general.

22. Feeding narratives appear in Mark 6:32–44 (= Matt 14:13–21 = Luke 9:10–17) and 8:1–10 (= Matt 15:32–39) and in John 6:1–15. It is generally agreed today that the second narrative is a different tradition of the same incident; Mark has put together two series of narratives, 6:32—7:37 and 8:1–26, each beginning with a feeding narrative and concluding with an uniquely Marcan healing narrative, the deaf mute in 7:31–37 and the blind man of Bethsaida in 8:22–26. Cf. Mann, Mark (AB 27) 325; Fitzmyer, Luke 762; P. Bonnard, L'Evangile selon saint Matthieu (Commentaire du Nouveau Testament 1; Neuchâtel: Delachaux & Niestlé, 1963) 217, 235. In John's account, the twelve are not distinguished from the disciples in general until 6:67; only Philip and Andrew play any significant role in the episode; Jesus himself distributes the loaves and instructs the disciples to gather the fragments.

23. Mark 14:17 and Matt 26:20 speak of "the twelve" and Luke 22:14 of "the apostles," which in his usage always refers to the twelve; cf. n. 20 above. If "the disciple whom Jesus loved" was not one of the twelve, the Johannine narrative of the last supper may imply a larger group. On the other hand, there is no institution narrative in John and some commentators think "the disciple whom Jesus loved" is always an addition to an earlier text. Barrett (John 446) identifies "the disciple whom Jesus loved" as one of the twelve but acknowledges that this portion of the narrative appears to be secondary.

24. The parallel text of Luke 22:24–27 is found in the narrative of the last supper where the audience is exclusively the twelve.

25. Sanders (Jesus and Judaism 103) accepts this text as authentic.

26. This interpretation may be confirmed in 20:24 by the identification of the absent Thomas as one of the twelve. With reference

to the presence of "the disciple whom Jesus loved" at the last supper, cf. n. 23 above. John 21 is an appendix and the disciples involved are explicitly named in 21:2; "the disciple whom Jesus
loved" must be one of "the two others," if he is not again an addition to the text. In the corresponding narrative of Luke 24, others
including the two disciples of Emmaus are present when Jesus appears to the eleven (24:33–49); on the role of these "others," cf. J.
Plevnik, "The Eleven and their Associates," *CBQ* 40 (1978) 205–11;
"The Eyewitnesses of the Risen Jesus in Luke 24," *CBQ* 49 (1987)
90–103.

27. Cf. the discussion below, 45–47, 51–53.

28. On the historicity of the choice of the twelve and of their
preaching mission during the lifetime of Jesus, cf. n. 17 above.

29. Since only Peter and John are remembered elsewhere in the
NT, it is easy to suppose that some confusion may have arisen about
the names of the others; cf. Sanders, *Jesus and Judaism* 101, 230.

30. The name "Matthew" appears only in Matt 9:9; the parallel
text of Mark 2:14 has Levi, the son of Alphaeus; Luke 5:27 also has
Levi, and a variant reading adds "the son of Alphaeus"; a variant
reading in Mark has "James, the son of Alphaeus."

31. Mark 1:16–20 = Matt 4:18–22; Luke 5:1–11; Mark 2:13–14 =
Matt 9:9 = Luke 5:27–28; such renunciation is also implied by the
parallel narratives of Mark 10:28–30; Matt 19:27–29 and Luke
18:28–30. Luke emphasizes the radical character of this renunciation by the use of the word "all" (*panta*), at 5:11, 28; 14:33. *Panta*
is also used, however, in Mark 10:28 (= Matt 19:27).

32. The choice of the twelve is taken for granted in Matthew
(10:1) and John (6:70).

33. Mark four times; Matthew five times; Luke four times; John
eight times.

34. Omitted from previous editions of Nestle, this clause has
been restored to the text by the editors of the 26th edition, but in
square brackets. If original, it would be an indication that Luke did
not coin the word "apostle" for the twelve!

35. On the role of eyewitnesses in the NT, cf. also John 15:27;
19:35; Luke 1:2; 24:48; Acts 1:8, 21–23; 2:32; 3:15; 5:32; 10:39, 41;
13:31.

36. The verb used by Luke in Acts 1:24, *anadeiknymi*, only appears again in Luke 10:1 for the appointment of the seventy by
Jesus.

37. "Preaching" (*kērygma*) is generally defined as the public
proclamation of the kingdom of God or of the risen Jesus to non-

believers; "teaching" (didachē) is the instruction of believers, comprising for the most part an interpretation of the Jewish scriptures in the light of the resurrection. In the Acts of the Apostles teaching is more prominent than preaching; didaskō appears of Christian teachers fourteen times; didachē four times; kēryssō six times; but euaggelizomai fifteen times, twice in parallelism with teaching (5:42; 15:35), teaching appearing first. On the biblical notion of "command," see G. Schrenk, "entellomai, entolē," TDNT 2.544–556, esp. 545; M.J. O'Connell, "The Concept of Commandment in the Old Testament," TS 21 (1960) 351–403.

38. Mark 6:7 = Matt 10:1 = Luke 9:1; Luke adds the word "power": dynamin kai exousian (cf. Luke 4:36). The gift of "authority" is also noted by Jesus himself after the mission of the seventy (Luke 10:19).

39. In parables, exousia is given to servants to exercise responsibility over others: A householder gives authority to his servants in his absence in Mark 13:34; in Luke 19:17 civil authority over ten cities is given to a responsible servant; cf. Luke 19:19 (the same idea is expressed without the word exousia). In John 1:12 all who believe in Jesus receive exousia to become children of God, but this is not a missionary text. Matt 9:8 speaks of exousia being given to men (anthrōpois) to forgive and to heal; cf. the discussion below, 44–45.

40. In 2 Cor 10:8 and 13:10 exousia is used of the apostolic authority given to Paul by the Lord; in 1 Cor 8:9; 9:4, 5, 6, 12, 18; 2 Thess 3:9 it means "right," "freedom" or "claim"; cf. W. Foerster, "exestin, exousia etc.," TDNT 2.560–575.

41. Cf. Matt 25:31–46 and John 12:26. A symbolic reference to the service of disciples may also be found in texts such as Mark 1:31; 15:41; Luke 8:3, texts which concern Peter's mother-in-law and the ministering women.

42. Cf. J.L. McKenzie, Authority in the Church (New York: Sheed & Ward, 1966).

43. Mark 6:7–13 (= Luke 9:1–6 = Matt 10:1–14) for the commissioning of the twelve; Luke 10:1–16 for the commissioning of the seventy. Matt 10:15–42 is a collection of "Q" sayings and some Marcan material drawn from Mark 13:9–13 and 9:41 on the themes of mission and/or discipleship; the missionary sayings in Matt 10:15–42 generally apply to the post-resurrection period; cf. n. 21 above.

44. The Lucan formulation, "The laborer deserves his wages" (10:7), more likely preserves the form of "Q". It reappears in this

form in 1 Tim 5:18. The Matthaean form reappears in the *Did.* 13:1. Matthew prefers the word *trophē* (four times; Luke once; John once). Cf. Fitzmyer, *Luke* 848.

45. Luke 9:1–2 reads, "And he called the twelve together and gave them power and authority over all demons and to cure diseases, and he sent them out to preach the kingdom of God and to heal."

46. Recall the way Matthew presents the preaching of John the Baptist and of Jesus in 3:2 and 4:17 respectively: "Repent, for the kingdom of heaven is at hand."

47. Luke 9:6: "And they departed and went through the villages, preaching the gospel and healing everywhere."

48. Compare Luke 10:2 and Matt 9:37–38; Luke 10:3 and Matt 10:16; Luke 10:4 and Matt 10:9–10a; Luke 10:5–6 and Matt 10:12–13; Luke 10:7 and Matt 10:10b; Luke 10:8–9 and Matt 10:7–8; Luke 10:10–12 and Matt 10:14–15; Luke 10:16 and Matt 10:40. The text of Luke 10:13–15 appears in Matt 11:21–23 where it applies to the work of Jesus.

49. Cf. I.H. Marshall, *The Gospel of Luke* (New International Greek Text Commentary; Grand Rapids: Eerdmans, 1978) 412–27; Fitzmyer, *Luke* 841–58. Both Marshall and Fitzmyer allow for some Lucan redaction of "Q".

50. Only the mission "two by two" of Mark's commissioning of the twelve (6:7) appears in Luke's commissioning of the seventy (10:1). The judgment on the cities in Luke 10:13–15 appears in Matt 11:21–23; cf. n. 48 above.

51. Matthew achieves the same effect by placing this saying before the commissioning of the twelve (9:37–38) and by including in the discourse instructions of Jesus concerning the post-Easter mission (10:16–42).

52. The phrase *apesteilen . . . pro prosōpou autou* occurs in 9:52 and 10:1. Fitzmyer, (*Luke* 845), is uncertain whether these messengers are identical with the seventy or not.

53. The nations of the world in Gen 10:2–31 number seventy in the MT and seventy-two in the LXX. The number seventy-two figures in the OT only in Num 31:38. For a detailed discussion of the possibilities, cf. Marshall, *Luke* 414–15. The textual variants may reflect the confusion of copyists with respect to the symbolism. Fitzmyer, (*Luke* 845–46), considers seventy-two as the *lectio difficilior*, and understands seventy as a copyist's change to a round number: "The number seventy is surely an approximation or 'round number' for a more original seventy-two" (846).

54. Luke may also have had in mind the presbyters of Acts, especially in the light of Paul's discourse to the presbyters of Ephesus (Acts 20:18–35, esp. v 28). It is more likely, however, that he is thinking of itinerant apostles and prophets rather than of residential leaders; cf. *Did.* 11–13. C.H. Talbert (*Literary Patterns, Theological Themes, and the Genre of Luke-Acts* [Missoula: Scholars, 1974] 16, 20) parallels Luke 10:1–12 with the missionary journeys of Paul to the Gentiles in Acts 13—14, 16—20; on p. 78 he attempts to justify the unbalanced length of the parallel texts.

55. Cf. Luke 6:40; John 13:16; 15:18–27; Matt 10:22.

56. Cf. Luke 10:16; John 13:20 and the rabbinic concept of the *shālîaḥ*; K.H. Rengstorf, "*apostellō, apostolos,*" *TDNT* 1.413–420.

57. Cf. n. 15 in chap. 1 above. In the preferred Greek text of Mark 2:10, the formula *epi tēs gēs* follows *aphienai hamartias*; in Matt 9:6 and Luke 5:24 it precedes the infinitive. The position of the phrase does not seem to affect the meaning: God's forgiveness is available here on earth through Jesus as a human being; cf. Mann, *Mark* 227. The Prayer of Nabonidus from Qumran Cave 4 speaks of a Jewish exorcist pardoning the sins of Nabonidus on God's behalf; cf. Fitzmyer, *Luke* 585. The shift to the plural probably indicates that 2:10ab is the evangelist's address to his readers; cf. Fitzmyer, *Luke* 579, 585; C.P. Ceroke, "Is Mark 2:10 a Saying of Jesus?" *CBQ* 22 (1960) 369–90.

58. Mann (*Mark* 225–28) argues that in this parenthesis the early church and Mark are identifying Jesus as the eschatological Son of man. Fitzmyer (*Luke* 585) agrees that the phrase is titular in the present text of all three gospels, but suspects a pre-Marcan form in which "the son of man" is simply a periphrasis for a human being. He refers to Matt 9:8 and the Prayer of Nabonidus from Qumran Cave 4 (cf. previous note). Caragounis (*The Son of Man*, 187–90) reads the text on the lips of Jesus and understands Jesus as claiming already to exercise the power of the eschatological judge.

59. Cf. J.D. Kingsbury, *Matthew: Structure, Christology, Kingdom* (Philadelphia: Fortress, 1986); J.P. Meier, *The Vision of Matthew: Christ, Church and Morality in the First Gospel* (New York: Paulist, 1979).

60. The narrative about the temple tax (Matt 17:24–27) is a Matthaean insertion into the Marcan sequence.

61. On Matt 18:15–20, cf. W.G. Thompson, *Matthew's Advice to a Divided Community: Mt. 17:22—18:35* (AnBib 44: Rome: Biblical Institute, 1970) 175–202; R.H. Gundry, *Matthew. A Commentary on*

His Literary and Theological Art (Grand Rapids: Eerdmans, 1982) 367–70.

62. *Halakâ* is the legal interpretation of torah (law), as distinct from *haggadâ*, its homiletic elaboration. On this interpretation of "binding and loosing," cf. Thompson, *Matthew's Advice* 189–93; the interpretation of the formula by Billerbeck (Str-B 1.738–39) which includes imposing and releasing from the ban (*shammetâ* = decree of expulsion) is based on only one rabbinic text (*b.Mo'ed Qat.* 16a) and an interpretation of Matt 18:17 which would include a formal judicial process and excommunication. The formula "loose and forgive" is well attested in the Targums and connects Matt 18:18 with John 20:23. The combined formula of binding and loosing is found in *Tg. Ps.-J.* Num 30:6, 9, 13 for binding oneself by vow and for releasing others from vows. Thompson concludes, "The parallel in Pseudo-Jonathan shows that the transferred meaning of 'bind and loose' in the Matthaean saying is not unique but the more precise connotation must be determined from the immediate context" (193).

63. It is interesting to notice how the rules for Vatican II called for a two-thirds majority, but in fact most documents were passed almost unanimously; cf. *Lumen Gentium* 12 on the infallibility and indefectibility of the whole church in A.P. Flannery (ed.), *Documents of Vatican II* (Grand Rapids, Eerdmans, 1975) 363–64.

64. The following texts concerning Peter are peculiar to Matthew: 10:2; 14:28–31; 15:15; 16:17–19; 17:24–27; 18:21. These texts all imply respect for the role of Peter well after his death.

65. Cf. R.E. Brown and J.P. Meier, *Antioch and Rome. New Testament Cradles of Catholic Christianity* (Ramsey, N.J.: Paulist, 1983) esp. 11–86; R.E. Brown, *The Churches the Apostles Left Behind* (Ramsey, N.J.: Paulist, 1984) 124–45.

66. In Matt 16:19b the saying is in the singular and connected with v 19a by the conjunction *kai*; in 18:18 the plural is used and the saying is introduced by the solemn *Amēn, legō hymin*, which suggests an independent saying added to vv 15–17. Thompson (*Matthew's Advice* 193–94) agrees that the thought sequence in 16:19 is more coherent but admits that the development could go in either direction. He does add, however, that "it is important to recall that in Matthaean doublets the same saying may have two different meanings (e.g., 10, 40 = 18, 6[sic]; 5, 29–30 = 18, 8–9)" (194).

67. Cf. Mark 8:29: "You are the Christ"; Luke 9:20: "The Christ of God." In Matthew the disciples have already acknowledged Jesus as the Son of God in 14:33.

68. Nicodemus concluded that Jesus was a teacher from God simply on the basis of his signs (John 3:2).

69. Cf. O. Cullmann, *Peter: Disciple. Apostle. Martyr* (New York: Meridian, 1958) 158–212, esp. 180–84 for the last supper setting; R.E. Brown, K.P. Donfried, J. Reumann (eds.), *Peter in the New Testament* (Minneapolis/New York: Augsburg/Paulist, 1973) 83–101, 105–07; esp. 85–86 for a post-resurrectional setting; this ecumenical consultation does not deal directly with the question of authenticity; they acknowledge a pre-Matthaean semitic tradition, reworked by the evangelist for insertion here. Denying authenticity, Marshall (*Matthew* 330–36) argues for Matthaean composition in Greek; F.W. Beare, (*The Gospel according to Matthew* [San Francisco: Harper & Row, 1981] 353–56), on the contrary, considers that the evangelist drew upon an Aramaic source which originated in debate within the Palestinian community.

70. The ordinary Pauline expression is "church(es) of God," usually with reference to the Jerusalem church or to local communities; 1 Thess 1:1; 2:14; Gal 1:13; 1 Cor 1:2; 10:32; 11:16, 22; 15:9; 2 Cor 1:1; cf. Acts 20:28. The universal sense may be detected in Gal 1:13; 1 Cor 15:9. "All the churches of Christ" appears only at Rom 16:16.

71. Cf. Matt 13:37–43; 16:28; 20:21. The same concept appears in Luke 1:33; 22:29–30; 23:42 and in the parable of the pounds (Luke 19:12–27); 1 Cor 15:25–28; Col 1:13. In these texts a distinction is drawn between the kingdom of God and the kingdom of the Son of man or of Christ. On the other hand, the kingdom of God and the kingdom of Christ are one in Eph 5:5; Rev 11:15.

72. Note that in addressing Peter in John 21:15–17 the risen Lord speaks of "my lambs" and "my sheep." Peter is only the caretaker of what properly belongs to Christ.

73. The RSV expression "the powers of death" conveys the sense of the Greek *pylai hǫdou*; the gate was the strong point of a city and Hades refers to the dwelling of the dead in general. It was a common Jewish idea that death would not have a permanent hold over God's elect; for the expression, cf. Is 38:10; Job 38:17; Pss 9:13; 107:18; Wis 16:13.

74. In the book of Revelation, the risen Christ speaks of himself as the one "who has the key of David, who opens and no one shall shut, who shuts and no one opens" (3:7). The fact that similar imagery—e.g., rock, shepherd, keys—is used both of Christ and of Peter, the apostles and the presbyters is another indication of the way the ministry of Jesus continues in them.

75. Luke 22:31–34 gives to Peter personally a post-Easter responsibility with respect to the other apostles, subsequent to the disappointing response of the twelve during the passion. The actual commissioning of Peter in John 21:15–17 is again personal.

76. Cf. Str-B 1.739–41; in the same sense, one text from *Sipre Deut* 32,25 § 321 (138[a]) also refers to Is 22:22 with reference to such authoritative decisions; also Thompson, *Matthew's Advice* 190.

77. Rengstorf maintains that *apostellō* emphasizes commissioning and responsibility more than *pempō*, but admits that in John the two verbs are used almost interchangeably; cf. *TDNT* 1.397–406.

78. Schnackenburg (*Johannesevangelium* 2.109) implies as much when he says that these departing Galilaean disciples are no longer mentioned in the gospel.

79. Thomas is also called "one of the twelve" at 20:24.

80. Jesus is the subject of the verb *eklegomai* only in John 6:70; 13:18 and 15:16–19; a participial form of the verb is also used in Luke 6:13 for Jesus' choice of the twelve.

81. Brown (*John* 345–55) would understand "Jews" in this text as the inhabitants of Judaea; Jesus is calling them to a deeper faith and they do not respond. Schnackenburg (*Johannesevangelium* 2.259–60) on the contrary, sees here a reference to Jewish Christians of the author's day whose faith is inadequate and under attack from fellow Jews. The development of the dialogue in the rest of John 8 favors Brown's opinion.

82. In no biblical text is the word *mathētēs* used unequivocally of a woman. The word *mathētria* is used of Tabitha in Acts 9:36; it is used of Mary Magdalene in the Gospel of Peter (12:50) and of female disciples in gnostic literature; cf. Moulton-Milligan 385. The word does not appear in *LPGL*.

83. Neither Jesus nor the evangelist is speaking at John 7:3. In John 8:31 Jesus invites the Jews to go beyond an inadequate faith to become true disciples. It has been argued that "the disciple whom Jesus loved" is always an addition to the text; "the other disciple" may be "the disciple whom Jesus loved," and also an addition to the text; cf. M.-E. Boismard and A. Lamouille, *Synopse des Quatre Evangiles en Français. L'Evangile de Jean* (Paris: Cerf, 1977) 3.341, 409, 453–56. As a secret disciple Joseph of Arimathea would not have been present either at the last supper or for the resurrection appearances.

84. Cf. C.H. Dodd, *Historical Tradition in the Fourth Gospel* (Cambridge: University, 1963) 343–47.

85. Barrett (*Gospel*, 243) lists a variety of opinions; he himself

opts for a generalizing interpretation: All missionary activity pre-supposes the unique eschatological activity of Jesus. Schnacken-burg (*Johannesevangelium* 1.485–88) agrees with O. Cullmann that the reference is to the Samaritan mission of the Hellenists in Acts 8 and its subsequent approval by the apostles of the Jerusalem church; also Brown (*Gospel* 183–84). Bultmann (*Das Evangelium des Johannes* [Göttingen: Vandenhoeck und Ruprecht, 1941] 147–48) understands *alloi* of Jesus and all others who at any time pre-cede Christian missionaries. Others have suggested the OT proph-ets, John the Baptist and Jesus, or Jesus and the Father.

86. Cf. 1 Cor 3:10–15 and Bultmann's understanding of John 4:37–38 in n. 85 above.

87. *Akoloutheō* is used fifteen times of discipleship in John, ei-ther directly or indirectly.

88. The verbs in John 17:18 are in the aorist tense as if the dis-ciples of Jesus have already been sent. The actual sending does not take place until after the glorification of Jesus (20:21) where the verb *pempō* is in the present tense. In the last supper discourses of the fourth gospel Jesus speaks as if he were already glorified. Cf. Brown, *Gospel* 581–82; Schnackenburg, *Johannesevangelium* 3.53–54; and especially Barrett, *Gospel* 449–50: "The true setting of these chap-ters is the Christian life of the end of the first century, but from time to time John, whose intention it is to bind the life of the church in his own age to the history upon which it was founded, consciously brings back his narrative to what is ostensibly its original setting, the night in which he was betrayed."

89. Cf. Brown *Gospel* 411, 765–67; Schnackenburg, *Johannes-evangelium* 3.210–14; Barrett, *Gospel* 510–11.

90. The notions of sacrifice and priesthood may be seen here, but in an entirely new and transferred sense, as in the letter to the Hebrews.

91. Cf. R.E. Brown, *Biblical Exegesis and Church Doctrine* (Mah-wah, N.J.: Paulist, 1985) 136: "The early Christian proclaimers of the Good News did more than preach, and we had better do more in this world than preach if we wish to be proclaimers of the word of God . . . the God of Israel is a God who acts and not simply a God who speaks . . . those who proclaim the God of Israel and the Father of Jesus Christ had better be as concerned about action as about preaching."

92. Judas Iscariot and Thomas were absent; cf. John 20:24.

93. Cf. John 1:33; 3:34; 7:39; 14:16–17, 26; 15:26; 16:7–15.

94. Although often attempted, there are no exegetical grounds for

harmonizing the gift of the Spirit in John 20 with Pentecost in Acts 2; cf. Brown, *Gospel* 1038–39: ". . . functionally each is describing the same event; the one gift of the Spirit to his followers by the risen and ascended Lord." Schnackenburg (*Johannesevangelium* 3.386–87) argues that the Lucan narrative does not represent the norm but a special manifestation of the Spirit; Barrett, (*Gospel* 570), also rejects any attempt at harmonization.

95. Cf. also Luke 24:47–49.

96. John 1:29 speaks of the Lamb of God who takes away (*airō*) the sin of the world, but *aphienai* and *aphesis* do not appear with reference to sins in this gospel except in 20:23. This vocabulary is found in the synoptic gospels ten times in Matthew, nine times in Mark and eleven times in Luke; five times in Acts.

97. *Krateō*, "to retain," is used with reference to sins only here in the NT.

98. Brown (*Gospel* 1039–45) studies John 20:23 in relation to Matt 16:19 and 18:18. Though the sayings are formally related, the context demands a different meaning in each case. "In many ways the Johannine formula is more kerygmatic and perhaps preserves more of the original import of the saying than does the juridic formula used in Matthew" (1041). Brown denies that the text can be related exegetically either to the preaching of the gospel or to admission to baptism. The discriminatory and reconciling work of the Spirit can and has been exercised in a variety of ways throughout the history of the church. Cf. 1 John and Forestell, *Word of the Cross* 184–89. Schnackenburg (*Johannesevangelium* 3.387–89) refuses as an exegete to settle later ecclesiastical and sacramental questions on the basis of this text, but does affirm that the community was concerned from the beginning with freedom from sin and its own purity, and had to exercise some form of discernment concerning those who belonged and those who did not belong; Barrett, *Gospel* 571: "The authority conveyed implies an extension of the ministry of Jesus through that of the Holy Spirit." Cf. John 16:8–11.

99. Although the observation need not be theologically or juridically significant, it is nonetheless morally certain that the disciples initially commissioned by Jesus during his public ministry and in the post-resurrection period were males.

Chapter III

1. Cf. Gal 1:18; 2:6–14; 1 Cor 1:12; 3:22; 9:5; 15:5.
2. The evangelist is generally considered to be other than "the

disciple whom Jesus loved," although the latter is most probably the eyewitness at the source of the tradition contained in the gospel. "The disciple whom Jesus loved" is more likely an otherwise unknown Jerusalem disciple. "The presbyter" who wrote 2 and 3 John is generally considered to be the author of 1 John also. Cf. R.E. Brown, *The Epistles of John* (AB 30; Garden City, N.Y.: Doubleday, 1982) 14–35, esp. 19, 30; *The Community of the Beloved Disciple* (New York: Paulist, 1979) 33–34.

3. If he was among the brothers of Jesus mentioned in John 7:5, he must have become a believer after the resurrection. He appears in Gal 1:19; 2:9, 11–14 and in Acts 12:17; 15:13–21; 21:17–26.

4. According to Eusebius (*Hist. eccl.* 2.1), Clement of Alexandria in the *Hypotyposes* identified Barnabas as one of the seventy; Eusebius (*Hist. eccl.* 1.13; 2.1) also mentions a Thaddeus as one of the seventy who evangelized Odessa. If the seventy are a literary and theological construct of Luke, it is not surprising that they have left no trace.

5. Cf. 1 Cor 15:7, 9; 9:5; 12:28, 29; Gal 1:17, 19; Rom 16:7; Eph 2:20; 3:5; 4:11; they may be among the associates of the eleven mentioned in Luke 24; cf. J. Plevnik, "The Eleven and their Associates," *CBQ* 40 (1978) 205–11; "The Eyewitnesses of the Risen Jesus in Luke 24," *CBQ* 49 (1987) 90–103.

6. Without prejudice to the contemporary discussion of the ordination of women, it is nonetheless explicity stated that a man was sought to replace Judas: *tōn synelthontōn hēmin andrōn* (Acts 1:21).

7. The proto-Pauline or certainly authentic letters are 1 Thessalonians, Galatians, 1 and 2 Corinthians, Philippians, Romans and Philemon. Although unanimous agreement is lacking among critical scholars, a wide spectrum of opinion considers Colossians, Ephesians, 2 Thessalonians and the pastorals (1 and 2 Timothy and Titus) to be deutero-Pauline; cf. J.A. Fitzmyer, *Paul and His Theology, A Brief Sketch* (Englewood Cliffs, N.J.: Prentice-Hall, 1989) 27.

8. Others are *doulos* (Rom 1:1; 2 Cor 4:5; Gal 1:10; Phil 1:1), *oikonomos* (1 Cor 4:1–2) and *leitourgos* (Rom 15:16). He also uses verbs associated with cult to describe his activity: e.g., *hierourgeō* (Rom 15:16), *latreuō* (Rom 1:9) and *spendomai* (Phil 2:17).

9. On Cor 2:14—4:6, cf. L. de Lorenzi (ed.), *Paolo. Ministro del Nuovo Testamento (2 Co 2,14–4,6)* (Serie Monographica di «Benedictina»; Sezione Biblico Ecumenica 9; Roma: Benedictina Editrice, 1987).

10. Cf. V.P. Furnish, *II Corinthians* (AB 32A; Garden City, N.Y.: Doubleday, 1984) 182; he translates *diakonētheisa hyph'hēmōn* as

"cared for by us" and considers Paul either as the amanuensis of a letter dictated by Christ or its courier; J. Murphy-O'Connor, "Ministry Beyond the Letter (2 Cor 3:1–6)," in de Lorenzi (ed.), *Paolo* 105–28, esp. 108–11, 122–25.

11. Murphy-O'Connor ("Ministry Beyond the Letter," 116–17, 125–29) argues that in 2 Cor 3:6 Paul is not contrasting the Mosaic covenant with the new covenant, but a Judaizing understanding of the new covenant with a spiritual understanding.

12. Cf. A. Vanhoye, "L'interprétation d'Ex 34 en 2 Co 3, 7–14," in de Lorenzi (ed.), *Paolo* 159–80.

13. The metaphor of "treasure" in 4:7 is applied to the *diakonia* of 4:1. Other interpretations mentioned by Furnish, *II Corinthians* 279, are the gospel itself or "the illuminating power of the knowledge of Divine glory."

14. Cf. below, 63–65.

15. Cf. 1 Cor 3:9: "For we are God's fellow workers (*synergoi*)"; Timothy is also God's fellow worker (*synergon*; RSV: servant; 1 Thess 3:2).

16. Note the concept of Christ as a *diakonos* of the circumcision in Rom 15:8.

17. Cf. 2 Cor 8:4, 9:1, 12, 13; Rom 15:25, 31. In the deutero-Paulines Paul is still presented as a *diakonos* of the gospel (Col 1:23; Eph 3:7) and of the church (Col 1:25), and his calling is presented as an appointment by Christ Jesus our Lord for *diakonia* (1 Tim 1:12). Paul uses the same vocabulary of his fellow workers and even of his rivals; cf. 1 Thess 3:2 (*l.v.*); 1 Cor 3:5; 2 Cor 11:23; Phlm 13; Col 1:7; Eph 6:21; 1 Tim 4:6. The technical sense of "deacon" as an office-bearer is found for certain only in 1 Tim 3:8–13 and probably in Phil 1:1; Rom 16:1; Col 4:17. Paul also uses the vocabulary of slavery (*doulos, douleuō*) of his apostolic ministry; he is both a slave of Christ (Gal 1:10; Phil 1:1; Rom 1:1) and of Christians themselves for Jesus' sake (2 Cor 4:5); in the deutero-Paulines, cf. Titus 1:1; 2 Tim 2:24; Col 4:12. Unlike the vocabulary of service, the language of slavery is also used in the Pauline letters of the Christian life in general; it is a slavery to God, to Christ and to one another; cf. 1 Thess 1:9; Gal 5:13; 1 Cor 7:22; Rom 6:16; 7:6, 25; 12:11; 14:18; 16:18; Col 3:24; Eph 6:6, 7; this slavery is not the same as slavery to other human beings (1 Cor 7:23); the same language is used of Paul's fellow workers; cf. Phil 1:1; 2:22; Col 4:12; 2 Tim 2:24.

18. He uses the word *diakonos* of himself only three times (1 Cor 3:5; 2 Cor 3:6; 6:4) in the authentic letters, as compared to twelve

times for *apostolos* (1 Thess 2:6; Gal 1:1; 1 Cor 1:1; 4:9; 9:1, 2; 15:9[2]; 2 Cor 1:1; 12:12; Rom 1:1; 11:13). In the deutero-Paulines the ratio is 2:7.

19. It also appears at the head of Colossians, Ephesians, 1 and 2 Timothy, and Titus.

20. W.F. Orr and James Arthur Walther (1 *Corinthians* [AB 32; Garden City, N.Y.: Doubleday, 1976] 322) suggest that the term "apostles" includes more than the twelve, such as missionaries and the seven of Acts 6:1–6. James, the brother of the Lord, seems to be included among "the apostles" by Paul in Gal 1:19. Andronicus and Junia(s) (Rom 16:7) are more likely Jerusalem apostles than emissaries of a local church. There seems to be no way of determining whether Junia(s) is male or female; commentators, both ancient and modern, are divided. *Jounias* could be the abbreviated form of a male's name, *Jounianus* (cf. Silas = Silvanus), but it is not attested elsewhere; *Jounia* as a female's name is attested. Only the accent decides the difference, and the earliest mss. did not use accents.

21. The fathers, Käsemann and Barrett understand "the superlative apostles" as the leaders of the Jerusalem church, namely, Peter, James and John, and so distinguish them from Paul's opponents at Corinth. Most modern commentators, however, identify "the superlative apostles" of 2 Cor 11:5 and 12:11 with the false apostles of 2 Cor 11:13 and the self-styled ministers of Christ of 2 Cor 11:23. Cf. Furnish, *II Corinthians* 502–505 for the arguments on both sides.

22. Cf. K.H. Rengstorf, "*apostellō, apostolos* etc.," *TDNT* 1.398–477, esp. 420–43. Rengstorf's attempt to give a univocal sense to the term "apostle" is not convincing. Missionary apostles appear in parallel with itinerant prophets in *Did.* 11.3–6; cf. J.-P. Audet, *La Didachè. Instruction des Apôtres* (EBib; Paris: Gabalda, 1958) 119, 251, 435–47.

23. Timothy was already a believer when Paul recruited him at Lystra (Acts 16:1). Silvanus is probably to be identified with Silas of Acts 15:22 who with Judas Barsabbas is called a leader (*andras hēgoumenous*), but is apparently not one of the presbyters; the same two individuals are called prophets in Acts 15:32. B. Rigaux, *Saint Paul, Les Epîtres aux Thessaloniciens* (EBib; Paris: Gabalda, 1956) 418, on the contrary, includes among the apostles Silvanus and Timothy from 1 Thess 2:6 and Apollos from 1 Cor 4:9.

24. Though a native of Cyprus, Barnabas was a member of the early church in Jerusalem (Acts 4:36–37). He was sent to Antioch to investigate the spread of the church to the Greeks (Acts 11:20–25), in much the same way as Peter and John were sent to Samaria (Acts

8:14). Barnabas may easily have been one of the Jerusalem apostles in the wider sense.

25. Cf. P. Benoit, "L'Ascension," *RB* 56 (1949) 161–203; Eng. tr. in P. Benoit, *Jesus and the Gospels* (London: Darton, Longman & Todd, 1973) 1.209–53.

26. Cf. D.M. Stanley, "Paul's Conversion in Acts: Why the Three Accounts?" *CBQ* 15 (1953) 315–38.

27. Paul does not refer explicitly in his letters to the mission which he and Barnabas received from the church in Antioch; this mission accounts for the use of the term *apostolos* of Paul and Barnabas in Acts 14:4, 14, contrary to Luke's practice of reserving the term for the twelve. It may also explain the claim Paul makes for himself and Barnabas in 1 Cor 9:6, but cf. n. 24 above.

28. Cf. 1 Cor 15:3–5; Rom 1:3–4; 1 Cor 11:23–26; 1 Thess 4:15–17; 1 Cor 7:10–11; 9:14.

29. Cf. Gal 1:16; 2:2, 7–9; Rom 1:5; 11:13; 1 Thess 2:16; it is also emphasized in the conversion accounts of Acts (9:15; 22:15; 26:16–18).

30. Cf. 1 Thess 1:5; Gal 1:11; 2:2; 2 Cor 4:3; Rom 2:16; 16:25; in the deutero-Paulines, 2 Thess 2:14; 2 Tim 2:8.

31. Eph 1:1; 3:1–21; Col 1:1; 1:24–29; 1 Tim 1:1, 12–17; 2 Tim 1:1; 4:6–8; Titus 1:1–13.

32. Cf. J.T. Forestell, "Christian Perfection and Gnosis in Philippians 3:7–16," *CBQ* 18 (1956) 123–36.

33. Cf. 1 Cor 9:16; 2 Cor 5:14 The genitive in the phrase "the love of Christ" should be understood as a subjective genitive; cf. Furnish, *II Corinthians* 309.

34. The Greek here is *charis*; the RSV has translated "commission."

35. Cf. J.T. Forestell, "St. Paul, Teacher of the Christian Life," *Clergy Review* 45 (1960) 456–65, esp. 457.

36. Cf. B. Ahern, "The Christian's Union with the Body of Christ in Cor, Gal, and Rom," *CBQ* 23 (1961) 199–209; Fitzmyer, *Paul and His Theology* 88–93 with bibliography.

37. The first person plural in these verses could refer to Paul alone, to Paul and his associates, or to all Christians. The context from 5:11 suggests that the first or second alternative is to be preferred. Although Furnish adopted the second alternative in the earlier part of this passage, he opts for the more inclusive sense in vv 16 and 18 because of the universal character of vv 14, 15, 17, and the universal character of God's reconciliation in Christ in v 18a. This argument is not entirely convincing, because v 18b is certainly

parallel to v 20 where Furnish necessarily reverts to the narrower sense of the Pauline apostolate because of the figure of speech being used ("ambassador") and the second person plural imperative in v 20b; cf. *II Corinthians* 312, 317, 339.

38. The RSV does not translate the *hōs* which precedes the final phrase of the Greek text. Furnish (*II Corinthians* 339) hesitantly paraphrases "the conviction that God is appealing through us"; cf. Blass-Debrunner-Funk § 425 (3).

39. Eph 6:20 speaks of Paul as an ambassador in chains for the mystery of the gospel. The idea is the same as 2 Cor 5:20.

40. Cf. Furnish, *II Corinthians* 338–39.

41. *Who is the Heir* 42 (205–206): "To His Word, His chief messenger, highest in age and honour, the Father of all has given the special prerogative, to stand on the border and separate the creature from the Creator. This same Word both pleads with the immortal as suppliant for afflicted mortality and acts as ambassador (*presbeutēs*) of the ruler to the subject. He glorifies in this prerogative and proudly describes it in these words 'and I stood between the Lord and you' (Deut. V. 5), that is neither uncreated as God, nor created as you, but midway between the two extremes, a surety to both sides; to the parent, pledging the creature that it should never altogether rebel against the rein and choose disorder rather than order; to the child, warranting his hopes that the merciful God will never forget His own work. For I am the harbinger of peace to creation from that God whose will is to bring wars to an end, who is ever the guardian of peace" (LCL 4.385–87); cf. also Bornkamm, *TDNT* 6.681–83, and above, 57.

42. 3.22.23: "Then if he is thus prepared, the true Cynic cannot be satisfied with this; but he must know that he is sent a messenger from Zeus to men about good and bad things, to show them that they have wandered and are seeking the substance of good and evil where it is not, but where it is, they never think . . ." (*Great Books of the Western World* [Chicago: Encyclopedia Britannica, Inc., 1952] 12.196).

43. *TDNT* 6.682–83; Bornkamm adds that the apostle's ministry is nonetheless not to be considered as a continuation of the work of Christ. It will be argued below that Paul's ministry is a continuing representation of the total ministry of Christ in a "sacramental" mode; cf. below, 65–66.

44. Cf. H.D. Betz, *Galatians. A Commentary on Paul's Letter to the Churches in Galatia* (Hermeneia; Philadelphia: Fortress Press, 1979) 131: "One of the goals of the ancient orator was to deliver his

speech so vividly and impressively that his listeners imagined the matter to have happened right before their eyes."

45. Cf. 1 Cor 2:1–2; although some commentators argue that Paul changed his manner of preaching after the failure of a philosophical sermon in Athens, J. Munck (*The Acts of the Apostles* [AB 31; Garden City, N.Y.: Doubleday, 1967] 172–74) finds no foundation in the text for failure in Athens, and Orr-Walther (*I Corinthians* 162) affirm that Paul's preaching was always Christ-centered. The Athens speech of Acts 17:22–31 may also be based on a model of the early Christian kerygma attributed to Paul by the author of Acts, although Munck (173) states that "Paul might well have delivered such a missionary sermon."

46. The variant reading, *dia rhēmatos theou*, though attested by a wide variety of witnesses, is not accepted by the editors of the 26th edition of Nestle. *Rhēma Christou*, occurring only here in the NT, is the *lectio difficilior*, *rhēma theou* being the more familiar expression; cf. Bruce M. Metzger, *A Textual Commentary on the Greek New Testament* (London/New York: United Bible Societies, 1971) 525. The exact meaning of the phrase is disputed; it should be connected with the use of *rhēma* in v 8 and with the use of *hou* in v 14; it is Christ himself who is heard in the preaching of his messengers; cf. C.E.B. Cranfield, *The Epistle to the Romans* (ICC; Edinburgh: T. & T. Clark Limited, 1979) 2.534, 537. H. Schlier (*Der Römerbrief*, Zweite Auflage [HTKNT 6; Freiburg: Herder, 1979] 318) allows an even stronger meaning; the preaching of the messenger is tantamount to the revelation of Jesus Christ himself: "das Tat-Wort Christi das sich dem Apostel nach Gal 1,2.16 durch die apokalypsis Jesou Christou eröffnet hat." For E. Käsemann (*Commentary on Romans* [Grand Rapids, Eerdmans, 1980] 295) the apostolic preaching is a means of Christ's revelation, the mission being traced back to the exalted Lord himself. The paraphrase offered by Max Zerwich and Mary Grosvenor (*A Grammatical Analysis of the New Testament* [Rome: Biblical Institute, 1974] 482), "word about Christ," is too weak for the present context.

47. Furnish (*II Corinthians* 570) interprets the *en* in 2 Cor 13:3 as instrumental, referring to 2 Cor 2:17 and 5:20a: Paul is the instrument of Christ in his ministry. Cf. Thomas Hopko, "On the Male Character of the Christian Priesthood," in Thomas Hopko (ed.), *Women and the Priesthood* (Crestwood, N.Y.: St. Vladimir's Seminary Press, 1983) 97–134, esp. 118–119; also "La place de la femme dans l'Eglise orthodoxe. Conclusions du Congrès théologique interorthodoxe de Rhodes," *Documentation Catholique* 86 (1989) 344–48.

48. The RSV may be misleading here. The anointing may be the gift of the Spirit proper to all Christians (cf. 1 John 2:20, 27), not just the grace of apostleship. In favor of the general sense, cf. Furnish, *II Corinthians* 136–37.

49. Commentators are divided as to whether the reference is to God or to Christ. Furnish, (II Corinthians 176), prefers God, but specifies that in the light of 4:6 Christ is the one through whom the knowledge of God is disclosed.

50. The cognates *hikanos* and *hikanoō* refer to worthiness or adequacy; when that worthiness or adequacy comes from another, we can talk of enabling or empowering; cf. Furnish, *II Corinthians* 184; K.H. Rengstorf, "hikanos etc.," *TDNT* 3.293–96.

51. All commentators agree that the referent here is Christ; cf. Phil 3:10; 1 Tim 1:12.

52. Cf. 1 Cor 3:9; 15:10; 2 Cor 1:17–20; 6:1, 4.

53. But cf. note 45 above.

54. Colossians, if Pauline, would be another exception. Cranfield (*Romans* 764–65) argues against such a rigid interpretation of Paul's words; Paul is simply reflecting on his commission to be a founder of churches and not preparing his visit to Rome; cf. Rom 15:24.

55. Cf. H.-J. Klauck, "Erleuchtung und Verkündigung. Auslegungsskizze zu 2 Kor 4, 1–6," in de Lorenzi (ed.), *Paolo* 267–97; C.E.B. Cranfield, "Ministry and Congregation in the Light of II Corinthians 4:5–7. An Exposition," *Int* 19 (1965) 163–67.

56. Cf. M. Carrez, "*Hikanotēs*: 2 Co 2, 14–17," in de Lorenzi (ed.), *Paolo* 79–95.

57. In Gal 4:12 Paul appeals to the Galatians as a true friend to remain free of the law as he was. Cf. Betz, *Galatians* 221–23; A. Viard, *Saint Paul, Epître aux Galates* (Sources Bibliques; Paris: Gabalda, 1964) 93.

58. Cf. e.g. Ex 7:5; Jgs 7:2; Deut 8:17–18; 9:4; 32:27; Amos 6:13–14; Hos 10:13; Is 10:12–19; Jer 16:21; Ez 25:5–7, 15–17; 28:22–26; 36:33–36; 37:28.

59. Cf. 1 Thess 1:6; 2:14–16; 1 Cor 4:16; 11:1; W. Michaelis, "mimeomai etc.," *TDNT* 5.659–74, esp. 666–73; D.M. Stanley, " 'Become Imitators of Me': The Pauline Conception of Apostolic Tradition," *Bib* 40 (1959) 859–77.

60. Cf. 2 Cor 11:17, 30; 12:1, 5–6.

61. Cf. J.T. Forestell, "Christian Perfection and Gnosis in Philippians 3, 7–16," *CBQ* 18 (1956) 123–36.

62. Cf. 1 Cor 4:9–13; 2 Cor 4:8–12; 6:4–10; Phil 1:13; Phlm 1.

63. 1 Thess 3:2; Gal 1:7; 1 Cor 9:12; 2 Cor 2:12; 9:13; 10:14; Phil

1:27; Rom 15:19; cf. "the gospel of our Lord Jesus" in 2 Thess 1:8 and "the gospel of Jesus Christ" in Mark 1:1.

64. The image used here is that of the father of the bride-to-be who was, according to the customs of the time, "responsible for safeguarding his daughter's virginity between the time of her betrothal and the time when he actually leads her into the bridegroom's house" (Furnish, *II Corinthians* 499).

65. On this interpretation of a critically uncertain text, cf. Murphy-O'Connor, "A Ministry Beyond the Letter," in de Lorenzi (ed.), *Paolo* 122–25; with Bultmann, he considers the better attested reading, *hēmōn*, to be nonsensical and an assimilation to *hēmōn* in the earlier part of the verse; the letter is written on the hearts of the Corinthians and is legible by others in the quality of their Christian lives.

66. The individual Christian is also a temple of the Holy Spirit (1 Cor 6:19).

67. Cf. H. Strathmann-R. Meyer, "*leitourgeō* etc.," *TDNT* 4.215–31, esp. 227–28.

68. The parallel text of Rom 15:27 demonstrates that *leitourgia* in 2 Cor 9:12 has its secular sense of public service; cf. *TDNT* 4.227. Nonetheless such effective provision for the material needs of others can be referred to metaphorically as cultic sacrifices of thanksgiving to God for the spiritual gifts received from Jerusalem.

69. Cf. 2 Cor 3:3. Thomas Aquinas (*Summa Theologica. Supplementum* 40.2) considers this aspect of a priest's ministry to be secondary to his principal function of consecrating the body of Christ. On the historical significance of this doctrinal position of Aquinas, cf. below pp. 125–126 and K.B. Osborne, O.F.M., *Priesthood. A History of the Ordained Ministry in the Roman Catholic Church* (Mahwah, N.J.: Paulist, 1988) 204–08.

70. *TDNT* 4.230: "R.15:16 also moves in the realm of priestly and cultic ideas. Paul describes himself as *leitourgon Christou Iēsou eis ta ethnē*. This does not have to include the idea of a sacral function. But if not, he might just as well have used *diakonos*. What follows shows that he is using *leitourgos* cultically almost in the sense of priest. For he construes it in terms of *hierourgein to euaggelion*. He discharges a priestly ministry in relation to the gospel. The final clause which follows shows how. He wins the Gentiles to the Christian faith and leads them to God. They are thus an acceptable sacrifice. The context thus shows that *leitourgos* had for Paul a sacral ring. This alone explains the phrases that follow." Cf. also E. Käsemann, *Commentary on Romans* (Grand Rapids: Eerdmans,

1980) 392–93: ". . . here he is calling himself the priest of the Messiah Jesus to the whole of the Gentile world" (392). H. Schlier (*Der Römerbrief* [HTKNT 6; Freiburg: Herder, 1977] 430–31) comments in the same vein. On *heirourgein*, cf. C. Wiener, "*Hierourgein* (Römer 15, 16)," in *Studiorum Paulinorum Congressus* 2.399–404. Cranfield (*Romans* 2.754–57) argues against the cultic interpretation of Rom 15:16. A cultic reference in 2 Cor 2:15 is not widely recognized by commentators; cf. Furnish, *II Corinthians* 176–77.

71. Cf. Furnish, *II Corinthians* 461–64; the imagery used by Paul is military.

72. The genitive in the phrase "the love of Christ" is a subjective genitive; cf. n. 33 above.

73. Cf. 1 Thess 1:2–10; 1 Cor 1:4–9; Rom 1:8–15; Phil 1:3–11; Phlm 4–7.

74. In addition to the introductory formulas mentioned in n. 73, cf. also 1 Thess 3:10; Rom 10:1; and in the deutero-Paulines, Col 1:3–12; Eph 1:15–23; 3:14–19; 2 Thess 1:11–12; 2 Tim 1:3.

75. 1 Thess 5:25; 2 Cor 1:11; Phil 1:19; Rom 15:30; Phlm 22; in the deutero-Paulines, cf. Col 4:3; Eph 6:18–20; 2 Thess 3:1.

76. Cf. 1 Thess 2:9; 1 Cor 9:12–18.

77. Cf. Gal 1:16; 2:2, 8–9; Rom 1:5–6, 13; 11:13; 15:15–20; 1 Thess 2:16.

78. 1 Thess 2:12; 4:1, 10; 5:14; 1 Cor 1:10; 4:13, 16; 16:12, 15–16; 2 Cor 1:4; 2:8; 5:20; 6:1; 8:6; 9:5; 10:1; 12:18; 13:11; Phil 4:2; Rom 12:1; 15:30; 16:17; Phlm 9, 10. The cognate noun *paraklēsis* also appears in all the genuine letters except Galatians, but not always with reference to Paul's own ministry: 1 Thess 2:3; 1 Cor 14:3; 2 Cor 1:3–7; 7:4, 7, 13; 8:4, 17; Phil 2:1; Rom 12:8; 15:4–5; Phlm 7. The personal noun *paraklētos* does not appear in the Pauline letters.

79. On *paraklēsis*, cf. O. Schmitz-G. Stählin, "*parakaleō, paraklēsis*," *TDNT* 5.773–99, esp. 794–99.

80. 1 Thess 2:2; 2 Cor 3:12; 7:4; Phil 1:20; Phlm 8; cf. H. Schlier, "*parrhēsia, parrhēsiazomai*," *TDNT* 5.871–86, esp. 879–84.

81. Cf. Acts 16:19–40.

82. Cf. 1 Cor 16:9; 2 Cor 10—12. For a summary of the extensive discussion of the identity of Paul's opposition at Corinth, cf. Furnish, *II Corinthians* 48–54.

83. 1 Thess 1:6; 2:14–16; 1 Cor 4:16; 11:1; Phil 3:17; 4:9; cf. Stanley, *Bib* 40 (1959) 859–77 (n. 59 above).

84. Cf. Furnish, *II Corinthians* 421–22.

85. RSV renders *exousia* as "right" or "rightful claim" in 1 Cor 9;

in 8:9 it is rendered as "liberty"; in 10:29 "liberty" renders *eleutheria* with a similar meaning; cf. W. Foerster, "*exestin, exousia* etc.," *TDNT* 2.570.

86. Cf. Furnish, *II Corinthians* 162.

87. The same verb (*kyrieuō*) appears in Jesus' instructions to the twelve on the exercise of authority in Luke 22:25; in the parallel texts of Mark 10:42 and Matt 20:25 a compound form (*katakyrieuō*) appears. This same compound form appears in the instruction to presbyters in 1 Pet 5:3.

88. The deutero-Pauline character of 2 Thess, Col and Eph is widely recognized today, even by Catholic interpreters, as well as the pseudepigraphal character of the pastorals. Fitzmyer, *Paul and His Theology* 27. For a positive assessment of the significance of this recognition for the development of the church and of theology from a Catholic perspective, cf. R.E. Brown, *The Churches the Apostles Left Behind* (New York: Paulist, 1984), especially 31–60.

89. Cf. Eph 1:1; 1 Tim 1:1; 2 Tim 1:1; Titus 1:1.

90. It is obvious from Col 2:1 that Paul does not know the addressees of Colossians personally and from Col 1:7 that Epaphras had founded the church at Colossae. Cf. Eph 1:15–23; 3:14–19.

91. *Diakonos* is used by Paul himself of his own ministry in 1 Cor 3:5; 2 Cor 3:6; 6:4.

92. The expression "the word of God" (*ho logos tou theou*) appears in the authentic Paulines at 1 Thess 2:13; 1 Cor 14:36; 2 Cor 2:17; 4:2; Phil 1:14 (*l.v.*); Rom 9:6. *Mystērion* is found in 1 Cor 2:1, 7; 4:1 (plural); 13:2 (plural); 14:2 (plural); 15:51; Rom 11:25; 16:25. The meaning is somewhat different in Col–Eph; the closest parallel is in the inauthentic doxology of Rom 16:25; cf. Cranfield, *Romans* 1.5–11; 2.808–14; Käsemann, *Commentary on Romans* 422–28; Schlier, *Der Römerbrief* 451–55; Schlier (452) points out the similarity of Rom 16:25–27 to Eph–Col.

93. The word *energia* which is used here appears only at Phil 3:21 in the authentic Paulines; *dynamis* which also appears in Col 1:29 is quite common in the genuine letters (thirty-four times *dynamis*; eight times *dynamis tou theou*).

94. Cf. Eph 6:19–20. The expression "to open a door," also appears in the authentic letters; cf. 1 Cor 16:9; 2 Cor 2:12.

95. The formula in 2 Tim 1:1 is exactly the same in Col and Eph (*apostolos Christou Iēsou dia thelēmatos theou*), as in 2 Cor 1:1 and 1 Cor 1:1 (*l.v.*); 1 Tim 1:1: *apostolos Christou Iēsou kat'epitagēn theou* . . . ; Titus 1:1: *doulos theou, apostolos de Iēsou Christou* . . .;

cf. Phil 1:1: *Paulos kai Timotheos douloi Christou Iēsou*, and Rom 1:1: *Paulos doulos Christou Iēsou, klētos apostolos.*

96. In 1 Cor 15:9–10 Paul presented himself as the least of the apostles; in Eph 3:8 he is presented as the least of all the saints; here in 1 Tim 1:15 he is the first of sinners!

97. In the authentic letters, *latreuō* appears in Phil 3:3 and Rom 1:9; *spendomai* only appears here and in Phil 2:17 in the NT.

98. For the arguments for and against authenticity, see W.G. Kümmel, *Introduction to the New Testament* (Nashville: Abingdon Press, 1975) 264–69.

99. Whereas the verb *paraggelō* appears only three times in the genuine letters (1 Thess 4:11; 1 Cor 7:10; 11:17) and the noun *paraggelia* only once (1 Thess 4:2), the verb appears four times in 2 Thess 3 and four times in 1 Tim; the noun appears only in 1 Tim 1:5, 18.

Chapter IV

1. Jonah's dire prediction of the destruction of Nineveh in forty days (Jonah 3:4) was not realized because of the repentance of the Ninevites (Jonah 3:10). The return of Christ, and the full realization of the kingdom implied thereby, are dependent upon the adequacy of the preaching of repentance (2 Pet 3:9). Cf. W.G. Kümmel, *Promise and Fulfilment. The Eschatological Message of Jesus* (2nd English ed.; London: SCM, 1961) esp. 141–55; R. Schnackenburg, *God's Rule and Kingdom* (New York: Herder & Herder, 1963) esp. 195–214; also "Kingdom of God," in J.B. Bauer (ed.), *Sacramentum Verbi* (New York: Herder & Herder, 1969) 2.461–64.

2. Cf. Mark 9:38–41 = Luke 9:49–50; Matt 7:15–23; 10:42; Luke 6:46.

3. The root of *prostatis* is *proïstēmi*, which can mean "to help" or "to preside" (cf. 1 Thess 5:12; Rom 12:8; 1 Tim 5:17). It is unlikely that Phoebe exercised authority over Paul; cf. the role of Lydia with respect to Paul in Acts 16:14–15.

4. Vanhoye, reviewing Schillebeeckx's *Ministry* in *Clergy Review* 68 (1983) 161–62, affirms the NT basis for a hierarchical structure of the church, which nonetheless is not to be identified with hierarchy on later Roman or feudal models: "Certainly, if the hierarchical structure of the Church is to be defined 'on the basis of later Roman models in the Roman Empire and even later of feudal structures' . . . things will be sufficiently confused to be able to

maintain the denials. But anyone who refuses to accept this con-
flation will have to recognize that the movement of the New Testament lies in the direction of a hierarchical structure. . . . But
hierarchy does not mean a system of domination. This word, which
among some causes an allergic reaction, expresses the idea of an
authority in conformity with the holiness of God. An authority of
this kind has to be exercised in a spirit of service, for while it is
effectively at the service of unity in Christ (Ep 4:11–13), it cannot
serve unity unless it remains authority."

5. This is the only place in Acts where Luke uses the expression
"the twelve." The term "apostles" is reserved for the twelve in Acts
(twenty-six times) except in Acts 14:4, 14 where it is used excep-
tionally of Paul and Barnabas, emissaries of the church of Antioch
(13:1–3). The phrase "the twelve" appears four times in the gospel
according to Luke (three times in Matt; ten times in Mark; four
times in John). H. Conzelmann (*Acts of the Apostles* [Hermeneia;
Philadelphia: Fortress, 1987] 44–46) suggests that the use of a
source may account for the rare use here of the expression *hoi
dōdeka*.

6. It should be noted that men (*andras*) are here chosen for a
ministry to women. This observation is of historical significance
only; Luke was hardly concerned with contemporary problems concerning the ordination of women.

7. It is tendentious to argue that the whole community laid on
hands; in the light of v 3, "whom we may appoint (*katastēsomen*)
to this duty," the obvious antecedent for "they" in v 6b is "the
apostles" in v 6a. Conzelmann's comment (*Acts* 45) is deliberately
vague: "The description of the installation (proposal, choice by the
congregation, and ordination under the direction of the congregation) reflects the custom of the church at the time of Luke and is not
to be used for the reconstruction of the polity of the early church."
Conzelmann's remarks are slanted in favor of a congregational polity as opposed to an apostolic polity.

8. Cf. Num 27:15–23; Deut 34:9. In sacrificial ritual, the laying
on of hands meant that the victim was being presented in the name
of and for the benefit of the offerer; in the rite of Yom Kippur (Lev
16) it symbolized the transfer of sins to the scapegoat which, however, was not sacrificed but sent into the desert; cf. R. De Vaux,
Ancient Israel. Its Life and Institutions (Toronto: McGraw-Hill,
1961) 461. In Num 8:10 the rite symbolizes the substitution of Levites for the first-born; the laying on of hands was not used for the

investiture of priests in post-exilic ritual; in post-biblical times it was used only for the installation of doctors: "These later Jews based their practice on the text which states that Moses laid his hands on Joshua (Nb 27:15–23), and they presumed that he had done the same for the seventy elders of Israel (Nb 11:16–17)" (De Vaux 347). Cf. also Ch. Maurer, "epitithēmi," TDNT 8.159–61; E. Lohse, "cheir," TDNT 9.431–34; D. Daube, The New Testament and Rabbinic Judaism (London: Athlone, 1956) 224–46.

9. Philemon is really addressed to Philemon, Appia, Archippus and the church assembled in Philemon's house; Philippians is addressed to "all the saints with the overseers and servants (syn episkopois kai diakonois)." Commentators are not agreed as to whether these words, episkopoi kai diakonoi, are used here in a simply functional sense, or in their later technical sense of bishops and deacons.

10. It is implied in 1 Cor 1:13–17 that Paul himself did not regularly baptize. On this passage, cf. Orr-Walther, 1 Corinthians 151–52.

11. Conzelmann (Acts 169) considers the references to the eucharist (vv 7 and 11) to be redactional intrusions into a miracle narrative: "In the original form the liturgical embellishment was absent. No conclusions about the course and the components of the liturgy can be drawn from the redactional additions, since they do not intend to provide ritual exactitude. The unusual position for the Eucharist in the sequence of events cannot be explained on the basis of the actual course of the celebration (neither at the time of Paul or of Luke). The note has simply been inserted in an awkward manner."

12. Note the use of this same verb in Rom 12:8; 1 Tim 3:4, 5, 12; 5:17. Prostatis, used of Phoebe in Rom 16:2, is from the same root but is generally rendered "patroness"; cf. n. 3 above.

13. Admonition (noutheteō) is a function both of the apostle or community leader (1 Cor 4:14; Col 1:28; Acts 20:31; 1 Thess 5:12) and of Christians in general (1 Thess 5:14; Rom 15:14; Col 3:16; 2 Thess 3:15). Encouragement (paramytheomai) is a work of Paul (1 Thess 2:12) and of Christians in general (1 Thess 5:14); paramytheomai is synonymous with but not as extensively used as parakaleō; paraklēsis is an integral part of the apostle's work; parakaleō appears twenty-one times of Paul himself in the proto-Paulines and five times in the deutero-Paulines; this work of encouragement is done by others for Paul (1 Thess 3:2; Col 4:8; Eph

6:22; 1 Tim 5:1; 6:2; 2 Tim 4:2; Titus 1:9; 2:6, 15). Encouragement is also the work of God in and through the apostle as well as being a charism in the community (2 Cor 1:3–7; 5:20; 1 Cor 14:31; Rom 12:8); it is the responsibility of Christians toward one another (1 Thess 4:18; 5:11) and the work of a prophet (1 Cor 14:31). *Antechomai* appears in the sense of helping or supporting only in 1 Thess 5:14.

14. Cf. H.D. Betz, *Galatians* (Hermeneia; Philadelphia: Fortress, 1979) 304–06. Most commentators think that material support only is involved; others would argue for both material and spiritual support.

15. H. Küng's otherwise excellent treatment of "The Church as the Creation of the Spirit" perpetuates this unjustified contrast between charism and office; cf. his *The Church* (New York: Sheed & Ward, 1967) 150–202, esp. 179–91. Cf. n. 24 below.

16. The same verb, *oidate*, is used here as in 1 Thess 5:12 (*eidenai*). The RSV does not translate the same verb in the same way in both texts, although the context demands a similar translation.

17. The Greek verb is *hypotassō*. Cf. Orr-Walther, *1 Corinthians* 362. The same verb is used elsewhere in the NT for the submission of Jesus to his parents in Nazareth (Luke 2:51) and to the Father (1 Cor 15:28), for the subordination of demons to the seventy (Luke 10:17, 20), for the subordination of citizens to the state (Rom 13:1; 1 Pet 2:13, 18), for the mutual subordination of Christians (Eph 5:21), for the subordination of wives to husbands (Eph 5:22; Col 3:18; 1 Pet 3:1, 5; Titus 2:5), of slaves to masters (Titus 2:9) and of younger men to older men or to the presbyters (1 Pet 5:5). Subordination to another may be voluntary or compulsory; not all forms of subordination are necessarily negative; it is concerned primarily with order in society and cooperation in view of a common goal; the correlative of subordination is not domination, but direction; cf. G. Delling, "*hypotassō*," *TDNT* 8.39–47.

18. The three Greek words used in 1 Cor 12:4–6, *charismata*, *diakoniai* and *energēmata*, are practically synonymous; according to 1 Cor 12:7 each is a manifestation of the Spirit; cf. Orr-Walther, *I Corinthians* 281.

19. Cf. E. Shils, "Charisma," *International Encyclopedia of the Social Sciences* (Crowell, Collier, Macmillan; 1968) 2.386–90.

20. Cf. BAG 878b–879a.

21. The Greek word *charisma* does not appear in this text, but it can be understood from the context of 1 Cor 12—14.

22. Cf. 1 Cor 14:32: ". . . the spirits of prophets are subject to prophets." Other uses of the word *charisma* in the NT are less specific in their precise connotation (Rom 12:6; 1 Cor 1:7; 12:4, 9, 28, 30, 31; 1 Pet 4:10).

23. Concrete nouns are given to these three groups, but abstract nouns are used for the other charisms in the list of 1 Cor 12:28. The reference is more likely to the apostles, prophets and teachers of the past and present than to any permanent provision for the future; cf. Acts 13:1; Eph 2:20; 3:5; 4:11.

24. R. Sohm was responsible for this dichotomy in *Kirchenrecht* I (Leipzig, 1892). Of this distinction Conzelmann wrote in 1973: "One cannot accept the well-known distinction between charismatics and office-bearers, or at least not in terms of the way that the early Church viewed itself. This distinction rests on an antithesis between office/law on the one side and Spirit on the other. The Spirit Himself posits law" ("*charisma*," *TDNT* 9.406); cf. also Markus Barth, *Ephesians* (AB 34–34A; Garden City, N.Y.: Doubleday, 1974) 435: "Gift and institution, charisma and office, are not mutually exclusive alternatives; they are combined and inseparable."

25. 1 Cor 12:4–11, 28–30; Rom 12:6–8; Eph 4:11; 1 Pet 4:10–11.

26. *Lumen Gentium* 7, 12 in A.P. Flannery (ed.), *The Documents of Vatican II* (Grand Rapids: Eerdmans, 1975) 354–56, 363–64.

27. For a summary of the discussion concerning the identity of Paul's opponents in 2 Corinthians, cf. Furnish, *2 Corinthians* 48–54.

28. Cf. the balanced presentation of F.W. Beare, *The Epistle to the Philippians* (Black's New Testament Commentaries; London: Adam & Charles Black, 1959) 48–50; also R.P. Martin, *Philippians* (New Century Bible: London: Oliphants, 1976) 61–62; J.H. Houlden, *Paul's Letters from Prison* (Harmondsworth, England: Penguin, 1970) 49–50; J. Murphy-O'Connor, *Scripture Discussion Commentary 11* (edited by Laurence Bright; London/Sydney: Sheed & Ward, 1971) 101. A vaguer translation, such as "guardians and assistants," or "overseers and servants," is to be preferred. The formula *episkopoi kai diakonoi* appears for local leadership in 1 *Clem.* 42.5, *Did.* 15.1 and coupled with teachers (*episkopoi kai didaskaloi kai diakonoi*) in *Herm. Vis.* 3.5.1.

29. BAG (707a) offers both meanings for each text with supporting bibliography.

30. Cf. p. 88 n. 3 and p. 58 n. 20.

31. The word is used of local leaders in 1 *Clem*. 1.3 and in the form *proēgoumenoi* in 1 *Clem*. 21.6 and *Herm. Vis*. 2.2.6; 3.9.7; elsewhere in 1 Clement, *hēgoumenos* is used of civil rulers.

32. Note the way the order of Phil 1:1 is reversed here, the leaders being greeted first!

33. 1 Peter has been dated prior to Nero's persecution of Christians in the 60s or prior to the persecutions of Domitian in the 90s. In the first case authorship by Peter is possible. In the latter case, we would be dealing with a pseudepigraphon, written possibly by Silvanus. Cf. K.H. Schelkle, *Die Petrusbriefe. Der Judasbrief* (HTKNT 13.2; Freiburg: Herder, 1961) 7–15; Kümmel, *Introduction* 421–25. The later date is preferred by Kümmel, while the earlier date is defended by Schelkle, with Silvanus writing under Peter's direction.

34. This word has been restored to the text in the 26th edition of Nestle, but in brackets. It is absent from Sinaiticus, Vaticanus, one other Greek ms. and from the Sahidic version, but is otherwise the more common reading.

35. These words, *kata theon* in Greek, have been restored to the text in the 26th edition of Nestle. They are absent from Vaticanus and from the majority of Greek mss.

36. This same verb appears in Jesus' instructions to the twelve in Mark 10:42 (= Matt 20:25); the simple form of the same verb, *kyrieuō*, is used in the parallel text of Luke 22:25 and by Paul in 2 Cor 1:24.

37. Cf. G.A. Krodel, *Acts* (Augsburg Commentary on the New Testament; Minneapolis: Augsburg, 1986) 40.

38. Cf. above 90–91.

39. Conzelmann (*Acts* 99) considers the laying on of hands here to be a blessing rather than an ordination; cf. Dibelius-Conzelmann, *Die Pastoralbriefe*. Vierte, ergänzte Auflage (HNT 13; Tübingen: Mohr, 1966) 56. Krodel (*Acts* 228) speaks of "a commissioning for carrying out the specific task described in chaps. 13 and 14."

40. Conzelmann (*Acts* 108, 111) considers the term "apostle" in these texts to have been taken over from a source. The word is absent from the western text of v 14. Krodel (*Acts* 253) assigns the word to a tradition used by Luke and understood by him in a functional sense.

41. Josephus writes of a famine in Palestine at the time of the procurator Tiberius Alexander (46–48 C.E.; *Ant*. 20.5.2. § 101), but there was no universal famine during the reign of Claudius; cf. Conzelmann, *Acts* 90–91 with bibliography. Agrippa I died in 44

C.E. (Acts 12:23). Of the presbyters, Krodel (*Acts* 210) writes, "Their presence anticipates a change in the leadership of the church in Jerusalem."

42. The literary and historical problems associated with Paul's journeys to Jerusalem in Gal 1—2 and in Acts 9:26–29; 11:30; 15:1–29 and the apostolic decree are notorious. For a detailed analysis with bibliography, cf. Conzelmann, *Acts* 114–22.

43. Although presbyters are mentioned out of chronological order in 11:30, James does not appear until chap. 15, except for a brief mention in 12:17. Of Acts 15 Conzelmann (*Acts* 115) writes, "It is not by chance that the Apostolic Council occupies the middle of the book. It is the great turning point, the transition from the primitive church to the 'contemporary' church. From this point on the apostles disappear, even in Jerusalem itself. . . . In Jerusalem continuity is represented by James, in the Gentile Christian church by Paul." By involving Paul with the apostolic decree of James, though historically unlikely because of Gal 2:6 and Acts 21:18–26, Luke may also be illustrating his thesis of harmony between Jerusalem and Paul.

44. Krodel (*Acts* 261–62) acknowledges the anachronistic terminology used here by Luke, but recognizes leadership roles in the early Pauline churches. Of such references in the earlier letters of Paul he comments, "While we cannot describe their functions adequately, their presence shows the need for structures within the community."

45. The verb used here, *cheirotoneō*, means "to select by a show of hands" or "to appoint or install" (cf. BAG 881a); the first meaning applies in 2 Cor 8:19; here, with Paul and Barnabas as subjects of the verb, the second meaning is required. Philo and Josephus use the verb of the appointment of a king by God. The verb is not to be confused with the later patristic verb, *cheirotheteō*, which means "to ordain by the laying on of hands"; cf. Conzelmann, *Acts* 112. In patristic literature the two verbs were sometimes confused; cf. *LPGL* 1522b–1523a.

46. The 26th edition of Nestle has accepted the rarer reading of Sinaiticus and Vaticanus: *tēn ekklēsian tou theou hēn periepoiēsato dia tou haimatos tou idiou*. This reading is preferred in later editions of the RSV and by Conzelmann, *Acts* 175 and Krodel, *Acts* 389. The first edition of the RSV followed the more common reading: "the church of the Lord which he obtained with his own blood."

47. Only here is the personal noun, *poimēn*, used of a charism or

of an ecclesial minister in the NT. Christ presents himself as the good shepherd in John 10 (cf. 1 Pet 2:25; Heb 13:20) and the imagery of shepherding is used for church ministry in John 21:15–17; 1 Pet 5:2 and Acts 20:28. Cf. Houlden, *Letters from Prison* 312–14; Barth, *Ephesians* 435–39.

48. These three phrases may be read coordinately or subordinately. Although the Greek preposition *pros* appears with the first and *eis* with the second and third, no significant difference in meaning can be discerned in the use of the prepositions. If read subordinately, all Christians are ordered to ministry, not just those with leadership roles; a coordinate reading would favor a more clerical understanding of ministry. Cf. Houlden, *Letters from Prison* 314. Barth's extensive treatment of these verses (*Ephesians* 439–40, 478–84) in favor of a democratic ministry is polemical in tone.

49. This is the common opinion of exegetes; Barth (*Ephesians* 314–17, 437), on the contrary, assigns them a permanent role in the church, understanding that the preaching of doctrine is the continuing foundation of the church.

50. The significance of Ephesians for the development of office in the church is extensively studied by H. Merklein, *Das kirchliche Amt nach dem Epheserbrief* (SANT 33; München: Kösel, 1973); on Eph 4:11, as constitutive for the church and the foundation of ecclesiastical office *iure divino*, cf. esp. 79–81, 401.

51. Cf. F. Mussner, *Der Jakobusbrief* (HTKNT 13.1; Freiburg: Herder, 1964) 218–25; on the relationship of healing to forgiveness, cf. esp. 223 n. 4; also H. Schlier, "*aleiphō*," *TDNT* 1.229–32.

52. Although recognizing some doubt with respect to 1 John, R.E. Brown (*The Epistles of John* [AB 30; Garden City, N.Y.: Doubleday, 1982] 14–19) accepts common authorship for all three letters; so also R. Schnackenburg, *Die Johannesbriefe* (HTKNT 13.3; Freiburg: Herder, 1965) 295–301, esp. 298). After discussing five possible interpretations of *ho presbyteros*, Brown, following Papias' terminology, prefers a disciple of the disciples of Jesus to an officeholder (647–51). Schnackenburg also favors a disciple of the apostles and a bearer of the apostolic tradition rather than the bearer of the presbyteral office (296–97, 305–06).

53. On the adversaries addressed in 1 and 2 John, cf. Brown, *Epistles* 47–68; also Brown, *Community* 93–144.

54. On Diotrephes, Brown (*Epistles* 715–20, 728–39), after discussing a variety of options, concludes that Diotrephes was the host of a house church: "Diotrephes is on his way to become a presbyter-

bishop in the style of the Pastorals, or even the sole bishop in the style of Ignatius" (738). The thesis of E. Käsemann, to the effect that Diotrephes was an orthodox bishop rejecting the gnostic tendencies of the presbyter and his community, is not widely accepted.

55. Brown, *Community* 151–62.

56. John 21 is widely recognized as an appendix added later by a redactor to a gospel which was already complete at 20:30–31. The matters treated in the appendix are not typical of the rest of the gospel, even though traditional materials may have been used.

57. Dionysius of Alexandria, in the middle of the third century, pointed out the difference in style between the gospel according to John and Revelation and rejected the earlier conviction that John the apostle was the author of Revelation. It is recognized today that Revelation and John are the work of different authors, neither of whom can be identified with John the apostle, the son of Zebedee. Cf. Kümmel, *Introduction* 469–72; G.R. Beasley-Murray, *Revelation* (The New Century Bible Commentary; Grand Rapids: Eerdmans, 1974) 32–37.

58. Cf. Beasley-Murray, *Revelation* 68–70; Brown, *Epistles* 715; J. Massyngberde Ford, *Revelation* (AB 38; Garden City, N.Y.: Doubleday, 1975) 384.

59. A. Feuillet, "The Twenty-Four Elders of the Apocalypse," in his *Johannine Studies* (Staten Island, N.Y.: Alba House, 1965) 183–214; cf. also Ford, *Revelation* 72–73.

60. Cf. N. Brox, *Die Pastoralbriefe* (Regensburger Neues Testament 7/2; Vierte, völlig neu bearbeitete Auflage; Regensburg; Pustet, 1969); Kümmel, *Introduction* 370–84; Fitzmyer, *Paul and His Theology* 27.

61. This is especially clear for Titus (Titus 1:5). Timothy may have enjoyed a similar responsibility over local communities in the region of Ephesus (cf. 1 Tim 1:3); cf. Brox, *Pastoralbriefe* 18–19, 102; 21, 282–83.

62. On the role of prophecy in the designation of missionaries, cf. Acts 13:1–3; for a discussion of Timothy's "ordination," mentioned in 1 Tim 1:18; 4:14; 2 Tim 1:6, cf. Brox, *Pastoralbriefe* 117–19, 180–82, 228–29. Brox speaks explicitly of Timothy's ordination as a sacramental act; cf. also J.D. Quinn, "Ordination in the Pastoral Epistles," *Communio* 8 (1981) 358–69.

63. The genitive, *tou presbyteriou*, in 1 Tim 4:14 may be subjective or objective; if objective, the meaning would be "the laying on of hands which made you a presbyter."

64. Cf. 1 Tim 1:3; 4:6, 11, 13, 16; 6:1–3; 2 Tim 2:1–2, 14, 24–25;

4:2, 5; Titus 2:1, 3–5, 15. Older women are encouraged to be good teachers (*kalodidaskaloi*) of the younger women in Titus 2:3–5.

65. Cf. 1 Tim 1:3–11; 4:1–5; 6:3–5, 10, 20–21; 2 Tim 1:14; 2:14–19, 23–26; 3:1–9; 4:3–4; Titus 1:10–16; 3:9.

66. *Meta pasēs epitagēs*: RSV translates "with all authority"; BAG (302a) recommends "with all impressiveness"; C. Spicq (*Les Epîtres Pastorales* [EBib; 4e éd.; Paris: Gabalda, 1969] 2.644) cites Thomas Aquinas: *cum fiducia auctoritatis*.

67. Such disciplinary action is also apparent in another deutero-Pauline; cf. 2 Thess 3:14–15.

68. Cf. 1 Tim 4:13; 5:1–2; 6:2; 2 Tim 4:2; Titus 2:6, 15.

69. Cf. e.g., 1 Tim 4:7–10, 12, 15–16; 6:11–12, 14; 2 Tim 2:3, 10–13, 22.

70. As Brox puts it (*Pastoralbriefe* 147–52) all bishops were presbyters, but not all presbyters were bishops. Spicq (*Epîtres Pastorales* 439–55), on the other hand, maintains that already in the pastorals the *episkopos* was an individual member of the presbyteral college but a first among equals. Some commentators have seen a parallel between the role of the *mĕbaqqer* or *pāqîd* at Qumran and that of the *episkopos*. The preeminence of James among the Jerusalem presbyters is often attributed to his relationship to the Lord. Cf. R.E. Brown, "*Episkopeō* and *Episkopos*: The New Testament Evidence," *TS* 41 (1980) 332–38; B.E. Thiering, "*Mebaqqer* and *Episkopos* in the Light of the Temple Scroll," *JBL* 100 (1981) 59–74.

71. The RSV translation supposes that the later office of a monarchical bishop is already operative here. A better rendering would be "If any one aspires to the task of guardian . . ."

72. If this indeed were true, church leadership today might simply hire more priests and not wait upon vocations!

73. Cf. also Titus 1:9: *hina dynatos ē kai parakalein en tē didaskaliạ tē hygiainousę kai tous antilegontas elegchein*. Timothy is personally encouraged to be *didaktikon* in 2 Tim 2:24.

74. The same verb, *proïstēmi*, is used here and in 3:4, 12 for governing one's household as is used for church leadership in 1 Thess 5:12; Rom 12:8 and 1 Tim 5:17.

75. The following phrases and ideas are parallel in both texts: *episkepsasthe* (Acts 6:3) and *episkepsastho kyrios ho theos* (Num 27:16); *anthrōpon, hos echei pneuma en heautǭ* (Num 27:18) and *andras . . . plēreis pneumatos kai sophias* (Acts 6:3, 5; cf. Deut 34:9 re Joshua: *eneplēsthē pneumatos syneseōs*); Joshua is installed in the presence of the priest Eleazar and the whole congregation (Num 27:19) and the seven are installed by the apostles in the presence of

the whole community (Acts 6:6); Moses lays hands on Joshua (Num 27:18, 23) and the twelve lay hands on the seven (Acts 6:6). De Vaux (*Ancient Israel* 347) says that the rabbis extended this rite to the appointment of the seventy elders in Num 11:16–17 (cf. n. 8 above). E. Lohse, ("*cheir*," *TDNT* 9.433 n.55), comments, "Since Nu. 27:15–23 serves as a basis of ordination for the Rabb., the intentional borrowing from Nu. 27 in Ac. 6:1–6 is designed to show that the institution of the Seven is meant as Chr. ordination." Conzelmann (*Acts* 44–46) suggests that Luke has reworked his sources "to avoid the impression of an internal crisis during the time of the apostles"; the seven appear to have been leaders among the Hellenists as the twelve were leaders among the Hebrews; the work of the seven was not limited to serving at tables as the sequel in Acts shows for Stephen and Philip. Luke places all developments under the control of the twelve apostles of Jesus.

76. In Num 11:16–17 God shares *some* of the spirit that is upon Moses with seventy elders (*andras apo tōn presbyterōn Israēl*) to help him in the governance of the people. In Num 27:15–23 and Deut 34:9 Moses lays his hands upon Joshua to confer *some* of his authority (Num 27:20) or the spirit of wisdom (Deut 34:9) upon him as his successor. Note that some mss. of the Hebrew text of Num 27:23 and some mss. of the Greek and Latin use the same verb (*ṣiwwâ*) in both parts of v 23, suggesting that Moses' commissioning of Joshua paralleled God's commissioning of Moses! Of Num 27, F.L. Moriarty (*Jerome Biblical Commentary* [Englewood Cliffs, N.J.: Prentice Hall, 1968] 1.97) comments, "Leadership was not hereditary but charismatic, and no one could assume its functions unless he had first received the gift of the spirit. The institution of charismatic leadership emphasized the providential guidance of Yahweh." J. Blenkinsopp (*Jerome Biblical Commentary* 1.122) also comments with respect to Deut 34:9, ". . . authority in the sacred community is not separable from charism."

77. The responsibility of the priesthood was the source of fear and flight for some of the church fathers (Gregory of Nazianzen, John Chrysostom, Theodore of Mopsuestia, Augustine, Gregory the Great) and not to be undertaken for worldly reasons. Cf. Agnes Cunningham, "The Holy Order of a Saving Ministry," *Chicago Studies* 22 (1983) 269–81.

78. Brox (*Pastoralbriefe* 154–55) interprets 1 Tim 3:11 of deaconesses rather than the wives of deacons, but admits that certainty is not possible. The fact that the text returns to deacons in 3:12–13 may imply that 3:11 concerns either the wives of deacons or the

women who assist them in their work; the absence of the possessive pronoun, "their," with *gynaikas* suggests the latter interpretation. An official position in church organization is given to widows in 1 Tim 5:3–16. Spicq (*Epîtres Pastorales* 1.460–61) agrees with Brox on the understanding of 1 Tim 3:11.

79. Many important mss., including the Vulgate, read v 13b: "Be at peace with them" (i.e., the leaders; *autois* in place of *heautois*).

80. Orr-Walther (*I Corinthians* 363), commenting on 1 Cor 16:15–16, speak of a hierarchy of service: "The apostle gives his approval to a kind of hierarchy of service in the church. Natural leadership is to be recognized, and this is to include more than casual acknowledgement: the membership is to *give recognition to such* people. Two characteristics of this serving leadership are identified: co-operation and hard work." The same comments could apply to 1 Thess 5:12–13.

81. This is said explicitly of the gift of prophecy in 1 Cor 14:29.

82. Peter: Acts 2:38, 41; 10:47–48; Philip: 8:12, 13, 16, 36, 38; Ananias: 9:18; 22:16; Paul: 16:15, 33; 18:8; 19:5.

83. The twelve (esp. Peter): Acts 2:43; 3:1–10; 4:10, 16, 29–30; 5:12; 9:33–42; the seven: 6:8 (Stephen); 8:6–8, 13 (Philip); Paul and Barnabas: 14:3, 8–11; 15:12; Paul alone: 19:11–12. The synoptic word for miracles, *dynameis*, is used in Acts 8:13 and 19:11.

84. Isaac's blessing of Jacob could not be withdrawn, even though Jacob had deceived his father (Gen 27:37). The Hebrew word *dabar* (Greek *rhēma* or *logos*) can mean both "a word" or "an event"; cf. Luke 2:15: "Let us go over to Bethlehem and see this thing (*rhēma*) that has happened, which the Lord has made known to us."

85. Cf. Forestell, *The Word of the Cross* 141–45.

Conclusions

1. The evidence of the Ignatian letters is valid for the churches of Antioch, Ephesus, Magnesia, Tralles, Philadelphia and Smyrna. No reference is made to the three-tiered hierarchy in the letter to the church at Rome; 2.2 refers to Ignatius himself as the bishop of Syria. On the recent discussion of the authenticity of the Ignatian letters, cf. W.R. Schoedel, "Are the Letters of Ignatius of Antioch Authentic?" *RelSRev* 6 (1980) 196–201, and *Ignatius of Antioch. A Commentary on the Letters of Ignatius of Antioch* (Hermeneia; Philadelphia: Fortress, 1985) 4–7, 22–23. For a more systematic study of

ministry in the various books of the NT, cf. P. Bony, E. Cothenet et alii, *Le ministère et les ministères selon le Nouveau Testament* (Paris: Seuil, 1973).

2. Cf. K.B. Osborne, O.F.M., *Priesthood. A History of the Ordained Ministry in the Roman Catholic Church* (Mahwah, N.J.: Paulist, 1988) 130.

3. Cf. H. Crouzel, "The Ministry in the Church. Reflections on a Recent Publication. II – The Witness of the Ancient Church," *Clergy Review* 68 (1983) 164–74, esp. 164–65.

4. Cf. A. Vanhoye, *Prêtres anciens, prêtre nouveau, selon le Nouveau Testament* (Paris: Seuil, 1980). Cf. n. 20 below.

5. The conciliar Decree on the Ministry and Life of Presbyters (*Presbyterorum Ordinis* 2) of the Second Vatican Council uses Rom 15:16 to integrate the celebration of the eucharist with the ministry of the word. This use of the text of Romans is an extension of its historical meaning. As F. Wulf says in his commentary on this text (H. Vorgrimler [ed.], *Commentary on the Documents of Vatican II* [New York: Herder & Herder, 1969] 4.223), "the Eucharist only makes plain, in symbolic and sacramental efficacy, the goal towards which the whole apostolic ministry of the priest is directed: preaching the faith and pastoral care as well as the administration of the sacraments. It makes plain that 'the whole society of the redeemed, the assembly and fellowship of the saints are offered as an all-embracing sacrifice to God through Christ the high-priest' (Augustine)." Cf. also Forestell, *The Word of the Cross* 199–200.

6. Cf. Jean M.R. Tillard, *What Priesthood has the Ministry?* (Grove Booklet on Ministry and Worship 13; Bramcote, Notts.: Grove Books, 1973).

7. Q. 40, a. 4; translation of the English Dominicans (New York: Benziger, 1948) 3.2704: *Respondeo dicendum, quod sacerdos habet duos actus: unum principalem, scilicet consecrare corpus Christi; alterum secundarium scilicet praeparare populum Dei ad susceptionem huius sacramenti . . .* " For an historical explanation of how this shift in theological understanding came about in the middle ages, cf. Osborne, *Priesthood* 161–218.

8. Cf. G.A. Lindbeck, "The Lutheran Doctrine of the Ministry: Catholic and Reformed," *TS* 30 (1969) 589–612.

9. Cf. Schoedel, *Ignatius of Antioch* 22–23; on the exercise of collegiality between the bishop, his presbyters and deacons, and on the consultation of the laity for approval of decisions taken by the bishops with his clergy, cf. *The Letters of St. Cyprian of Carthage.*

Vol. I (translated by G.W. Clarke; ACW 43; New York: Newman, 1984) Letter 14.2 & 4 (pp. 87–89); Letter 19.1–2 (pp. 99–100); Volume II (ACW 44; New York: Newman, 1984) Letter 49.2 (pp. 76–79).

10. 1 Clem., 42:4.5; 44:5. Clement's citation of Is 60:17 is either adapted to his purpose or derives from another textual tradition; his citation uses episkopous and diakonous. Irenaeus' citation of the same text in Adv.Haer., 4.26.5 follows the more accepted text in Rahlfs, using archontas and episkopous.

11. There is evidence for elders (presbyteroi) in pagan Hellenistic communities as well; cf. G. Bornkamm, "presbys, presbyteros, etc.," TDNT 6.653.

12. Cf. R. Dillon, "Ministry as Stewardship of the Tradition in the New Testament," Proceedings CTSA 24 (1969) 10–62.

13. J.L. McKenzie, Authority in the Church (New York: Sheed & Ward, 1966) 176: "In all theological reasoning the danger of rationalism is always present. It would not be too grossly simplified to say that all heresies ultimately were efforts to reduce the mystery to something reasonable. Not all rationalism issues in formal heresy or even in material heresy; but the normal and expected issue of rationalism is theological error, a misconception of the mystery which may be no less damaging because it falls short of full and formal heresy. Authority in the Church may be one of the points where rationalism is more subtle. Of theological interpretations of authority one may say that if they leave Church authority entirely comprehensible, they fail to present its reality."

14. Cf. Osborne, Priesthood 89–160, esp. 145–48.

15. In Hebrews the word archiereus is applied to Jesus in 2:17; 3:1; 4:14, 15; 5:5, 10; 6:20; 7:26; 8:1; 9:11; the simple form hiereus is applied to Jesus in 8:4 and 10:21. In all cases, however, it is clearly affirmed that Jesus is not a priest in the levitical sense, but "according to the order of Melchisedech."

16. Cf. J.H. Elliot, The Elect and the Holy. An Exegetical Examination of 1 Peter 2:4–10 and the Phrase basileion hierateuma (NovTSup 12; Leiden: Brill, 1966); E. Schüssler-Fiorenza, Priester für Gott: Studien zum Heerschaft–und Priestermotif in der Apokalypse (NTAbh N.S.7; Münster: Aschendorff, 1972).

17. Osborne (Priesthood 96) writes of the comparison of the episkopoi/presbyteroi in 1 Clem., 40.5 to the archiereus and the hiereis of the OT, ". . . the ministry of presiding over the eucharist was associated with the ministry of presiding over the community, and is a part of the latter, rather than vice versa. It is not a special ordination to 'priesthood' which is the root of presiding over the

community; rather, it is the commission to preside over the community which allows for a presiding over the eucharist." Of Ignatius Osborne writes (*Priesthood* 101), "Ignatius speaks only of Old Testament prophets, and for him there is only one teacher, Jesus Christ (Eph 15,1)."

18. Cf. *Oxford English Dictionary* (Oxford: Clarendon, 1933) 8.1352.

19. Cf. J. Lécuyer, "Decree on the Ministry and Life of Priests. History of the Decree," in H. Vorgrimler (ed.), *Commentary on the Documents of Vatican II* (New York: Herder & Herder, 1969) 4.183–209. The title of the decree was changed from *De Clericis* to *De Sacerdotibus* to *De Vita et Ministerio Sacerdotali*, and finally *De Presbyterorum Ordinis*; also F. Wulf, "Commentary on the Decree" in Vorgrimler 4.210.

20. A. Vanhoye, *Prêtres anciens, prêtre nouveau selon le Nouveau Testament* (Paris: Seuil, 1980). Eng. tr. *Old Testament Priests and the New Priest according to the New Testament* (Petersham, Mass.: St. Bede's, 1986).

21. The figure of "bridegroom" is used of Christ in Mark 2:19–20 (= Matt 9:15 = Luke 5:34–35); John 3:29; and in the parable of the ten virgins (Matt 25:1–13). The same imagery is implied in the parable of the wedding feast in Matt 22:1–10; in Paul, cf. 2 Cor 11:2; in Eph 5:22–33 the relation of Christ to the church is compared to that of husband and wife; the church is portrayed as both the new Jerusalem and as the bride of Christ in Rev 21—22.

INDEX OF AUTHORS

184

INDEX OF BIBLICAL REFERENCES

(Only references in the text are included in this index.)